On Your Own

On Your Own

A Widow's Passage to Emotional and Financial Well-Being

Alexandra Armstrong, CFP
& Mary R. Donahue, PhD

 Dearborn
Financial Publishing, Inc.

This book is intended to provide general information. The publisher, author and copyright owner cannot assume responsibility for individual decisions made by readers.

Should assistance for these types of advice and services be required, professionals should be consulted.

References to tax provisions in this books are based on current laws and regulations. Revisions in tax law, if adopted, might affect the tax consequences.

Publisher: Kathleen A. Welton
Associate Editor: Karen A. Christensen
Editorial Assistant: Kristen G. Landreth
Interior Design: Irving Perkins Associates
Cover Design: Dan Christmas

Published by Dearborn Financial Publishing, Inc.

Printed in the United States of America

93 94 95 10 9 8 7 6 5 4 3 2 1

Library of Congress Cataloging-in-Publication Data

Armstrong, Alexandra.
On your own : a widow's passage to emotional and financial
well-being / Alexandra Armstrong and Mary R. Donahue.
p.   cm.
Includes bibliographical references and index.
ISBN 0-79310-515-3
1. Widows—Finance, Personal.   2. Financial Security.
I. Donahue, Mary R.   II. Title.
HG179.A724   1993
332.024'0654—dc20   93-18639
                                                          CIP

Dedication

This book is dedicated to my Mother, who taught me how to be a survivor by her example, and to the Religious of the Sacred Heart at Stone Ridge, who gave me the education that enabled me to write this book.

—ALEXANDRA ARMSTRONG

This book is dedicated to my parents, who, in an age when it was not the norm, established for me the concept that it was a woman's right to reach her potential, whatever it might be. To my late husband, George, whose unconditional love and support enabled me to expand my horizons and better define my personal goals, and to my daughters, Laurie and Rachel, with whom I mourned, grew and thrived.　　　—MARY R. DONAHUE

Acknowledgments

We would like to thank the following people for their assistance in making this book a reality: Roy Alexander, Beverly A. Anderson, Tracy A. Berriman, Michael J. Curtin, Esquire, Susan Davis, Laurie Donahue, Rich Dubroff, Gregory A. Foster, Susan B. Fredrickson, Maureen Geimer, Greg and Rhoda Hackler, Gertrude Jacobs, Hannah Kaufman, Kitty Kelley, Donna Kozuch, Ph.D, Tillie Lehrer, Terri Ann Lowenthal, Robert E. Madden, Esquire, Virginia McArthur, Esquire, Jerry J. McCoy, Esquire, Millicent Neusner, Michele O'Hare, Pam Ormond, Ed and Jeannie Pechin, Virginia Phillips, Esquire, Jean Romeres, Lori Smith, Mark Tibergien, Sylvia Tull, Bob Wilkerson, Susan Winston.

Special thanks to Rachel Donahue, who typed the manuscript, and to Karen Preysnar, who prepared the financial planning numbers.

Contents

Introduction

Terror, fear, pain, loneliness, paralysis, anger, numbness, sadness, panic, weakness, helplessness . . . These are some of the all-too-familiar emotions that crash and swirl around the fragile ego of a woman who has just become a *widow*.

The loss of your husband is likely to be the most traumatic event of your life. You did not choose to be a widow, you don't like being a widow and you are overwhelmed by the enormity of the issues you are required to handle due to the changes in your personal circumstances.

We have written *On Your Own* to help you cope better with this dramatic alteration in your personal situation. Viewing your recovery as a series of building blocks, we start the book with your initial grief response, then move through various stages to an ultimate state of emotional and financial well-being. This book reflects our belief that there is a connection between your financial and psychological recovery. The better able you are to come to terms with your loss emotionally, the better able you will be to address the financial consequences. Similarly, the more you understand about your financial situation, the less anxious you will be, which in turn will contribute to your emotional healing.

Our primary goal in *On Your Own* is to provide you with information that will enable you to cope better with your life. We hope our book will not only help you deal with the enormity of your loss but will also guide you along the path to emotional and financial health. We have purposely made it basic yet comprehensive. We presented the material so that you can read it from cover to cover or select individual chapters for specific information. Our ultimate goal is to enable you to be emotionally and financially self-reliant.

While *On Your Own* is designed specifically for widows, we believe any woman seeking control of her future will find it useful. Recent statistics indicate that most women will find themselves alone at some time, whether by choice or due to divorce or widowhood. Ignoring the possibility of bereavement or estrangement and the emotional and financial consequences is to deceive yourself. The reality is that you need to know what to do in your time of crisis, to whom you should turn, the questions you should ask and the help available to you when you find yourself "*On Your Own.*"

To start this project, we read several books written for widows. Many helpful ones are available, but they seem to fall into three categories— those books written by one woman about her particular experiences, those books written by a financial advisor who is not a widow telling widows what he/she thinks they should do or those books written by a mental health expert on the grief experience. We were unable to find one book that considered the psychological and financial impact of widowhood concurrently.

In discussing what we thought should be included in this book, it became obvious that you cannot put all widows in one category. There are young widows and old widows. There are those with dependent children, those with older children and those without children. Some husbands died after a long-term illness and others died suddenly. Some widows had been very dependent on their husbands, others independent. The marriage might have been happy or happy only when viewed in retrospect.

We also realized that the healing process cannot be put into specific time frames. Different widows heal in different periods of time depending on the circumstances of the husband's death, the widow's preexisting mental health, the available emotional support from friends and family and her financial knowledge. Progress cannot be charted on a straight upward line. Just when a widow thinks she has it all together, she may have a relapse.

It is difficult to recover from the loss of anyone close to you. However, there is no death that has so many psychological and financial implications and that leaves the survivor feeling so helpless and alone as the death of a spouse.

Our personal experiences contributed to our decision to write this book. Each of us was forced to cope with the major consequences of death in our families. Here are our stories:

Alexandra Armstrong's Story

Although I am not a widow myself, my mother was widowed when she was 48 years old and I was eight. Dad had been ill for some time, and taking care of him had depleted the family's resources. In order to make ends meet, Mother went to work for the first time as a clerk in a dress store two years before he died.

By the time Dad died, there was very little money left, but there was a small life insurance policy ($10,000). Mother used this money as a down payment on a small house in Georgetown (Washington, D.C.) costing $18,000. My sister and brother, who were just starting to work, assumed responsibility for the mortgage. Although I took their generosity for granted at the time, in retrospect I realize how tough that must have been for them on their own limited budgets.

My mother and I lived principally on the income that came from VA benefits, Social Security and Mom's salary. My grandfather had set up a small trust fund that provided some extra income from time to time. The checks from this fund often made it possible for us to get through the end of the month. After a while, Mom noticed that the checks were smaller and their payment was sporadic. Since she was not knowledgeable about financial matters, she asked Dad's brother to help her investigate what was happening to this important source of income. After he looked into it, he brought her the bad news that she had been the victim of white-collar crime. The person who managed the trust fund for her had "borrowed" the money to cover his own expenses. He intended to pay it back to the fund but wasn't ever able to do so. By the time my uncle had taken an inventory of what was in the trust fund, very little money was left.

Although I was young when it happened, I understood the ramifications of this discovery—we didn't have this much-needed income. When I was older, I realized that if Mother had known more about investments, she might have been aware of the problem earlier and might have been able to avert the disaster. This event had a profound impact on my life. I resolved I would learn as much as I could about how money worked so I would have financial control of my own life.

We might not have had much money left after Dad died, but Mom certainly made up for any loss of income by the abundant love and care she gave me when I was growing up. She talked the nuns at the convent school I was attending into giving me a scholarship because she believed a good education was essential to my future and it seemed clear that I would have to pay my own expenses.

In school, I discovered that I actually liked and had an aptitude for mathematics. I majored in math my first two years in college and then switched to history when I realized that I did not enjoy theoretical math as much as applied math. After completing college in 1961, I found a job as a secretary in the research department of a regional New York Stock Exchange firm located in Washington, D.C. (In that era, most female college graduates chose to be either teachers or secretaries.)

After two years in that department, I requested a transfer because I wanted to work more directly with people. Initially, I was assigned to two partners—one of whom was a woman (which was highly unusual in the '60s). In 1965, I became the personal assistant to another woman partner at the same firm, Julia Montgomery Walsh. When I started working for Julia, she was a young widow supporting four sons. It seemed that I was destined to be involved with widows, whatever I did!

In 1966, at Julia's request, I passed the test to become a stockbroker and worked with her until we started our own firm in 1977. By that time, I had completed the courses to become a Certified Financial Planner (CFP). This course taught me about various aspects of financial advice, not just investments. Financial planning was a relatively new concept, but one that seemed logical to me. Looking at all aspects of a person's financial situation before giving investment advice made more sense to me than giving investment advice in a vacuum. With the CFP designation, I started the Financial Planning Department of the new firm.

In 1983, I started my own financial planning firm in Washington, D.C., and in 1991, I started still another firm with two partners. Today, we have 15 employees providing individuals with financial planning and investment advice. Although our firm never focused particularly on single women as clients, many have gravitated to our firm. Our female clients indicate they want to learn more about investments and to work with advisors who don't act as if their questions are "stupid."

Today, about 50 percent of my clients are widows. In view of my experience with my mother and others like her, I have enjoyed helping women learn more about investments. Raising the level of their financial consciousness is personally satisfying. I believe that this knowledge will enable them to better control their financial futures. The more these women know, the less apt they are to make mistakes. The old adage "money can't buy happiness" might be true, but I have found that it sure can make life more comfortable.

Mary Donahue's Story

I was a professional and supposedly enlightened woman when my ostensibly healthy husband, almost 22 years my senior, collapsed and died on January 21, 1980. Up until his death, I had never been an active participant in our family's financial decision making, nor did I believe I needed to be.

My childhood and teenage years were relatively uneventful and monetarily trouble-free. I attended a private school through eighth grade and a public school through high school in the New York City area. My father, a physician, provided a comfortable life-style for us although we were never indulged. I never gave much thought to money. It was there if I needed something, but it was not limitless. College was a given and not a privilege.

In this age of enlightenment for women, I often reflect on how it was that my traditional dad imbued in me the sense that I could accomplish whatever I chose to accomplish while simultaneously telling me that my professional choices were nursing or teaching. I chose the latter as a springboard to my present career in psychology.

My young adult years were spent attending graduate school working first towards a master's degree and subsequently a doctoral degree in psychology. During this time, I was employed initially as an elementary school teacher and then a school psychologist. This latter position led to a special assignment on a project funded by the National Institute of Mental Health. The project focused on establishing educational programs for seriously disturbed and learning disabled children utilizing the skills of supervised paraprofessionals. My husband-to-be was one of the project coordinators.

Prior to our marriage, we had many in-depth conversations about the implications of the disparity in our ages and its potential impact on our intention to have a family. Since we were in allied professions that focused on the well-being of the individual, we were sensitized to this area in our personal lives in contrast to financial matters. This sensitivity was reflected in our lengthy, probing conversations. Conversely, we spent hardly any time discussing financial matters.

My husband's personal background included working from the age of 11 through the Depression years to earn money to obtain a higher education, including graduate degrees. There was no family money. Whatever he accrued was the result of his own earning power.

As time went on and we had two daughters, we discussed how to divide our available time to maximize their time with both of us. We made a conscious decision to shift our work loads. At this point in our lives, I had begun to develop a private psychological practice. By mutual agreement, he took a consulting job that provided him with considerable flexibility in terms of committed time, and I gradually increased my private patient hours from a few hours a week to two-and-a-half days a week. We shared equally in the raising of our daughters. However, again by mutual agreement, he managed our home and our finances. On innumerable occasions, he would say, "Mary, we really need to find time to review our financial structure because you need to be more familiar with this area of our lives." I would predictably reply, "Yes, you are absolutely correct," and equally predictably never made the time to do so. The last time this all-too-familiar script was replayed was January 1, 1980.

I was therefore totally unprepared to steer our financial ship following his death on January 21, 1980. At that time, our daughters were 10 and 15. My husband had no life insurance, and there were no provisions for the girls other than Social Security. So there I was on my own without warning: a single parent with total responsibility for my daughters. I would have to assume their financial support in full, run our house and expand my part-time practice if we were to survive financially. I was overwhelmed! Where to start? Where to turn? I had most familiarity with parenting, some familiarity with running the house and no financial knowledge.

I chose to start in the area in which I had the least knowledge. In this case, it was with our financial planner, who is now a valued friend and collaborator in this endeavor. There were several reasons. First, my husband and I had decided to consult a financial planner to help us look at this area of our lives. We had been recommended to Alex, met with her, liked her philosophy and felt she could be of assistance to us. It should not come as any surprise to the reader to learn that the work with Alex was almost exclusively handled by my husband. Second, she knew more about my finances than I did. Third, and perhaps of greatest importance, she had the comprehensive financial knowledge I knew I needed. In the process of sorting out where I stood, she was invaluable.

I often remind Alex of the time when, discussing some point with me over which I was equivocating, as usual trying to determine what George—my husband—would have wanted me to do, she turned to me and in a somewhat stern, frustrated, teacher to pupil manner said, "For heaven's sake, Mary, you make decisions every day in your work. What prevents you from making them in this area?" In a sense, at that moment I grew up monetarily. Although I have regressed on occasion, I have for the most part forged ahead rightly or wrongly as a responsible adult, not second-guessing myself or trying to do what I thought my husband or parents would want me to do.

Knowing in retrospect the mistakes I had made in resisting knowledge on a financial level and understanding some of the psychological factors responsible for my resistance, I wanted to join Alex in providing to widows, at a time when they are most vulnerable, some sort of guidance that integrates the psychological and financial aspects of this painful period in one's life.

Each of us has practiced in our chosen profession for over 25 years. This book is an outgrowth of personal and professional experiences with numerous widows during this time. From our experiences, we created the stories of four widows. The hypothetical profiles that follow were created to illustrate various personality traits, financial situations, ages and family circumstances. We hope these composites will help you identify factors in your own life that are likely to play a role as you move through the various stages of grief.

If your personal financial circumstances are very different from those of our hypothetical women, do not feel this book has no relevance for you. We have attempted to present financial problems that most widows have to address to some extent. Your personal finances may be different, but your needs are the same. Our composites are just that—"composites."

You might identify with the reactions of more than one or possibly all of these widows. The purpose of the profiles is to make this book not just a textbook or a helpful handbook but one to which a recent widow can relate in terms of her own experiences. As you read the ensuing chapters, you will follow the progress of these four widows as they rebuild their lives. In the process, you will be rebuilding your own life. We wish you the best on your personal journey to emotional and financial well-being *On Your Own*.

PART ONE

Picking Up the Pieces

CHAPTER 1

Reacting to Your Loss

And a woman spoke, saying, "Tell us of pain."
And he said, "Your pain is the breaking of the shell that
encloses your understanding."

KAHLIL GIBRAN

Introduction

According to the United States Census Bureau, in March 1990, there were 11,477,000 identified widows in this country out of an adult female population of 99,838,000. One can become a widow at any age. The 1990 census data indicate the age at which one becomes a widow and the numbers within each age range as follows:

Widows	Numbers
Under 25	10,000
25–29	47,000
30–34	86,000
35–39	145,000
40–44	202,000
45–54	688,000
55–64	1,931,000
65–74	3,597,000
75–84	3,593,000
85+	1,177,000

No married woman likes to dwell on the likelihood of becoming widowed, but it is a state or stage of life that any of us might be forced to assume without warning, whether or not we are ready to do so. A widow reacts to the loss of a spouse, regardless of cause of death, with certain emotional responses. The individual circumstances surrounding the death of a loved one will have an impact on the bereaved's response to the loss as well as the individual's personality characteristics. Both common denominators and individual circumstances need to be understood by the grieving woman. For example, universally experienced emotion may be manifested in different ways depending on the personality structure of a given woman. In this book, we will discuss two widely accepted theories of the grief process: the stage theory and the tasks of mourning theory. The bibliography at the back of this book lists several books that elaborate on these theories and the grief experience.

Prior to discussing the "stage theory," it is important to keep in mind that, although we refer to the emotions about to be described as stages, you might not experience them in a manner that moves smoothly from one step to another with no overlaps or regressions. For some, the grieving process is experienced as waves cresting and pounding against the shore, while for others it is experienced as climbing an endless, steep staircase with the top imperceptible.

The stages referred to are not defined by days, weeks or even years. Most individuals go through them in sequence, although the time required to move from one stage to the next varies with the individual. The amount of time you require to go through the various stages is the one that is right for you.

Stage One: Initial Shock Phase

The initial response to the death of a loved one is usually shock, disbelief, denial and a kind of numbness, regardless of the circumstances leading to the death. Most widows are aware of having experienced these emotions upon learning of the death of their spouse; however, the manner in which widows display these emotions varies considerably. For example, one woman may go through the time leading up to and through the funeral in what superficially appears to be a detached manner, responding calmly to questions and making decisions. Another woman may be incapable of making any decisions, leaving the arrangements to others while weeping ceaselessly. Surprising as it may be, despite the external differences, both women may be experiencing the same emotion.

This may be unexpectedly revealed months or years later when a friend or relative comments on something that occurred during the days immediately following the spouse's death. The widow may have no recollection of the incident even though she thought she had been in control and was functioning rationally. Often, she is surprised by this personal revelation.

The numbness or state of shock experienced in the generally brief initial stage of grief is the body's way of protecting itself. It is as if the body's emotional immune system had "kicked in" in an attempt to protect you from major emotional or physical illness. Unfortunately, the emotional trauma one experiences in response to the death of a loved one lowers one's total resistance on both the physical and emotional level. Following the immunized initial grief phase of the mourning process, it is not at all uncommon for widows to experience a recurrence of symptoms related to a previously diagnosed physical problem of their own or to develop either a physical or an emotional illness. These may include sleep disturbances, excessive fatigue, visual difficulties, eating difficulties, irritability, drastic mood swings and changes in bowel and bladder functioning. Some women even feel they are developing the symptoms their spouse experienced in the early part of his illness if an illness was the cause of death.

Stage Two: Sorting Out Phase

When you emerge from the initial stage of grief, many conflicting and rapidly changing emotions are frequently experienced. In this phase, the woman is beset by myriad emotional responses, including guilt, anger, frustration, yearning, betrayal, bitterness and sadness. Sometimes it is difficult for a widow to sort out just what she is feeling. If she is unable to locate an item for which the deceased spouse had primary responsibility, she may experience anger and/or frustration. These feelings may be directed toward the deceased spouse or turned inward toward herself. If it is the former, she may become guilt ridden for having such a response, whereas if it is the latter, she may become increasingly depressed. Alternatively, she may become unreasonably irritated with a family member and berate herself for doing so. One widow described herself as often feeling like an emotional yo-yo during this second stage of the grieving process.

Stage Three: Rebuilding Phase

The last stage of the mourning process is the time one begins to experience the dimension of self in a new way. It is a rebuilding process that leads to a redefined self-image. When you were first married, you brought to this stage in your life your background as a child, adolescent, daughter or young woman, and then you developed an identity of wife and perhaps mother. So, too, to this new stage of growth you will bring the totality of your past. Your previous self-image is maintained, but is reshaped by the needs and life-style of the new you.

Tasks of Mourning

A more recently proposed explanation of what takes place following the death of a loved one defines the grieving process in terms of "tasks." J. William Worden, author of *Grief Counseling and Grief Therapy*, and others suggest there are four tasks of mourning. Tasks are thought of by some as more in keeping with the process since by definition the word "task" does not imply a given time frame.

The first task of mourning is the acceptance of the loss. This task is impacted upon by a number of factors. If one's spouse dies from a lingering illness in which there was identifiable pain and a gradual decline in the ability to enjoy life, acceptance of the death often takes less time. If the death was sudden or occurred under questionable circumstances, such as an accident, homicide or suicide, this first task may take longer to accomplish. The age of the deceased and other significant losses endured within the recent past will likewise affect the first task.

For some, the quality of the marriage may be a factor. If your spouse never fulfilled your expectations, you may feel tremendous emptiness when he dies. It may be exceptionally difficult to accept that he is gone and your hope of someday realizing your dreams with him is no more.

For most women, the acceptance of the loss, which is the first task of mourning, occurs within two or three months. For others, it takes longer. The acceptance of the death of your spouse opens the door to the second task of mourning, which is responding to the pain of grief. This is similar to the second stage in the stage theory.

Many strong emotions are experienced at this time, including anger, rage, guilt, depression, withdrawal and feelings of isolation. Some widows report being overwhelmed by one emotion, while others report having some or all of these feelings. These rapidly changing emotions often leave them feeling frustrated and out of control. It is common to hear a widow express her concern about what she is now experiencing. This is often in contrast to her earlier reaction, which may have been less emotional.

If a widow feels she is recovering because she is experiencing minimal pain and begins the second task of mourning, in which pain is truly realized, she may feel she is regressing. This is not the case. It is rather a component of a process. If one is unable to complete any task, there is reason for concern. If such is not the case, recognize the pain you are currently experiencing is a healthy part of the grief process.

Sometimes well-meaning family members or friends encourage you to keep occupied and to become involved in a number of activities to prevent you from having these feelings. Although well intentioned, this is not good advice. It is very important and necessary to be allowed to express your loneliness, your pain and your rage as well as to be provided with an opportunity to talk about your loved one. You need to be able to express these feelings for as long as you need to in order to move on to the third task of mourning. Sometimes your friends and family may appear to be unwilling to listen to you. This usually reflects their discomfort. If this is the case, seek an appropriate individual or group with whom you are able to share your feelings (see chapter 2).

The third task of mourning is described by Worden as "adjusting to an environment in which the deceased is missing." Basically, this translates to how well you function as an individual without your husband. Are you appropriately handling the demands of daily life? While working on this task, it is necessary to address many details related to your husband's estate. This may include financial items, such as your budget and his investments as well as the more mundane aspects of daily life such as walking the dog or caring for the lawn. This is the time you begin to think about yourself as an individual woman rather than a wife.

In task four, you acknowledge that you are in a different place while realizing the role your deceased spouse played in your life. Although this person is no longer physically present in your life, he has become an integral part of the present you. You would not be the person you are today if you had not been his wife. In dealing with this task, you realize you are alive and continue to have needs, wants and desires. These human needs now have to be met in a different way than they were in the past.

When you reach this task, you need to evaluate such things as what you would like to do, what you need to do and how you would like to spend your time. You may have to acquire new skills or adjust to a different quality and style of life. It is a time when you emotionally withdraw from the deceased and focus on the living. Some widows feel renewed guilt when contemplating moving on or experiencing new things because their husbands are not there to share it with them. This is a feeling you need to overcome.

It is hard to suggest time frames in which these tasks of mourning are accomplished. However, it is unlikely that they will be completed in less than four seasons because you tend to reflect upon aspects of your life with your spouse in every season. You usually need to review special and ordinary events which occurred each season. The fourth task may not be completed until the end of the second year or the beginning of the third year of mourning. There are many emotions you experience while you are completing the fourth task. Sometimes you may feel so uncertain about what you would like to do or think you could do you become frustrated with yourself.

Conclusion

In summary, try to remember that you are engaged in a process: a painful process that must be experienced from beginning to end in order to reach a healthy new place. Both your individual characteristics and the degree to which you were happy in your marriage impact your recovery.

Death has been described by several as man's final stage of growth. As a widow, you, too, are in a growth phase. This growth phase is not of your own choosing, but one that is yours to mold following the healthy process of grieving.

We will now introduce you to our four hypothetical widows as they go through the various stages of recovery.

Scenario One: Diane

Diane, age 42, was contacted by Larry, a partner in her husband's law firm, who advised her that her husband had slumped forward in his seat in the midst of a partnership meeting and lost consciousness. When efforts to revive him had failed, the rescue squad was called and he was rushed from his downtown Washington, D.C., office to George Washington University Hospital. Larry said he would pick her up and take her to the hospital.

In a fraction of a second, Diane's world turned black. She felt paralyzed, rooted to where she stood in the familiarity of her kitchen with her hand on the phone. She didn't know what she had told Larry. Her three children, Alice (age 7), Jeremy (age 11) and Erin (age 15), were due home from school in an hour, and Jeremy had soccer practice. How long had she stood there? The next thing she knew, Larry was at the door.

Her next awareness was of being at the hospital in a small room, where a somber doctor stood before her. She really didn't know what he said other than Mark, her husband of 20 years, had had a massive heart attack and was dead. Even that she was uncertain about. Larry was there beside her talking in a rational manner to the doctor. Both of them pressed tissues into her hand to stem what she later realized was a flood of tears.

A nurse moved her to the room where Mark lay with things still attached to him. She supposed she should do or say something, but she felt only numb as she dabbed hopelessly at the tears that kept pouring from her eyes. Without warning, Diane's world had changed forever. Somehow, some way, Larry took her home after she had signed some papers. The children were huddled together in the family room, looking toward her for something. In her current state, she was unable to comprehend what.

Friends and family seemed to materialize out of nowhere and began to take over. Gratefully, she let them. Mark had always handled everything. She had felt so protected and cared for by him. Gradually, over the next several days, she comprehended that people expected her to make certain decisions and provide certain information. In her current emotional state, she was not capable of making decisions, nor did she have the information she was expected to have.

Before she married Mark, she had always been taken care of by her dad. She had moved from her parents' home to an apartment with Mark. At some point, Diane realized that her dad once again had resumed his parental role with her. It allowed her to feel somewhat safe, yet simultaneously uncomfortable. Somehow she got the message that Mark had not had a will. Apparently that was not good. Her dad was particularly critical of Mark for not having attended to this matter. She was hurt and angered that her father could think poorly of him at this moment.

Before marrying Mark, Diane had been a paralegal. She had prepared herself for this work in a college program. In fact, that is how she met Mark. They both worked for the same firm, the very one he was working for at the time of his death. He had risen to partnership status in seven years and the firm had grown from 10 people when they met to more than 100 today.

Over the years, with Mark's approval, Diane had spent increasing amounts of money on the household and the children. They lived in a $500,000 house, and she learned for the first time that she was responsible for a mortgage of about $300,000. She felt overwhelmed on all levels. She had always been supported by Mark, and now she didn't know where to turn. She was willing to accept help, advice, kindness from anyone who offered it.

In her initial response to the loss of her husband, Diane was incapable of comprehending the implications of her new state. She felt as though she was in some timeless place surrounded by fog and mist. She felt disconnected to life. Sometimes she was aware of saying something to her mom, dad, the children or Larry, but she felt detached from the woman who walked through the rooms of her home and responded to questions or comments.

There were so many people at the funeral. She was not certain who was responsible for the funeral arrangements. She knew she had been asked a great many questions, but other than selecting the clothes Mark was to be buried in while crying hysterically, she couldn't remember her answers to any of the questions.

Friends and relatives commented on what a beautiful funeral it was and how well liked Mark had been. Diane restrained herself from beating on them with her fists for their well-meaning but, for her, empty comments. She felt numb and alone—lost in her own disconnected world.

Diane's Profile

PERSONAL PROFILE WHEN WIDOWED

Age: 42
Occupation: homemaker (paralegal prior to marriage)
Husband: Mark
Age at time of death: 45
Cause of death: heart attack
Occupation: partner, law firm
Years married: 20
Place of residence: Bethesda, Maryland
Children: Erin (15)
            Jeremy (11)
            Alice (7)
Parents: Mother (65)
         Father (68)
Will: none

PERSONAL AND PROFESSIONAL SUPPORT PEOPLE AT THE TIME OF DEATH

Stockbroker: Scott Truitt
Insurance agent: Jack Blafford
Estate planning lawyer: Mary Sue Ryan
Mark's friend at the firm: Larry
Larry's wife: Gail

NEW PERSONAL AND PROFESSIONAL SUPPORT PEOPLE

Financial planner: Dorothy Trumbull
Firm benefits person: Karen Hutchinson
Erin's friend's widowed mother: Jennifer Greenberg
Jeremy's friend's divorced mother: Nancy Martin
Support group friends: Robyn, Marcy

Scenario Two: Susan

Susan, a 50-year-old executive with a nonprofit association based in Seattle, Washington, could not believe she was once again single. She had about given up the idea of marriage when she met Lance 13 years ago. They had been married for 12 years now and, despite their individual family demands, had been happy. She hadn't been able to process the events that led to his death. It didn't seem possible that it was only two weeks ago that she had been informed of his accident. A teenager ran a red light and plowed into his car. He had been taken to the hospital, where they identified internal bleeding as well as several broken bones. It was the complications stemming from the internal bleeding that subsequently caused his death in the early hours of the morning.

She was not feeling up to dealing with Lance's two children from his first marriage. They had never really accepted the fact that their father had married her. Adam, age 25, had recently begun to talk with his father about going to graduate school. Leslie, age 21, was a senior in college.

Lance, with his accounting background, had managed their finances. He always told Susan what he was doing, but she "tuned out" his lengthy explanations as to why he selected one investment over another. Due to her previous experiences, she considered herself a woman with a fundamental understanding of money matters even if she did not know the specifics of their current financial situation. Although she was dreading it, she knew she had the ability to take charge of her financial life.

In light of their individual financial responsibilities prior to their marriage, they had worked out a premarital agreement that left their respective assets to their dependents—his children in his case, her mother in her case. However, recently they had amended this agreement. Lance had decided to leave his $400,000 insurance policy in trust for his children. Susan would receive the income from this insurance trust until she died, and then the children would receive the principal. Lance's will stipulated his children would receive $20,000 each when he died. The rest of his assets were left to Susan. She assumed that once Adam and Leslie were apprised of these financial facts, they would be very upset and threaten to contest the will.

On this chilly morning, Susan's thoughts turned to the impact of Lance's death on her 74-year-old mother, who had considerable financial needs. She and Lance had recently begun to explore retirement communities for her after rejecting the idea of bringing her to live with them in their condo.

Upon learning of Lance's death, Ron, her 55-year-old brother, offered to help in any way possible. She had her doubts as to how much help he could really be. Funny, although he and Lance were the same age, she didn't think of them as contemporaries because Lance was so much more knowledgeable when it came to financial matters and had accomplished so much in his lifetime.

Susan needed to do something to remind herself that Lance was really gone. The last time she spoke to him was just before he left work the day of his death. They talked on the phone in the late afternoon as they usually did to discuss their plans for dinner and the evening. Lance had volunteered to pick up the milk and bread they needed on his way home from the office. She said she would start dinner, and they ended the conversation with their usual "I'll see you in a bit." Little did she know these would be the last words he would say to her. Nothing profound or unusual—just normal and comfortable. Now everything was abnormal and unreal.

Although others had offered, she had insisted on making all of the funeral arrangements herself. Ron had accompanied her, but she needed to make all of the decisions, down to the most minute details. This process helped her realize Lance would not be walking through the door at any minute. Ron had said at some point that he didn't know how she could deal with everything and remain calm. He said, although he had never been married, he didn't think he could handle such a trauma as well as she was handling Lance's death.

"If he only knew—I'm probably not handling it at all. I can't even believe it's real. I need to remind myself all of these arrangements are for my husband. It's just something to occupy my time that feels familiar." Susan felt Lance would have been pleased with the funeral. "How macabre," she thought.

Lance had wanted to be cremated, so at least she hadn't had to deal with selecting a coffin. She kept feeling her reactions were strange, but she was not prepared for such an event. Her husband had been a healthy man—why should she have given any thought to the likelihood of his death? Susan didn't like the lack of control of her thoughts and feelings.

Susan had much to do in the days ahead and she knew it, but she wasn't ready to face it. She kept telling herself she needed to focus on one day at a time and get through it. She just hoped and prayed that she would find the internal strength to meet the demands about to be made of her. She had no professional advisors of her own. She thought this was something she needed to correct in the ensuing weeks.

Susan's Profile

PERSONAL PROFILE WHEN WIDOWED

Age: 50
Occupation: executive, nonprofit
Husband: Lance
Age at time of death: 55
Cause of death: auto accident
Occupation: partner, CPA firm
Years married: 12
Place of residence: Seattle, Washington
Stepchildren: Adam (25)
                Leslie (21)
Parents: Mother (74)
Siblings: Ron (55)
Will: yes, plus premarital agreement

PERSONAL AND PROFESSIONAL SUPPORT PEOPLE AT THE TIME OF DEATH

Lance's friend: Harry
Harry's wife: Emily
Attorney: Tim Longwood
Stockbroker: Bob O'Brien
Lance's assistant: Sarah Stone

NEW PERSONAL AND PROFESSIONAL SUPPORT PEOPLE

Trust officer: John Stepstone
Assistant trust officer: Ms. Peabody
Psychologist: Dr. Catherine Coleman

Scenario Three: Audrey

Audrey, age 62, had spent the past year, as she had in previous years, trying to meet her husband's needs. John was 65 when he died following a protracted struggle with lung cancer. The majority of the last year of his life had been spent in the hospital. She had not missed a day of visiting him in the three months prior to his death. A part of her was relieved that the agony was over. Another part looked with apprehension at the tasks ahead.

John had been an executive with a major corporation in St. Louis, Missouri. He took early retirement at 62 due to his poor health. The couple had health insurance through his company. He had managed their personal finances and she had managed the home, particularly the entertaining, at which she was a master. She sometimes wondered how far John would have gone in the company if she hadn't been the excellent hostess she knew she was. As she and her daughter left the hospital this last day, the doctor commented on what a support she had been to John, and she realized just how draining the last few weeks had been. She was exhausted. She was confident that John Jr., age 40, would arrive shortly to give advice and take over any task requested of him and some that were not.

She had been married for 47 years. Where had the years gone? She and John had never really been happy. She had stayed with him because life never seemed that bad, there were children to consider and one just didn't divorce a man who had always provided for you!

Audrey knew that John had a will. She remembered they had met with the attorney to review it. Other than that, she knew practically nothing about their finances. John managed that aspect of their lives and told her on what specific items she could and couldn't spend money. She thought about the day they purchased their home for $50,000 22 years ago and what a major financial outlay it had seemed at the time. It was now worth about $200,000. She was glad that they had so little left to pay on the mortgage ($20,000).

Her thoughts moved to her daughter, who drove her home on this memorable day. Joanne, at 35, had three young children, and she and her husband Keith never seemed to really make ends meet financially. How different her children were, much like herself and John. She wasn't looking forward to dealing with John Jr. in the days ahead. She knew he meant to help, but she resented his patronizing manner. At one time, they had been really close, but since he had become successful as a physician, their relationship seemed to be different.

What would she do with her life? She had never worked. There were many unanswered questions that made her somewhat anxious, but at the same time she was experiencing something else, a new sense of being on her own for perhaps the first time in her life. In a way, that was appealing. She thought she would understand it all much better in the days ahead.

One thing that surprised her was her inability to realize that it was over. John had actually died. He had been ill for such a long time that the finality of it seemed somewhat unreal. She was having more difficulty accepting his death than she had thought she would. She couldn't get in touch with what she was feeling. Sometimes she thought she felt loss, yet other times she just felt numb. How odd, she mused.

Joanne, John Jr. and Audrey worked out the funeral arrangements. The children were both willing to do anything she felt unable to handle. She didn't really find the details of the funeral too taxing. The staff of the funeral home was most helpful, which made the process less painful. Their minister knew them very well, so it was relatively easy to discuss the eulogy and format.

Actually, what she found most difficult was talking to their many friends and John's coworkers. This was an unfamiliar feeling for Audrey. She was such a social person, yet she didn't quite know what to say to these people. On the one hand, she was sorry John had died, but on the other hand, she was relieved that the agony of this long, drawn-out illness was over. Somehow it didn't feel quite right to express these feelings even though they were very real to Audrey. She found she left most of the initial conversations with other people to the children.

She selected what she would wear to the funeral without weighing one outfit over another. It was almost as though she had previously made this decision, although she was not conscious of doing so. What an unfamiliar experience, thought Audrey. It was very different from her feelings when her mother and father had died. She didn't feel it necessary to sort it all out in the present, but she knew she would spend many hours reliving and reviewing her reactions.

Audrey's Profile

PERSONAL PROFILE WHEN WIDOWED

Age: 62
Occupation: homemaker
Husband: John
Age at time of death: 65
Cause of death: lung cancer
Occupation: corporate executive
Years married: 42
Place of residence: St. Louis, Missouri
Children: John Jr. (40)
        Joanne (35)
Grandchildren: Casey (14)⎫
          J.T. (12)⎭ John
          Jamie (6)⎫
          Heidi (4)⎬ Joanne
          Noah (2)⎭
Parents: deceased
Will: yes

PERSONAL AND PROFESSIONAL SUPPORT PEOPLE AT THE TIME OF DEATH

Lawyer: Mr. Humphrey
Mr. Humphrey's assistant: Sally
Physician: Dr. PaPadisio

NEW PERSONAL AND PROFESSIONAL SUPPORT PEOPLE

Financial planner: Mr. Silver
Cold call broker: Mr. Postman
Real estate agent: Georgia Brown
Friends: Lionel Dawson, Janet Pine

Scenario Four: Elizabeth

Elizabeth and Ben had been married for 55 years. She could barely remember a time when she hadn't been married. Now she was 75, and Ben had been 83 when he died. Eighteen years had gone by since he had sold his small business in the Boston suburbs. Ben's health had been deteriorating over the past several years, and she had become frustrated by his memory lapses and confusion. He had always been somewhat of a hypochondriac, but she thought it was his way of guaranteeing him of her attention. She wondered whether he would still be alive if she had taken his physical complaints more seriously. Yesterday morning, she had been unable to wake him. It had been only 24 hours since he had died, yet it felt like so much longer.

At 75, she had her own problems. She didn't know how she would manage alone. She had been depressed periodically over the last 15 years and had some heart problems, "nothing terribly serious," according to her doctor.

She and Ben never had any children. They had lived a simple life—a few friends, some entertaining and church suppers. Their comfortable home was worth approximately $150,000 now. It didn't seem possible it was worth so much. They had paid off the mortgage years ago, so they owned it free and clear. Ben always said he didn't want her to have any financial worries when he "kicked the bucket."

She knew Ben had some financial advisors, although she had never met them. She wondered how competent they were and how they would deal with her. She had no knowledge of their financial situation whatsoever. She thought Ben had a will. At some point, she remembered him telling her that they were worth half a million dollars, but she wasn't sure if she had understood him correctly. She wondered where it was and what it would mean to her.

Elizabeth knew she had to make arrangements for Ben's funeral. She had called her older sister, Abigail, as soon as the rescue squad told her they could not revive Ben and that he had passed away peacefully during the night. She had also called her pastor, who appeared almost immediately after her call.

Pastor Appletorn had been so considerate. He had contacted the funeral home and spoken to the director, who arranged to have Ben's body removed from the house. He told her which papers she had to sign and why they were necessary. He also insisted on contacting her closest friend, Mabel, and making sure she would be able to spend the night at her house so Elizabeth would not be alone. He promised to return when Abigail arrived to finalize plans for the funeral.

Elizabeth was frightened, yet numb. She didn't know what she was supposed to feel. She had never been alone. She had always had a role: daughter, sister and then wife. What was she supposed to do in this new role? Who would take care of her? She had always clung to the thought that Ben would be there to take care of her if anything happened to her, even when she knew he really couldn't do that any more. Now she could no longer even pretend he would be there. She had been so involved in caring for him that she had never given any thought to the fact that he might die. "Why hadn't I?" she mused. There must be something wrong with her.

Elizabeth was very nervous. It seemed she couldn't eat, or sit still or think about anything for more than a few minutes. She cried a lot, but she wasn't sure she knew why she was crying. She was just scared. She felt a little better after Abigail arrived because she had always looked out for her when they were young. She recalled Abigail teasing her about being "afraid of her own shadow."

Elizabeth let Abigail participate in making all the arrangements for the small church funeral for Ben. In fact, if she were really honest with herself, Abigail managed it all. She couldn't even decide what to wear. Abigail patiently looked through her closet and selected something dark and conservative. In the evening, Abigail tried to console Elizabeth, sometimes patting her hand and encouraging her to relax a bit. Part of Elizabeth felt as though she were lost someplace. It reminded her of the way she had felt following some minor surgery years ago when she was regaining consciousness—there, but not there. She hoped she would feel better soon.

Elizabeth's Profile

PERSONAL PROFILE WHEN WIDOWED

Age: 75
Occupation: homemaker
Husband: Ben
Age at time of death: 83
Cause of death: age
Occupation: retired business owner
Years married: 55
Place of residence: Boston, Massachusetts
Children: none
Parents: deceased
Siblings: Abigail (77)
Will: yes

PERSONAL AND PROFESSIONAL SUPPORT PEOPLE AT THE TIME OF DEATH

Pastor: Pastor Appletorn
Brash young lawyer: Mr. Carroll
Friend: Mabel

NEW PERSONAL AND PROFESSIONAL SUPPORT PEOPLE

New lawyer: Mr. Grossfeldt
Church friends: Sam and Julie Weatherly
Trust officer: Mr. Samuels
Assistant bank manager: Ms. Riley
Accountant: Mrs. Greenfield
Friend: Abe
Real estate agent: Mr. Winthrop

CHAPTER 2

Identifying Your Personal Characteristics

Polonius: This above all, to thine own self be true,
And it must follow as the night the day
Thou canst not then be false to any man.
                                                WILLIAM SHAKESPEARE

Introduction

In addition to those emotions experienced by all widows, there are individual differences that are the result of many factors, such as the circumstances surrounding the death of the loved one, your individual personality, your health, economic factors, your age, the ages of your children and whether or not you considered yourself happily married. For example, do you feel emotionally fragile in your current state? Are these feelings unfamiliar
to you, or are they compatible with your psychological functioning prior to your loss? Based on your knowledge of yourself, are these feelings likely to be of short duration or long-standing? Are you so emotionally distraught you would be reluctant to trust yourself to appropriately absorb information presented to you by a lawyer, an accountant or a financial advisor? You need to make this determination to enable yourself to move ahead in the manner that is best for you.

In contrast to the woman who is unable to mobilize herself from her emotional paralysis following her loss is the one who needs to be busy. Such a woman might feel the need to respond to her grief by occupying her time with making lists or itemizing things in order to regain a sense of control in her life. If you are such a woman, is this a pattern with which you are comfortable and familiar? Are concrete tasks helpful to you in meeting your emotional needs? Only you will be able to determine what is right for you.

It is desirable for each widow to develop an awareness of the personality characteristics that will impact her ability to handle stress, make decisions, take risks and function independently. In assessing yourself, take into consideration your basic personality traits and previous as well as present functioning. These individual personality differences will affect to a large extent your ability to steer your personal ship to psychological and financial independence.

It is important at this point in responding to your loss to identify those personal qualities that have played a dominant role in your life to date. The way in which you interacted with others and solved problems is determined in part by your personality characteristics. Perhaps you never gave this much thought and are unfamiliar with the qualities that dominate your decision-making processes. To help you in your self-analysis, we will describe three personality characteristics to which we believe all widows will relate. The ones we have selected are common to everyone. These individual factors are significant and will help you understand your reactions as you go through this experience.

1. Are You Primarily a Thinking or a Feeling Person?

Do you respond to your world on primarily a thought basis? In other words, prior to making a decision, do you gather as much information as you are able to obtain, weigh the alternatives, speak with a variety of people and develop flow charts or whatever else will allow you to make an informed decision? If so, you primarily utilize thinking or cognitive processes to reach conclusions.

Others are more spontaneous in their decision making. These individuals may wake up in the morning and decide on a given course of action based on the temperature, the sun or a mood. The differences between these two types may be illustrated in the manner in which they would place bets at a track. One individual studies the conditions of the track, the odds and the past performance of the horse, the jockey and the trainer, while the other places a bet on the horse's name, the colors of the jockey's shirt, the color of the horse or other item to which the individual has a personal response. This is not meant to suggest you never have any emotional responses if you describe yourself as primarily utilizing thought processes or vice versa. All of us have both components within us. What makes us different is the degree to which we utilize one characteristic or the other.

2. Are You Primarily Extroverted or Introverted?

It is also important to understand yourself in the area of extroversion and introversion. For example, if you are a woman who is outgoing, enjoys socializing with others, seeks the company of others and is frequently described as very friendly, companionable and active in any number of areas, you would be described as extroverted. If you are extroverted, you are more likely to seek out others for advice, support, information and even direction.

An introverted woman is one who tends to engage in more individual pursuits, such as reading, crafts, music or any activity one can do by oneself. If you are introverted, you are likely to look within yourself, obtain printed matter or consult a single trusted friend or spiritual leader in the formulating of a course of action or direction. Again, few of us fall exclusively in one category or the other. However, upon reflection, you will be able to identify that you lean toward one behavior pattern more than the other.

3. Are You Primarily a Dependent or Independent Individual?

Another important characteristic the widow needs to be aware of is her need to be dependent or independent. Some women have been conditioned or allowed themselves to believe that it was preferable to leave major decisions to their spouse. They were pleased to be taken care of by their husbands, protected and treated as though there was no need for them to be involved in any decision making outside of the home. Perhaps to the widow it was a statement of the spouse's love.

Others, regardless of their involvement with financial decision making, carved out an area of independent functioning for themselves. This may have been on a professional level, job, volunteer activity or artistic pursuit. These women may have wanted to be involved with the financial aspects of their married lives but felt it would be hurtful to the spouse or the marriage to challenge an economic decision or request inclusion when investments were made.

Research tells us that the loss of a spouse is the single most stressful event in an individual's life. For most of us, the task of managing our finances by ourselves follows the most significant event of our lives. This is basically true, regardless of one's personal circumstances at the time of death. For those few individuals who have managed the family finances during the course of the marriage, these statements are somewhat less applicable, although when interviewed, these women reported that their ability to function effectively even in this area of familiarity is somewhat diminished immediately following their loss. Obviously, the more familiar you are with your family's finances, the better able you will be to take charge of your situation following your initial adjustment to your loss.

Understanding which characteristics have dominated your personality throughout your life will assist you in determining the most helpful approach to your new personal situation. The following simple questionnaire (see figure 2-1) is designed to help you identify in a very general way those characteristics that dominate your decision-making processes.

Check the answer that best describes you. Do not spend a great deal of time agonizing over your answers. If any of the choices listed represent something you would participate in now, as a result of your present emotional state, but would not have participated in normally, respond with the choice you would have made in the past. This will more accurately represent you as a person.

Personal Characteristics

FIGURE 2-1

QUESTIONNAIRE

1. If I could select an activity that I would particularly enjoy, it would be to:

   [ ] A. Have an opportunity to attend or host a fairly large social gathering.

   [ ] B. Work on a craft project, garden or read a book.

   [ ] C. Participate with a few others in an area of interest such as a gardening club, church/temple or volunteer activity.

2. When deciding how to spend my time, I would most likely:

   [ ] A. Look to another person to come up with an idea.

   [ ] B. Identify what I want to do and do it or look through the newspaper for ideas if I had nothing specific in mind.

   [ ] C. Waver between doing something or waiting for someone to approach me with an idea or a plan.

3. When a friend approaches me with a personal problem, I:

   [ ] A. Identify with my friend's problem and get caught up in what he or she is feeling.

   [ ] B. Identify the nature of the problem and either obtain appropriate information for the friend or encourage him or her to adopt a practical approach.

   [ ] C. Would prefer not to get involved.

4. When a group with which I am affiliated takes on a project, I:

   [ ] A. Allow others to define the necessary tasks to complete the project.

   [ ] B. Usually assume a leadership role in relation to others.

   [ ] C. Prefer to work with others on a specified aspect of the project without assuming a leadership role or taking on a great deal of responsibility.

5. It is important for a woman to:

   [ ] A. Reflect in her behavior what she thinks others expect of her.

   [ ] B. Do what she wants, regardless of the opinions of others.

   [ ] C. Balance her personal needs and desires against her family's and friends' expectations.

6. When I see a TV program or watch a movie that depicts people having to deal with personal problems, I:

   [ ] A. Predictably identify with the victim and usually find myself feeling overwhelmed and in tears.

   [ ] B. Find myself creating a plan to deal with the problem, which includes fact finding and gathering of information.

   [ ] C. Try to imagine what it would feel like to be in that situation and determine what I would have done to deal with the crisis or problem.

7. When it comes to financial matters, I would most likely:

   [ ] A. Assume that everyone is more knowledgeable than I am and take the advice of almost anyone rather than trust my own judgment.

   [ ] B. Rely upon my own judgment after doing some research on the subject.

   [ ] C. Rely on my own judgment for simple decisions and rely on an expert for more complex ones.

8. If I had the opportunity to plan an ideal vacation for myself, I would:

   [ ] A. Prefer to take a trip with others to an unfamiliar place.

   [ ] B. Relax and stay at home.

   [ ] C. Find one place to vacation and return to it every year.

9. When I go shopping, I:

   [ ] A. Feel badly if a salesperson has been particularly nice to me, and I buy something from her whether I like the item or not.

   [ ] B. Make a list of what I need and follow it without allowing a salesperson to flatter me into a purchase I don't need.

   [ ] C. Attempt to buy what I need but allow myself to buy something that strikes my fancy.

10. When it comes to being with other people in a social setting, I:

    [ ] A. Enjoy both large and small social gatherings whether work related or close friends.

    [ ] B. Have never felt the need for much socialization outside my home.

    [ ] C. Prefer being with a few people focused on an area of mutual interest.

11. My friends think I:
    [ ] A. Cry over the slightest thing (e.g., sad movies).
    [ ] B. Am strong because I tend to be solution-oriented when it comes to problems.
    [ ] C. Sometimes am too emotional but at other times don't get easily rattled.

12. If I find myself with some free time, I:
    [ ] A. Immediately call a friend.
    [ ] B. Find something to do at home.
    [ ] C. Depending on my mood, would read a book, work on my current project, go to a concert, etc.

Now record your responses to these questions keeping in mind there are no right or wrong answers. This is merely to give you an idea of which characteristics tend to play a greater or lesser role in your individual personality structure. Score yourself on the table below.

	A	*B*	*C*
1.			
2.			
3.			
4.			
5.			
6.			
7.			
8.			
9.			
10.			
11.			
12.			

Questions 1, 8, 10 and 12 refer to the qualities of extroversion and introversion. Pure extroverts will answer A to questions 1, 8, 10 and 12. Pure introverts will answer B to those questions. An individual with characteristics of both extroversion and introversion is likely to respond with C on questions 1, 8, 10 and 12 or with a combination of A, B and C.

If we viewed this on a scale from 1–10 of pure introverted to pure extroverted characteristics, most women would fall more to one side than the other. Few individuals are purely introverted or extroverted. Determine where you would fall in an effort to better understand yourself.

Questions 3, 6, 9 and 11 refer to the qualities of thinking and feeling. Those who use primarily feeling processes in problem solving will answer A to questions 3, 6, 9 and 11. Those primarily responding on a thought level to problem solving would answer B. Those utilizing both feelings and thought, dependent on other variables, are likely to answer C to questions 3, 6, 9 and 11 or a combination of A, B and C.

Again, if this area were viewed on a scale of 1–10 of pure thinking to pure feeling characteristics, most women would fall more to one side than the other. Few individuals are purely thinking or feeling. Determine where you would fall in an effort to better understand yourself.

Questions 2, 4, 5 and 7 refer to the qualities of dependence and independence. Essentially dependent women will answer A to questions 2, 4, 5 and 7. Essentially independent women will answer B. A woman with characteristics of both dependence and independence is likely to respond with C to questions 2, 4, 5 and 7 or with a combination of A, B and C.

Here, too, if this area were viewed on a continuum from 1–10 of pure dependence to pure independence, most people would fall to one side or the other. One more reminder: There are no rights and wrongs.

Conclusion

To summarize, the brief and simple questionnaire you just completed was designed to help you identify for yourself those personality traits that are likely to influence the way you react to the demands made of you in your newly widowed state. Other factors and characteristics will affect your adjustment, but we have selected those that we have found to occur frequently in our work with widows. The characteristics described may occur in different combinations within an individual.

Check the description that most closely represents your primary characteristics in the three areas we have discussed.

thinking   ( )   feeling   ( )   mixed ( )
introvert ( )   extrovert   ( )   mixed ( )
dependent ( )   independent ( )   mixed ( )

Diane's Responses to the Questionnaire

	A	B	C
1.	X		
2.	X		
3.	X		
4.			X
5.			X
6.	X		
7.	X		
8.	X		
9.	X		
10.	X		
11.	X		
12.	X		

As you can see from Diane's responses to our questionnaire, she is primarily an extroverted, feeling woman who tends to be more dependent than
independent. As you also will see, in the months ahead, family issues will
motivate Diane to function more independently than at any previous time
in her life.

Diane's way of approaching life had primarily been on a feeling level.
She is extroverted, likes people and tends to utilize her senses when
formulating opinions. She is sometimes described as artistic. If she per-
ceives something to be a particular way, she accepts her perception and
rarely seeks objective information to corroborate her impression. She is the
one among her friends who is described as having a sympathetic ear when

her friends need to talk. She would often tell Mark her feelings about an individual, an event or even a movie, which would lead him to affectionately describe her as "wearing her heart on her sleeve."

Significant personality characteristics: extroverted, feeling, dependent.

Susan's Responses to the Questionnaire

	A	B	C
1.			X
2.		X	
3.		X	
4.		X	
5.			X
6.		X	
7.			X
8.	X		
9.		X	
10.	X		
11.		X	
12.			X

Susan is relatively independent. She has both extroverted and introverted qualities but leans toward the latter. She has always been an excellent organizer. Sometimes she doesn't pay sufficient attention to the feelings and ideas of others in her desire to get the task completed in the most efficient fashion. She is effective and relentless in her ability to accomplish a stated goal. She has always been viewed as an excellent executive in her organization. Within her company, she was known to have both innovative ideas and the skills to implement them. Her need to get the job done and look at the facts concerning a given issue is one of the qualities with which her stepchildren have always had difficulty. Nothing about her has endeared her to them.

Significant personality characteristics: mixed features of extroversion/introversion, thinking/feeling, dependence/independence.

Audrey's Responses to the Questionnaire

	A	*B*	*C*
1.	X		
2.			X
3.		X	
4.			X
5.			X
6.			X
7.			X
8.	X		
9.			X
10.	X		
11.		X	
12.			X

Audrey has always been somewhat outgoing. She is also realistic regarding her life. She has been described as having a great deal of common sense. Her friends sometimes look to her for assistance because of her matter-of-fact approach to their problems. She has made it a practice to base decisions in her area of the marriage on known facts. There is a part of her that analyzes facts without realizing she is doing so. She possesses a capacity to look at herself realistically, an openness to new ideas and the ability to change.

Significant personality characteristics: mixed features of extroversion/introversion, thinking/feeling, dependence/independence.

Elizabeth's Responses to the Questionnaire

	A	*B*	*C*
1.		X	
2.	X		
3.			X
4.			X
5.	X		
6.	X		
7.	X		
8.			X
9.	X		
10.		X	
11.	X		
12.		X	

Elizabeth has always been a somewhat dependent person in need of a great deal of support. She is usually happier by herself or with small groups. Throughout her life, she has placed a high priority on loyalty and consideration for the welfare of those closest to her, particularly her husband Ben. She tried to make sure their home was a very comfortable place. The activities she enjoys the most are her various arts and crafts projects. She has been particularly proud of her needlepoint and quilting. She cares deeply about the misfortunes of others, whether it is someone she sees on TV or a personal acquaintance. She relates simplistically to her world, usually relying on her feelings and her senses in her assessment of others. She has tried to follow the golden rule: "Do unto others as you would have them do unto you" with considerable success.

Significant personality characteristics: introverted, feeling, dependent.

CHAPTER 3

Dealing with Your Emotional Needs

"Mourning is essentially a process of unlearning the expected presence of the deceased."

ELIZABETH KUBLER ROSS

Introduction

At some point, the finality of one's loss becomes real. It might be in a matter of days, weeks or even a month or more. It is at this moment that you realize your husband is no longer there to protect you or to rely upon for emotional or financial support. It is a painful awareness, one often accompanied by an emotional response. In order to move forward and act productively upon this awareness, you must assess the degree to which your emotional state is affecting your actions and judgments.

Your response to the death of your spouse has at least three components. The first relates to the way in which you experience the grief process. Mental health professionals have identified that there are stages to your response to your loss. The second is dependent on your specific personality characteristics and personal circumstances—for example, the extent to which your spouse has financially provided for you. The third has to do with the nature of the marital relationship. Was it conflicted or fulfilling?

Family and Friends

If you are surrounded by family members and close friends when your husband dies, they will undoubtedly make every effort to be there for you in whatever way will be helpful. This may include preparing food, assisting with the funeral arrangements, contacting out-of-town relatives and friends or anything else you may request of them. You are fortunate if you have your loved ones around you during this painful period, but keep in mind that they may not continue to be available to you in this way for any extended time.

In our highly mobile society, at the time of loss, you may find yourself in a city in which you have no close family members or friends. Being surrounded by loved ones at a time of personal loss is both emotionally supportive and helpful. Somehow it is easier and safer to express your feelings within your family unit or to long-standing friends than to others.

Thus, when one is alone or isolated from family at the time of loss, it is important to find a substitute for what the family would have provided in a different era. Don't feel embarrassed because you are feeling weak and need the support of others. It's normal! Simply allow yourself to act upon your realization of this need.

If you are uncomfortable displaying emotion, it may be difficult for you to allow your friends to know you need support. Perhaps you do not know how to ask for help. Sometimes, although willing to help, friends don't know what to do or how to approach you. If your support group consists primarily of friends, allow them to be there for you. Don't think you are imposing on them. Friends, by definition, are there for both the good and bad times. Allowing yourself to depend on existing friends does not preclude the advisability of seeking new people in your life. You may even feel more comfortable sharing your feelings of loss with someone in similar circumstances than with those with whom you have previously been close.

Following their loss, many widows find themselves in need of some special assistance beyond that available from family and friends. Those first contacted for additional help or support are usually the personal physician or spiritual counselor. Keep in mind, however, this person's role.

The roles of a physician, spiritual advisor or mental health professional are disparate and unique.

Physician

If you find your behavior, for what appears to be an excessive period of time, to be uncharacteristic of you and simultaneously you do not feel connected to your life, seek some help. Sometimes it is difficult for you to determine whether what you are experiencing is within the norm or beyond it. It is advisable to inquire. It is likely to be more harmful to remain miserable and uncertain.

Your physician is an excellent individual with whom to discuss whether or not what you are experiencing is normal for the grief process. He or she is aware of what you have recently gone through and is in a good position to help you understand what you are experiencing. The physician can prescribe medications if needed or make referrals to others who can help. He will also work with you to identify the type of help likely to be most beneficial to you and refer you to the appropriate individual or facility to provide this support.

Spiritual Advisors

Because some widows feel unable to move forward without coming to some personal terms with the death of their spouse, they may feel the need for private talks with a spiritual advisor. This might be a minister, a priest, a rabbi or another designated person. Spiritual advisors have considerable experience counseling people who have suffered a loss.

In addition to the physician and spiritual advisor, there are others available to provide more specialized assistance in the areas of grief and loss. Included in this group are widow support groups and mental health practitioners familiar with the specifics of loss and grief.

Widow Support Groups

Some women feel the need for the companionship of others who have gone through a similar experience for comfort in contrast to seeking the support of a spiritual advisor or physician. If, for example, prior to your loss you were essentially a gregarious individual who enjoyed the company of others, you might benefit most from a widow support group. Having an opportunity to share your feelings with other widows is often very reassuring.

As indicated, your existing friends, although wanting to help, may be unfamiliar with what you are going through. You and your husband probably socialized primarily with other couples. Now, as a widow, you may feel less comfortable with your coupled friends. When they invite you to join them in an activity, you may feel it is not because they truly enjoy your company, but because it is "the right thing to do." Another common problem is what to do about the bill in a restaurant. The husband(s) might insist on paying your portion of the bill, which might make you uncomfortable.

Joining a widow support group will provide you with an opportunity to share your feelings with others in similar circumstances. You will hear from other widows how they responded to these situations and how they solved the problem for themselves. Here, too, you will be in a position to develop new social contacts without the awkward aspects of associating with couples.

Widow support groups vary in format from place to place, and within areas, but they are basically widow-to-widow, woman-to-woman group situations. Some groups have a professional leader, or leaders, while others do not. Some have a defined number of sessions, while others are more open and ongoing. The cost varies. Some base their fees on a predetermined number of sessions, while others allow one to pay a nominal fee per session attended. Some groups focus on the widow with minor children at home, others on the older widow, while still others have a broad age range.

Customarily, the groups are small, providing an opportunity for the widows to get to know each other well. In fact, many women extend these contacts beyond the group. It is not uncommon for strong bonds to develop among the widows. These friendships long outlast their active participation in the widow support group. Some women have told us they don't know how they would have made it through the first months of widowhood without the support of the women in their group.

No one agency or facility sponsors such groups. For the most part, one finds out about them from a friend, physician or spiritual counselor. If you don't know of any in your area, consult the American Association of Retired Persons (AARP) *Directory of Widowed Persons Services* (see Bibliography). Few widow support groups have an outreach program.

Sometimes churches and synagogues offer groups for the recently bereaved. You might like to attend such a group in lieu of a widow support group. For information regarding such groups, it is best to contact someone at your own church or synagogue. If they do not have any groups of this nature, they will probably be able to direct you to a facility that does.

Mental Health Professionals

If you are not inclined to consult your primary care physician or a spiritual advisor about what you are experiencing, but feel or fear you are in a dysfunctional state, here are some guidelines to assist you in determining whether or not you might benefit from some professional help.

If, for example, you don't understand much of what you are experiencing, feel emotionally out of control a great deal of the time, have rapid and extreme mood swings, find yourself having difficulty organizing and sustaining any thought pattern, you may want to consider consulting a mental health professional or grief counselor. Do not feel embarrassed or "crazy" if you decide you would like to seek the services of such a professional. Like your physician, this individual will help you determine if what you are experiencing falls within the usual range of emotions experienced following a loss or if there are more serious issues that need to be addressed.

There are many types of counselors available to help one through this difficult period. There are psychiatrists, psychologists, social workers and counselors specializing in issues of loss or grief. We are presenting an overview of the background and training of these specialists to help you understand the differences among them.

Psychiatrists

A psychiatrist is a doctor who has gone to medical school, completed a medical internship and then completed a psychiatric residency, frequently at a hospital specializing in the care of the mentally ill. He or she may have obtained additional training in a given treatment technique. Psychiatrists are the only mental health practitioners allowed to prescribe medication to alleviate the debilitating feelings associated with depression and other disorders.

Psychiatrists may also provide psychotherapy on an individual or a group basis. They bill you for their professional time on a fee-per-session basis, with the fees for individual sessions being somewhat higher. Make sure you understand the fee structure and office policies of the individual practitioner you select. He or she will be pleased to share this information with you. Some even have the information in writing so you will have an opportunity to review it at home. (Health insurance coverage for these sessions will be discussed later in the chapter.)

A qualified psychiatrist is licensed to practice in the state in which you live. He or she will have met the requirements to practice medicine with a specialty in psychiatry. As with other physicians, the psychiatrist will probably have licenses and training certificates displayed on the wall. If not, inquire.

Psychologists

After completing four years of college, psychologists enter a master's or a straight doctoral program to study both normal and abnormal behavior. After completing this part of the training, those who decide they want to work with people on a therapeutic level or clinically move to an appropriate internship program in an approved treatment facility. Here, training under supervision in psychotherapy is provided. Many undergo additional training in a particular therapeutic approach. In terms of providing therapy to clients, there is considerable similarity between that provided by a psychiatrist and a psychologist. Presently, psychologists are unable to prescribe medication for their clients, but they do provide both individual and group therapy.

Psychologists' fees are charged on a per-session basis. The psychologist will clarify the fee structure and office practices either before or at the time of your first session. Many give their clients a written statement of policies and practices as well as answer any questions you may have.

Psychologists are licensed to practice by the state in which they work. They have qualified to perform the service they provide by satisfactorily completing a licensing exam. Evidence of training and licensure is usually visible in the person's office. Never hesitate to ask if you are uncertain.

If you do not know anyone in a position to provide you with a referral, contact the State Psychological Association.

Social Workers

Licensed social workers also have a specific training program. These individuals, following the completion of a college course of study, frequently proceed to a master's level and sometimes to a doctoral level, with an emphasis on individual and community services. Social workers also complete an internship in their particular area of interest. Here, too, many licensed social workers find themselves working with individuals or groups in a manner similar to psychologists or psychiatrists. Social workers do not need to complete a doctoral program to treat individuals with emotional problems.

Social workers bill their clients for professional time in the same manner as psychiatrists and psychologists. The social worker's fee is based on his or her background and training, and is usually lower than that charged by a psychologist or psychiatrist. There are always individual differences, but in general, a psychiatrist would charge more than a psychologist, and a psychologist would charge more than a social worker.

Professional Counselors

There are other counselors who are not psychiatrists, psychologists or social workers but have a master's level education specializing in a given area, such as grief counseling. These individuals are recognized as "certified professional counselors" if they have completed the course of study and internship required by the jurisdiction in which they work. They are licensed by the state in which they practice and display their license in their office. These individuals would charge a fee for services rendered comparable to that charged by social workers.

Licensing for mental health professionals as well as physicians and dentists is handled by the department of health and mental hygiene in the appropriate jurisdiction. All of the above disciplines require continuing education credits on an annual basis in order for one to maintain a license to practice. Continuing education requirements are determined by each profession.

Medical Insurance

Many health insurance policies include coverage for mental health services. In general, psychiatrists and psychologists are recognized mental health providers, while there is considerable variation in the coverage for the services provided by social workers and counselors. If you have any questions about your insurance plan, contact your carrier to clarify your coverage. If you are unable to deal with this yourself, ask a family member or close friend to obtain the information for you. If your health insurance plan provides coverage for such consultations, the mental health provider will assist you in obtaining the appropriate reimbursement for the services rendered. Those of you who have managed care plans must contact the group for information as to how to obtain service for mental health issues.

Conclusion

Regardless of how you have viewed yourself in the past, this may be a time to seek out the services of someone with experience in the area of behavior and loss or the support of others experiencing what you are experiencing. Do not feel that if you decide to talk to someone, you will have to lie on a couch and go into extensive detail about your childhood before you are able to discuss your present problems. You may want a few sessions with a specific focus or a more open-ended process. Whatever you seek, keep in mind that the choice is yours, and the purpose is to help you through a time of maximum stress in your life.

In general, when seeking the services of a mental health professional (because it is such an interactive relationship), it is desirable to interview more than one individual before deciding on a given person. The mental health professional's sensitivity to what you are experiencing, and his or her receptivity to helping you with what you feel you need to address, should be your primary focus. If your first contact does not feel right for you, seek another referral.

A friend, relative, doctor or spiritual advisor may be of help providing you with a referral to a specific therapist with whom he or she has had a positive experience or knows of someone who did. This mental health advisor should be familiar with women's issues and/or the grief experience. Regardless of what you are feeling, make an effort to identify what you need and try to locate the appropriate individual, group or agency for help.

In large measure, your personality type and the way you dealt with emotional issues in the past will determine the approach that best meets your needs. Some widows need time alone to work through what they are feeling. Those of you in this category might find yourselves taking long walks, listening to music or engaging in some other solitary activity. If this approach works for you, use it. If this is contrary to your normal way of responding to stress and represents withdrawal and depression, seek outside help.

Last, but certainly not least, in this discussion of initial emotional needs is the role of exercise. Exercise is an excellent way not only to stay fit but also to reduce tension and stress. Many widows who were involved in an exercise program before their husbands died have found themselves increasing the time they devoted to their exercise program after they were widowed. They found that it helped them deal with the grieving process. If you are not currently involved in an exercise program, this is a good time to begin one. You can start such a program gradually with something like walking on a regular basis.

Despite the fact that you have little or no energy to devote to something unfamiliar in your daily life, try to do something that will bring new people into your world. It might be something as simple as engaging in a short conversation with someone you've met in conjunction with your new responsibilities or talking to a salesperson.

We cannot sufficiently stress the point that there is no one right or wrong approach for all widows. This is the time for you to assess the desirability of managing on your own versus seeking the assistance of someone else. In making this decision, consider your basic personality traits and present emotional state. Whatever you do, make yourself and your needs your priority. Even if you feel others need you, keep in mind that your ability to help anyone is dependent on your ability to help yourself.

Whether or not you decide to seek additional support on a group level or an individual level will be shaped in part by cost considerations and by your own personality characteristics. Your knowledge of yourself, your current emotional state and your responses to the short questionnaire you recently completed should help in making this determination.

Here are some suggested organizations that may be able to assist you:

Directory of Widowed Persons Services
American Association of Retired Persons
601 E Street, NW
Washington, DC 20049
(202-434-2260)

American Psychiatric Association
1400 K Street, NW
Washington, DC 20005
(202-682-6000)

American Psychological Association
750 First Street, NE
Washington, DC 20002-4242
(202-336-5500)

National Association of Social Workers
750 First Street, NE
Washington, DC 20002
(202-408-8600)

Bereavement and Loss Center of New York
170 East 83rd Street
New York, NY 10028
(212-879-5655)

National Self-Help Clearinghouse
Graduate School and University Center
City University of New York
33 West 42nd Street, Room 620N
New York, NY 10036
(212-642-2944 or 212-642-1600)

THEOS (They Help Each Other Spiritually)
1301 Clark Building
717 Liberty Avenue
Pittsburgh, PA 15222
(412-471-7779)

In subsequent chapters, you will follow the choices our hypothetical women made in obtaining the help they needed in dealing with the loss of their husbands.

Diane: Reactions to Dealing with Her Initial Emotional Needs

At some point, without the widow necessarily realizing it, enough time passes or something happens that moves her out of her sense of numbness into a more mobile state. One of the more common factors leading to revitalization following the initial impact of personal loss is concern for one's offspring. This is more true for women with dependent children under the age of 18, but it applies to those with older children as well. This is understandable since concerns about children attach to a more familiar role based on the past, yet they take on new form in your present situation. Whether or not your children are minors, you tend to be concerned about the impact of the loss on them both financially and psychologically.

Diane had a hard time focusing on anything in the initial stage of grief. She was so disoriented and upset as the result of the sudden death of her husband she could not think clearly. She was using all her energies just to stop crying. However, several weeks after Mark's death, she awakened one morning and, after her initial familiar feelings of terror and vulnerability had subsided, for the first time, she thought about what her children must be going through.

Up until this point, she had functioned in an automatic manner, going through the motions of daily responsibility and signing some papers that her dad and Larry said needed to be signed. On this particular morning, she thought about the children. She really had not had the emotional strength to address their needs at all. She contemplated what they must have been going through without their father, even though they never really had much of an opportunity to spend daily time with him, and a nonfunctional mother. In a sense, the children had been forced to manage without either parent following Mark's sudden death.

She had to become more functional, but what could she do? If only she knew someone who had had a similar experience. As a couple, she and Mark did not know anyone whose spouse had died. Clearly, their friends would be unable to relate to her present situation. Then she remembered Erin mentioning that her friend Nicole's dad had been killed in a boating accident a few years ago. She didn't even know Nicole's mother's name.

Diane felt somewhat ashamed of herself when she recalled her matter-of-fact, casual response of "Oh, that's too bad" when Erin told her about it. Here she was some years later in the same situation.

Diane determined to ask Erin for the name of Nicole's mother. She wanted to talk to her and find out how she had dealt with these unbearably painful feelings. When Erin returned from school, she gave her Nicole's mother's name, Jennifer Greenberg, and the phone number. Diane wasted no time in contacting her. She even surprised herself in not being concerned about how this would appear to Nicole's mom. Jennifer turned out to be very understanding and helpful. She spent almost an hour talking to Diane.

For the first time since Mark had disappeared from her life, Diane felt there was someone out there who understood what she was feeling. Perhaps it was just that she didn't feel quite so alone in the world. Jennifer had many helpful suggestions. She told Diane she didn't know how she would have survived without the help of the women in her widow support group. Diane shivered at the mere use of the word "widow." That's what she was, though, a WIDOW, so she had better try to accept it.

A widow support group—she had never heard of such a thing. Jennifer explained how they worked. The one she went to met once a week for eight weeks in nearby Chevy Chase. Jennifer knew that the coordinator, Lisa, would be able to provide a great deal of support to Diane. She told Diane she had become very close to two of the women in her group. They had even gone on a vacation together this past summer. She said she was working now but would be available to Diane to provide support and information. Diane thanked her profusely. "What a warm, caring person she is," Diane thought. She called Lisa immediately upon hanging up the phone and left a message on her answering machine. For the first time since she learned of Mark's death, Diane felt calmer, but she wasn't sure why.

As we have noted earlier, Diane is primarily a feeling, extroverted and relatively dependent woman. Therefore, it is consistent with her previous patterns for her to turn to others for advice.

She and Mark had decided to place the children in private schools because they believed they provided a better educational environment. Would they be able to continue at these schools? Diane had no idea. With her feeling approach to life, she was able to get in touch with what the children were likely to be feeling. Emotionally, the children had been left to fend for themselves. She resolved to listen to what they were expressing on an emotional level. She also needed to pay attention to what was being told to her about her economic situation because it would have an impact on all of them. If at all possible, she wanted to maintain the children in their present schools, even if it meant making some sacrifices.

Although a logical and pragmatic approach to life was not part of Diane's personality structure, her strong feelings about what she wanted for her children would, in the weeks ahead, be helpful in mobilizing her and enabling her to comprehend what steps needed to be taken in order for her to assess her total financial situation and eventually make this decision which she believed would have a major impact on the development of her children. At this moment, they were the most important consideration in Diane's life.

She resolved to ask her friends how to go about assessing the viability of the private schools for the children. On an emotional level, she knew she didn't want to get into this with her dad or Larry. Surely her friends would be helpful in this area.

Susan: Reactions to Dealing with Her Initial Emotional Needs

Susan had a hard time accepting that Lance was dead. The fact that he had died suddenly complicated her situation. This was not surprising since dealing with sudden death, particularly in a healthy person, compounds the early phases of the mourning process. Techniques she had used in the past to deal with difficult times were not working for her. However, she had never had to deal with something so traumatic. She thought she could have handled Lance's death if he had been older or had had a long-term illness. In fact, he had always been healthy, so his death was totally unexpected. The only way she could move from her current state of disbelief and shock to some semblance of functioning was by resuming patterns of behavior she had utilized throughout her life. As observed in her responses to our questionnaire, she had always had a pragmatic approach to life and been attentive to details. In her work experience, she had always found it helpful to make lists of matters with which she needed to deal and possible ways to approach issues.

Shortly after the funeral, Susan began to compile lists of matters she needed to deal with related to Lance's death and the order in which they needed to be addressed. It was helpful to do something which felt familiar, something beyond her emotional paralysis. This activity enabled her to feel more in touch with the world and daily events. It was as if her emotional life existed in its own orbit, separate from the requirements of daily life.

While the list making allowed Susan to feel more in touch with life, it also made her realize she was spending her time writing and rewriting her lists, prioritizing and reprioritizing, but she couldn't get started. She was becoming frightened. This was not characteristic of her. She had always been able to act on that which needed to be done in a timely manner. It was one of the qualities Lance appreciated most in her. She wondered how long she would be in this state of inactivity, unable to move.

She had to do something to come to grips with what was happening to her, but what? She recalled a TV talk show she once saw that focused on various mental health professionals dealing with different aspects of grieving. At the time, she had commented to Lance, "I wonder why anyone would want to spend every day dealing with death." Now she thought this very type of person might be able to help her better understand what was happening to her. Was what she was experiencing normal for women in her circumstances, or was something more serious happening to her?

Susan reflected on the time 14 years ago when she had considered seeing a mental health professional to better understand her feelings about never having married. Actually, it was shortly before she had met Lance. She wondered if she still had the name and address of the woman she had been referred to by one of her coworkers. At the time, her coworker had indicated this was a therapist interested in dealing with women and women's issues. Susan wasn't sure her present situation as a widow was one with which this doctor had any familiarity. On the other hand, she was a woman and this was an issue for her. She guessed this doctor would tell her whether she had the skills to work with her or not. Susan thought she'd feel better if she could talk to someone about what was happening to her who was familiar with these kinds of feelings.

Although she hadn't wanted to admit it to herself, she had begun to feel symptoms of menopause prior to Lance's death. She based this on her realizing she had been feeling hot or cold for no apparent external reason, and more irritable, which was out of character for her. She was also experiencing other signs, including unfamiliar mood swings, increased fatigue, changes in her sleep patterns and, what she was most afraid to acknowledge, memory lapses. She knew she needed to discuss her fears about her total functioning with a professional. Was what she was experiencing her response to Lance's death, or was it menopause, or did the two impact on one another? Susan knew she could not explore this with a man, even though she accepted that there were competent male doctors. How she hated feeling this way!

Susan didn't want to burden her mother with her worries because she had her own problems, and her brother Ron wouldn't know how to help her.

Since Lance's death, she had had considerable difficulty sleeping through the night. It had been helpful to her to have her trusty note pad at her bedside to jot down her thoughts and feelings. It was clear to her from reviewing these notes she needed some professional help.

She thought she still had the doctor's name and phone number in her office Rolodex. She'd look it up and see if she was still in practice. If she couldn't locate her, Susan thought she would ask another woman in her office for the name of the person she'd taken her daughter to see when her daughter had had a miscarriage.

Susan knew she needed to get beyond her present state. There was too much to do, and she didn't have the luxury of remaining immobilized. She acted on these feelings that very day. She located the doctor's name, and as she stared at the number in her Rolodex, she realized her palms were sweating. Slowly, she tapped the numbers on her touch-tone phone and heard the phone ringing. A woman answered, "Dr. Coleman's office." Susan was pleasantly surprised—this was like calling any other doctor's office. She wondered why she had anticipated this phone would be answered in a very different manner from any other doctor's office phone. She was taken so off guard the woman had to repeat, "Dr. Coleman's office." Susan asked if Dr. Coleman dealt with grief issues. The woman told her Dr. Coleman was a psychologist familiar with grief counseling, but her practice was not limited to this area. She suggested Susan make an appointment to meet with Dr. Coleman and discuss her specific needs. She gave her the address and a lunchtime appointment for the following Thursday.

Susan was glad she finally had found the strength to see Dr. Coleman.

Her office wasn't at all intimidating. It was in an office building not far from where she worked. Dr. Coleman was very reassuring and comforting without making Susan feel there was something wrong with her for seeking professional help in dealing with Lance's sudden death. She explained to Susan she could help her address what she was experiencing emotionally. She confirmed that her emotional responses were indeed intensified because she had begun to experience normal physical and emotional changes related to menopause.

Dr. Coleman said she had worked with other widows in Susan's situation and appreciated how difficult it was for anyone in such a vulnerable state to begin to deal with all the necessary paperwork. They would, therefore, also focus on the demands of daily life. When Dr. Coleman used the word "widow," Susan was taken aback. Her image of a widow was someone her mother's age. She'd have to look at why she had such a negative response to this word. She should probably discuss it with Dr. Coleman, but there was not time for that today because her session was just about over. She thought it would be important to start with these feelings in her next session.

When Susan left Dr. Coleman's office, having scheduled her next appointment, she felt not quite so alone for the first time since Lance had died. She knew this was an important step for her.

Audrey: Reactions to Dealing with Her Initial Emotional Needs

It was about three weeks after John's death, but it felt to Audrey like the first morning since the funeral. She sat at the scarred wooden breakfast table and had her morning coffee by herself. She allowed herself to think about her future. She had come to appreciate such private moments during the particularly demanding last months of John's life.

Audrey, without realizing it, had given a good bit of thought to her needs following John's death. She had accepted life without John as something more than an existence to be endured. Her new status would allow her to explore as yet unidentified avenues she would not have had the courage to investigate while John was alive. She didn't know why that was so, but she was sure that it had been the case. She was determined to take personal charge of her situation and not allow her son to assume the role of primary advisor and decision maker, which, knowing him, she felt confident he intended to do.

She had not met with John's attorney in years but knew that he would be the one to handle John's will. She determined to make an appointment with him to see him by herself. If she found herself able to relate to him and understand what he told her, she would move ahead on her own. If she didn't feel ready to move forward on her own, she would ask her daughter Joanne to accompany her and later John Jr. She wanted him to know that she appreciated his caring and concern but was not a feeble basket case unable to think or act on her own.

Audrey's pragmatic yet thought-oriented approach to life enabled her to think reasonably well in her approach to her new circumstances. Perhaps more so than in the situations of our other widows, John's lingering illness had gradually accustomed her to her new state.

Audrey stretched and moved to the sink to place her coffee mug in the dishwasher. In doing so, she caught a glimpse of herself in the large hall mirror. She was startled to see how much thinner she appeared. She went upstairs to her colorful yellow and blue bedroom and took a good look at herself in the bedroom mirror. She certainly had lost weight. She hadn't even realized it. She wasn't really feeling sick. She was more tired than usual, but she had attributed her fatigue to the toll John's illness had taken on her. What about her weight? It was clear her clothes didn't fit right anymore. She wondered when all this had happened. The green plaid skirt she removed from her closet this morning was at least an inch too big around the waist. Why hadn't she realized this before? It certainly didn't just happen. She couldn't remember when she had last prepared a meal for herself. She usually grabbed some crackers and cheese or other snack in the evening with a cup of tea.

Audrey didn't want to overreact or underreact. Certainly weight loss was one of the first symptoms of what was subsequently diagnosed as lung cancer in John. She had a positive attitude about life and the future but didn't feel comfortable ignoring these health concerns. Better to be safe than sorry. She didn't even need to look up Dr. PaPadisio's phone number. It was engraved in her mind. She dialed the all-too-familiar number, identified herself to the receptionist, who expressed her sympathy about John's death, and asked for an appointment for an annual physical. As she did so, she recalled she hadn't had a physical since John's cancer had been diagnosed two years ago.

Elizabeth: Reactions to Dealing with Her Initial Emotional Needs

Elizabeth, at 75, with few outside interests or support people, was emotionally very needy. She had really never been on her own before. Her older sister, Abigail, had come up from Florida to be with her for the funeral. Elizabeth felt safer having her in the house with her but was embarrassed by her dependency on her older sister for support. It should have been the other way around. She wondered if Abigail was more confident because she had never married and had been forced to make so many decisions for herself. She was dreading her departure and begged her to extend her stay. Abigail did stay for a few more days but finally had to return to her retirement home in Florida. She encouraged Elizabeth to give some serious thought to moving to Florida to be closer to her, and Elizabeth promised to consider it.

After Abigail left, Elizabeth felt alone. She was terrified, panicked, and she didn't know where to turn. How would she survive? Her thoughts raced in all directions. Suddenly, she remembered that her minister, Pastor Appletorn, had made a home visit shortly after Ben's funeral. It had felt good to see his familiar, friendly face. He had encouraged her to come see him at the church. She felt safe with him, too, and in her loneliness determined to accept what she viewed as his ministerial but kind offer to make an appointment to see him. She hoped that he would be able to provide her with some guidance regarding the steps she needed to take in her newly widowed state. She knew she needed to meet with Ben's lawyer, whom she had never met. Perhaps he would know someone who could accompany her on this dreaded trip—she was so stupid about financial matters!

Elizabeth's dominant personality characteristics, as indicated in her questionnaire and the way she had led her life, made it difficult for her to cope with her newly widowed state. She was emotional, dependent and introverted, which did not provide her with good coping skills. Elizabeth had a considerable need to decrease the anxiety and stress of being alone.

She knew she would be required to deal with lawyers or other business advisors regarding Ben's will and estate, but she had no idea how this process began. Did someone contact you, or were you supposed to know you had to contact the lawyer? She was desperate for support and help. In order to obtain it, she was willing to risk initiating the contact with the minister. Her timidity would have prevented her from taking such a step in the past. However, she did feel comfortable with him, and he was the one person she could think of who might be able to help her with what lay ahead.

PART TWO
Getting Organized

CHAPTER 4

Organizing Your Finances

"You've got to be careful if you don't know where you're going, because you might not get there."

YOGI BERRA

Introduction

You may not have been involved in the financial process at all during your marriage. On the other hand, you may have handled everything financial, including investments. Perhaps you were somewhere in between—you paid the household bills and balanced the checkbook for the house but weren't involved in the investment selection process.

Many people have the misconception that if a woman worked outside the home for pay, she was familiar with family finances as well. Often the opposite is true, and the working wife is less involved in finances than the nonworking spouse. The reason is that she feels she has no time to spare after coping with her job, the household, her children and her husband. This works relatively well until the husband dies and the spouse finds herself with insufficient financial experience and knowledge.

Traditionally, money has been considered the male province. However, many men do not know a lot about money management or investment. Further—and this is much more dangerous—they might think they know more than they do. This problem is compounded if the husband dies prematurely. He might have thought he had plenty of time to accumulate money for a comfortable retirement, and, therefore, he may have invested in some riskier ventures with the idea he had plenty of time to shift to more conservative investments later.

Regardless of how financially knowledgeable you are, the numerous tasks you are currently facing can be overwhelming. How do you start to make order out of chaos? In the next few chapters, we will discuss the basics of determining where you are financially. This chapter will cover how to organize the information you currently have available. In chapter 5, we will discuss how to work with your three key advisors: your lawyer, accountant and financial planner. Chapter 6 presents a list of other people and agencies that can give you additional information you will need to construct an accurate picture of your situation. In chapter 7, you will develop a budget, and in chapter 8, you will calculate your net worth.

If you are unable to handle any or all of these jobs, ask someone to help you—but at least review these chapters so you have an idea of what has to be done. The sooner you understand your financial picture, the sooner you will be able to move toward recovery. The anxiety caused by uncertainty will be removed.

A word of caution: In this initial stage, a widow may feel compelled to take some kind of action—any kind of action—to demonstrate to herself and others that she is in control of her life. If this is what you feel, resist the impulse. Take no drastic action such as selling your house, quitting your job, moving in with or closer to your family, buying insurance, loaning money to a family member or friend or making a major investment. There is no need to make major decisions immediately. In fact, there are compelling reasons not to make any decisions that are not absolutely necessary at this time. **Now is not the time for irrevocable action.** Having said this, do not carry this advice to an extreme. There will come a time when action is wise and necessary. If you take no action, you are in fact making a decision not to take responsibility for your financial life. Now is the time to determine what your situation is so that you can intelligently plan your future.

The following tasks need to be accomplished in the first few months after your husband's death. Do not let the list overwhelm you. Assign yourself one job at a time, and don't get discouraged if it takes longer than you anticipate to do each task.

Locate Your Important Papers

Hopefully, you and your husband had a file cabinet in which all important records were kept. We say hopefully because this is the sort of thing that everyone means to do and never gets around to—or your husband may have set up an elaborate system and never explained it to you—or you didn't pay attention when he did. The records might also be in a computer, in a safety-deposit box or in an old shoe box. In some states, the jointly held safety-deposit box is sealed as soon as a spouse dies and cannot be opened without a court order.

Wherever your important papers are located, you need to look for a copy of your husband's will, his and your Social Security cards, your marriage certificate, his military discharge papers, insurance policies, his birth certificate and birth certificates of your minor children. These papers will be needed to establish claims for Social Security income, life insurance proceeds and veterans benefits.

Don't panic if you can't find your husband's will. Your lawyer or banker may have a copy. If there is no will, then the estate will be settled by the laws of the state in which you live. Contact the probate clerk in your county (see your Yellow Pages under local government listings) to find out what action to take. We recommend that you use a lawyer to help you because it is easy to omit something unintentionally that could cause subsequent problems. See chapter 5 for more on this topic.

Set Up a Work Area

Designate a special area—preferably a desk—to be devoted specifically to your financial affairs. If you have a file cabinet, fine. If not, go out and buy a basic two-drawer fireproof file cabinet with file folders inside it. Some people prefer the accordion file approach, which enables you to carry multiple files with you. Others use both. Do whatever is easiest for you.

Set Up Files

Label the files. If in doubt, make another file. If you can't locate a document, make the file with the idea that you will fill the file eventually. If you use a file cabinet, one drawer can be devoted to papers you need in order to settle the estate and the other to more current financial issues.

The "estate" drawer would include files for:

- safety-deposit box location and key
- your husband's will
- copies of your husband's death certificate*
- Social Security records for every member of the family
- your husband's life insurance policies
- last year's tax return
- birth certificates for each member of the family
- your marriage certificate
- his military discharge papers
- naturalization papers (if applicable)
- divorce agreement (if applicable)
- passports for each member of the family
- trust agreements for any trusts he might have set up or been the beneficiary of
- most recent statements for checking, savings and money market accounts
- accounts in his or joint names
- listing of credit cards in his or joint names
- listing of certificates of deposit in his or joint names
- stock brokerage statements both joint and in his name
- his retirement asset statements (IRA, Keogh, company pension plan)
- real estate titles and deeds for property owned
- most recent mortgage statement
- prenuptial or postnuptial agreement

* You may need copies of your husband's death certificate several years hence, so make sure that you request several more copies than you think you need for present use. We would suggest a minimum of 20 death certificates.

- title insurance
- auto registration or lease agreements
- recent statement of managed portfolio (if applicable)
- recent statements of mutual fund shares in his or joint names
- stock option plans
- property insurance policy
- casualty insurance policy
- health insurance policy
- auto insurance policy
- partnership agreements

Hopefully, you have most of the files available to you, if not in one place, in several places throughout the house. Your job is to get them into one central location so they are easily accessed during the next year. Once you no longer need them to settle the estate, some of them will become part of your personal files, but for now it is a good idea to segregate the past and the future.

The "personal" drawer would have a file for your:

- current bank statements
- stock brokerage statements
- charge account bills (one for each creditor)
- life insurance policies
- health insurance policies
- retirement asset statements (IRAs, etc.)
- will
- living will
- powers of attorney
- trusts
- burial instructions
- naturalization papers (if applicable)
- cemetery deed
- list of credit card numbers
- safe combination
- safety-deposit box location and key
- birth certificate
- divorce agreement (if applicable)
- military discharge papers (if applicable)

You will also need a file in this drawer for information relating to your current tax return and one for current bills. We realize these are a lot of files and what may appear to be an overwhelming amount of paperwork. If you feel unable to cope with all of this, ask a family member or friend for help. The most common complaint we hear from widows is the amount of paperwork involved in settling an estate. This is a legitimate complaint, but it has to be dealt with in order to figure out where you are financially.

Set Up a Book To Record Estate Income and Expense

We will discuss this in greater detail later (chapter 6), but any income you receive that was due your husband prior to his death (such as dividend checks) should be kept in an estate account separate from the rest of your money. When you visit your local bank, discuss the mechanics of setting up the estate account. Meanwhile, write down any checks you receive, the date received, the amount of the check and the payer. Similarly, ask for receipts and keep a record of any expenses incurred settling the estate.

Organize and Pay Appropriate Bills

Gather all your bills in one place and then divide them into three groups— yours, your spouse's and joint debts. You are responsible to pay your own and joint debts. Your spouse's debts should be paid from the estate account you will set up.

If a bill you receive for your husband is not a familiar one, write the creditor asking for proof that this is a proper claim. If any bill seems unfamiliar, do not pay it. There are unscrupulous types who take advantage of widows by sending them bills for items or services they claim the husband ordered and demanding payment. Refer these people to your lawyer if you have one.

Itemize these current bills making clear whose debt it is. If you have a high cash reserve, you may have no trouble paying all of them. If your reserve is not high, you will have to decide which bills must be paid and which can be delayed. Mortgage payments, utilities, health and property insurance premiums should be paid first. If you don't think you have enough money to pay all your bills, it is best to write the creditors explaining your situation— that you know you owe them money and plan to pay it, but you will have to pay a lesser amount until you have a better picture of your total financial situation. If you have difficulty doing this, ask someone to help you do this.

Set Up a Financial Diary and a Monthly Calendar

Buy a five-by-seven-inch spiral notebook and a "month at a glance" calendar. The notebook serves as a financial diary for you to list what you need to do and to record what you have done and when. Don't buy the larger size because it will be cumbersome to carry with you. On the other hand, the very small size that would fit in your purse is too small to keep all the information you need. Your financial diary will be a helpful reference book should you want to recall a conversation you had with one of your advisors or with anyone else. Most recent widows think they are operating perfectly rationally at the time of a meeting but, as we mentioned earlier, may have no memory of what happened a month later.

On the first page of your financial diary, make a list of projects you want to or must accomplish. Then look at your "month at a glance" calendar and decide when you are going to do each task.

In your financial diary, keep a daily account of whom you see and what was accomplished. In this book, record all conversations (phone calls or in person) that relate to your financial affairs. When your advisors see you keeping notes, they will know you are serious! A phone call from you that starts: "On June 6th, we agreed that you would do such and such. It is now July 15th. How are things progressing?" puts your advisor on notice that you expect results in a timely fashion.

A typical "to do" list for the first month would read:

1. Get 20 certified copies of the death certificate.
2. Make appointments to see lawyer, accountant and financial planner.

3. See your bank to open a new account in your own name (if you don't already have one) and to establish an "estate" bank account.
4. Notify all insurance companies involved and file claims.
5. Report death to Social Security and Veterans Administration and apply for benefits.
6. Notify your husband's employers to file for benefits.
7. Transfer jointly held securities to your name.
8. Notify IRA and Keogh accounts and any other retirement plans.
9. Consider donating your husband's clothes to a worthy charity. (There is no rush to do this.)

Buy a Three-Ring Binder To Keep Financial Statements

When you buy the notebook, the month at a glance and the file cabinet, also buy a three-ring binder, a three-ring punch and a set of dividers. In this binder, make a divider for each of the financial statements you receive. For instance, have a divider for each bank and savings account you have. Put the most recent statement behind each one. If you own mutual funds, the statements you receive may be cumulative. If this is the case, you only need to keep the most recent one. The purpose of this binder is to have a record of all financial transactions that take place during the year. This will be helpful to you when working on your taxes.

Conclusion

After you have set up your home office and financial records, you need to contact your key professional advisors. In the next chapter, we will review the role of each of your primary advisors and what you need to accomplish at the first meeting. We will also discuss how to select one if you don't have one.

Diane: Reactions to Getting Organized

Diane had a very difficult time dealing with this initial financial requirement. The idea of setting up files did not appeal to her. Here she was with
her world turned upside down, and she was being asked to spend her
energies on paperwork. However, she realized that getting her paperwork
in order might help her figure out how she was going to keep the children in
private school, and that was a motivating factor.

She was looking forward to meeting the women in the widow support
group Lisa had discussed with her. She was pleased the group consisted
of women in various stages of dealing with their loss. Maybe one of
these women could relate to what she was feeling. Lisa said there was at
least one woman in the group close to Diane's age. She wondered how the
other women dealt with all this paperwork. On the other hand, maybe she
should call Jennifer Greenberg again. Nicole was still a classmate of Erin.
Jennifer was obviously able to manage to pay her tuition. It was time for her
to focus on what had been requested of her but ignored, and set up financial
records. Maybe if she were better organized, she could begin to look at
whether or not she could afford the children's tuition.

She vaguely remembered that Mark had told her that their important
papers were in his desk. It was difficult for her even to go over to the desk
and open the drawers—it brought back so many memories of his sitting at
the desk working. She wished that she had paid more attention to what he
said.

She knew that they had some insurance besides the kind the firm
provided. Maybe there was something in his file drawer. She pulled the
drawer open and then found herself crying again as she recognized his neat
handwriting on the labels. Not only was there a file for life insurance but
also for auto, household and health insurance. She pulled out the life
insurance file and found there were five policies in it—all from different
companies. It was not clear how much money they represented or what she
had to do to get it.

She found another file marked "Estate Planning." Maybe this was where
the will was. Unfortunately, it contained only some handwritten notes he
had made on the subject. She knew that lawyers always joked about the fact

that they were the last people to get wills, even though they insisted their clients have them. She wished she understood the implications of not having a will.

It was becoming obvious to her that she needed someone to help her sort all this out. Perhaps someone in the widow support group could be of help.

DIANE'S TO DO LIST

1. Go to widow support meeting.
2. Call Jennifer regarding tuition.
3. Find out about life insurance policies.

Susan: Reactions to Getting Organized

Before marrying Lance, Susan had handled her own financial affairs. However, since they had been married, Lance had managed all the family's finances because he was an accountant and he enjoyed it. This had been a relief to her because she had had her hands full working full-time, taking care of the house, worrying about her mother and dealing with her stepchildren.

In her initial session with Dr. Coleman, Susan presented her anxieties regarding her inability to act on any of the items she currently had on her many lists the way she would have in the past. Dr. Coleman had suggested that she take the most important item from each list and place it on a single piece of paper. In this way, each sheet of paper would be devoted to the most important item. When she completed that item, she could cross it off and add another. Dr. Coleman suggested that for Susan this approach would be similar to the way she had functioned in the past and minimize her present sense of being overwhelmed. If it didn't help, she would discuss other approaches with her in their subsequent meetings.

Susan was relieved to find that Dr. Coleman was addressing her practical concerns as well as trying to learn about her background. In their first meeting, Dr. Coleman had explained that her therapeutic approach could best be described as "eclectic." This meant that she utilized aspects of various schools of psychological thought in her approach to her clients as opposed to only one. Dr. Coleman told Susan she felt it was essential to know something of a client's personal history in order to better understand the basis for what he or she was feeling or why he or she might be reacting in a particular way. However, she stressed that with Susan this would not preclude their focusing on her immediate needs, and she wanted Susan to make her aware of these concerns as they arose.

After her visit with Dr. Coleman, Susan decided her initial task was to set up a work area at home in her spare bedroom. She stopped at an office supply store to buy a two-drawer file cabinet and arrange for its delivery. Although she intended to set up computer records herself eventually, she thought she had better start by organizing the papers in the file cabinet. She also picked up a steno note pad and a calendar. She thought these would help her to move ahead in the manner Dr. Coleman had suggested.

Her next task was to visit Lance's office and talk to Harry about Lance's personal computer records. As an accountant, Lance had set up an elaborate computer program for their personal finances. She had no idea how to access this information, although she did know how to operate a computer. She would need some help with this matter. She would ask Harry about the various computer programs on the market so she could find one to use at home. She was sure that Lance's program would be too complex, but she liked the idea of having all the financial information she needed in one place on the computer. Hopefully, someone at the firm could show her how to get started. Given her personality type, she was sure she could manage it on her own after some instruction if she was able to focus on it.

Meanwhile, she made a list of their bills and divided them into those she knew she had to pay, like the mortgage and condo fee, and those she was not as clear about, like their VISA bill, which included some client dinners Lance had hosted before his death. She needed to discuss these with Harry because she knew Lance was usually reimbursed for these bills. Harry had given her Lance's month-end paycheck, but she wasn't sure what to do with it, so she had not cashed it.

She realized she had a lot of accounts to keep track of, and she needed to devise a system to keep track of all the statements. She had Lance's pension plan, her pension plan, Lance's stock account and the new trust account that was being established. The idea of putting the statements chronologically in a three-ring binder appealed to her organized style.

Susan needed to pull herself together and get on with the tasks ahead of her. Dr. Coleman's approach seemed to be working pretty well. Getting the files in order and making progress on the list of tasks she needed to accomplish made her feel a lot better.

SUSAN'S TO DO LIST

1. Organize files at home.
2. Visit Harry regarding Lance's personal computer records.
3. Ask Harry regarding the computer program on which to keep her records.
4. Discuss with Harry business expenses incurred by Lance and his final paycheck.

Audrey: Reactions to Getting Organized

Audrey had spent most of the past year visiting John in the hospital and had barely had time to keep their bills paid. However, the idea of creating order out of current chaos appealed to her. It was something concrete she could do to demonstrate to herself she was "in control."

John had already set up a pretty good file system in the big desk he had in his den. She knew that he had set up files for all the important papers. Over the past two years, she had started using his desk to pay the bills, so she had a pretty good idea of what their expenses had been. She decided to start keeping a notebook of her current expenses as well as people she needed to see. However, she also realized that knowing the expenses of the past two years wouldn't be very helpful to her in estimating future expenses. She had been so wrapped up in taking care of John that she had had no time to spend money on anything except the basic necessities and the medical bills. Fortunately, his health insurance had been wonderful. They had to pay very little out of pocket, but filing those insurance forms was so time-consuming and tedious!

Audrey was glad she had decided to have a physical, which had been first on her list of things to do. Dr. PaPadisio's staff had always been helpful and considerate of her as well as attentive to John during the ordeal of his illness. It felt odd to Audrey to be focusing on herself in Dr. PaPadisio's all-too-familiar consultation room—the same room in which he had informed them of John's prognosis. Dr. PaPadisio had her sit down and tell him how she was doing both emotionally and physically. He listened carefully to what she reported and asked questions about her weight loss. He was pleased with her mental attitude and said they'd talk further after he completed his physical examination. Audrey thought Dr. PaPadisio was unusually thorough in his exam. She wasn't sure whether he suspected something or was just being careful. While getting dressed to return to his office, Audrey found that she was quite nervous. She dreaded what he might say. Dr. PaPadisio seemed to sense her anxiety and was quick to say he hadn't found anything suspicious, but would wait until he received the results of the blood work and other tests he had ordered to finalize his medical report. However, he did tell her that, based on what she had told him and his knowledge of the demands made on her time and energy in the last months of John's illness, he wanted to review her eating and exercise or lack of exercise habit patterns with her.

He gently admonished her about the way she was eating and made several specific recommendations. He told her he wanted her to make a practice of eating regularly. He gave her suggestions as to which foods to consider for breakfast to assist her in gaining weight without increasing her cholesterol level. He suggested she have lunch with a friend or Joanne whenever possible. He thought it would force her to take the time to sit and eat in a more leisurely fashion and concentrate on what she was having. He advised her to think about making the midday meal her largest meal of the day for the present. He knew from other patients how difficult it was to make the effort to cook for oneself, but he wanted her to make herself something to eat in the evening, even if it was a frozen, microwaveable, "all-in-one" meal.

Next, he asked if she was exercising. She admitted she wasn't. He asked if she still had her German shepherd. She assured him she did, adding that poor Achilles still looked for John and looks at her as though he is awaiting his return. Saying that made Audrey realize how comforting it was to have had Achilles in the house with her all this time. She had really been neglecting him, she thought, by leaving him in the backyard. She couldn't remember when he'd last been walked, although she or John used to walk him at least twice a day.

Dr. PaPadisio wanted her to make it a practice of walking the dog once a day if the weather was suitable, gradually increasing the length of time she spent walking. He wanted to wait for the lab reports before discussing a more total fitness program with her. He commented that unfortunately many things had been neglected in her own care because of the demands of caring for John. He told her he'd have his receptionist schedule a follow-up visit with her for the next week. When Audrey left his office, she felt she had taken an important step in caring for herself. She really had given up all of the things she enjoyed and felt were important in maintaining her health. She vowed to make an effort to focus on her physical health again, beginning with walking Achilles and eating more nutritiously.

Audrey decided she was ready to put together an agenda of what to accomplish in the next month. She needed to meet with the lawyer and the banker, check with John's company about his pension, find out about the insurance and find someone to tell her what to do about his stock. When she drew up the list, it seemed a lot to do, but she had learned a long time ago that if you tackle a big task a piece at a time, you can get through it all. She was determined to start her new life as soon as possible! The sooner she got started, the sooner she would be able to have an intelligent conversation with her son about where matters stood. She was sure he would want to have a serious financial discussion with her in the near future.

AUDREY'S TO DO LIST

1. Call Joanne regarding lunch.
2. Eat breakfast regularly.
3. Walk Achilles daily.
4. Gain weight.
5. See lawyer.
6. See banker.
7. Call company regarding pension.
8. Call regarding insurance.
9. See John Jr. eventually.

Elizabeth: Reactions to Getting Organized

At Ben's request, Elizabeth had gradually assumed more responsibility for paying the bills. In the past few years, Ben's increasing loss of memory had caused some problems. However, she was finding her own memory wasn't what it used to be. If she didn't write down an appointment in a book, she was inclined to forget it, and sometimes she didn't remember everything that was said. In fact, it seemed that everyone was speaking in lower voices recently. She was having difficulty hearing what they were saying, and she felt awkward asking them to repeat themselves.

Although their checkbook was in pretty good order, the same could not be said of Ben's papers. The file cabinet she opened appeared to be crammed with old, out-of-date records. She wasn't sure what to keep and what to throw out. She needed someone to help her figure out which papers were important.

She did find a file labeled "Safety-Deposit Box," and in it were an envelope and a key from their local bank, that was clearly marked "safety-deposit box." Elizabeth intended to visit their bank anyway to talk with the manager about their accounts so she could also ask about opening the safety-deposit box. She had no recollection of Ben telling her about the contents.

Mabel, a close widow friend, had given Elizabeth a spiral notebook and had told her that it had been a lifesaver to her in the early months after her husband's death. Elizabeth stared at the clean white page in front of her and felt overwhelmed with all that was ahead of her. She had trouble keeping the checkbook balanced—how could she handle any more complex financial issues? Women of her generation never were taught much about money. In fact, it was not considered "ladylike" for women even to talk about money. She was really lost; however, she knew she had to start the process so that she would have some idea of her financial situation.

She knew she should make an appointment to see Ben's lawyer, but she really didn't know him very well. She decided to ask Pastor Appletorn if he knew someone who could go with her to the lawyer's office.

When Elizabeth met with Pastor Appletorn, he seemed to know what her worries were even before she explained them. He told her he had taken the liberty of speaking to a couple in the congregation about her. The husband, an attorney, had recently retired, and both he and his wife gave a great deal of time to the church. In fact, this man, Sam Weatherly, had joined the church's finance committee. If Elizabeth was willing, Pastor Appletorn wanted to ask this couple to join them for tea. He thought Sam might be able to help Elizabeth deal with her financial questions.

Elizabeth was so grateful she began to cry. Just knowing someone was there was a big comfort. She was sure Ben would not have wanted strangers to know anything about their finances, but she determined to meet this couple and draw her own conclusions. She really wanted some help in dealing with Ben's attorney. It felt good to have made even this small decision.

Pastor Appletorn arranged the tea for the following Sunday afternoon. Elizabeth felt guilty because she was looking forward to it. She didn't think she was supposed to look forward to anything at this point in her adjustment to her new state of widowhood. She even thought about what she might wear. She and Ben had practically stopped seeing people because it was so difficult to predict when Ben would be coherent during the last year of his life.

She dressed very carefully and was ready considerably earlier than necessary. Elizabeth wanted to make a good impression, and doing anything in a hurry tended to fluster her. She was neatly dressed and arrived at the rectory punctually at 4:00 P.M. The Weatherlys arrived shortly after she did, and she liked them at once. They made her feel comfortable and talked about many things she could relate to before they got into her business affairs. Sam Weatherly seemed very knowledgeable, and she thought she could trust him, so she gratefully accepted his offer to accompany her when she met with Ben's attorney.

ELIZABETH'S TO DO LIST

1. Visit bank about safety-deposit box and bank accounts.
2. Make appointment to see Ben's lawyer when convenient for Weatherlys.

CHAPTER 5

Working with Key Financial Advisors*

You gain strength, courage and confidence by every experience in which you really stop to look fear in the face. . . . You must do the thing which you think you cannot do.

ELEANOR ROOSEVELT

Introduction

Settling an estate is not an easy task, regardless of the size of the estate. Even if you or your husband never used professional advisors before, this is a time you should seriously consider using their services. We have observed that widows who seek professional help with various aspects of their emotional and financial situations progress more quickly to a state of well-being than those who try to do it all themselves.

Many widows initially may rely on their husband's advisors if he had them. After your husband's estate is settled, you may want to find your own advisors, but at this stage, it is easiest to work with those people familiar with your situation. However, if you find them unresponsive to your requests (assuming they are reasonable), replace them. The advisor's job

---

* Some of the technical and legal terms and procedures we refer to here will vary from one state to another. We will use generally accepted terminology in the interests of readability.

is to help you, and if you are not being helped, they are not doing their job. At the end of this chapter, we have included guidelines for selecting advisors.

Well-meaning family members and friends may offer legal or financial advice. Keep in mind they don't know the specifics of your situation, and as successful as they might be at managing their own affairs, their strategies may not be appropriate for you. So listen to them, but wait until you meet with your professional advisors before taking action.

Most advisors expect you to be accompanied by a family member or friend at your initial meeting. Your companion may help you by asking questions you might not think to ask. Be sure to ask questions. There is no such thing as a stupid question—it is a lack of knowledge in a particular field, and the advisor welcomes your questions.

Reading the Will

If you are able to locate your husband's will, read it. The will names a person to settle the estate, who is commonly called an *executor*, or *personal representative*. The first thing you or the personal representative or the lawyer who is representing either party must do is file this will with the probate court. Most states require you to file the will within a certain number of days of your husband's death. Your lawyer can tell you how soon it must be filed, or you can call the probate court and ask them yourself.

Sometimes more than one person is named, but the first one named is the person who usually takes care of the estate. If there is no will, the probate court will appoint an *administrator* to perform the same function. Hereafter, we are going to refer to this person as the personal representative. This may be a person such as yourself, your lawyer, a member of the family or someone else. If the personal representative is not experienced in settling estates, he or she should contact someone who is. Settling estates is not for amateurs unless your situation is very simple, and even then the rules and regulations are confusing. You could easily miss one of the deadlines involved through ignorance, and this could cost you some money.

Many people don't understand what *probate* means. It is simply the legal process whereby a court assures itself that a will is valid (or that there is no will) and oversees the distribution of property to creditors and legal beneficiaries.

Not all of your spouse's property will have to pass through probate. For instance, property owned in joint tenancy with right of survivorship will not be probated but will go directly to the survivor. U.S. savings bonds that are co-owned or payable to a beneficiary are not included in the probate estate. Life insurance policies, deferred annuities, IRA and other retirement plan benefits (unless the proceeds are payable to your husband's estate or the beneficiary has died) will be paid to the named beneficiary. Assets held in a living trust also escape the probate process. There are other examples, but a lawyer or another professional advisor can help you sort through all the assets owned or partially owned by your husband.

The probate court will issue *letters of appointment* certifying the authority of the personal representative, which you will be required to supply in order to transfer assets. The various banks, brokerage firms and other entities you contact usually require a recently dated letter of appointment (within the last 60 days). Therefore, you may have to go back to the probate court for more copies later. It depends on the complexity of your situation, but it is usually advisable to request 20 copies initially. When in doubt, provide the parties requesting the letter of appointment with a copy. If they need an original, they will tell you.

The personal representative's responsibilities include:

- File an inventory with the court of all money and property owned on the date of death (normally three months after being appointed).
- File periodic reports with the court showing property received and amount spent from the estate.
- Open a bank account in the name of the estate.
- Set up a separate account for each minor child who is a beneficiary.
- Obtain court permission to spend estate's money.
- Obtain court permission to sell, lease or invest property of the estate.
- Have the value of the property of the estate appraised.
- Deal with the creditors.
- File any necessary income, estate or inheritance tax returns.
- Account fully for all assets collected and expenditures made from the estate.

As you can see, this is no easy task and one that is often best delegated to the professionals in the lawyer's office. They know what to do and can do it faster than you can. If you are anxious to reduce the costs of settling the estate, ask what you can do to help. But unless you are skilled in this type of activity, you may be more hindrance than help.

The Lawyer's Role

Your lawyer's function is to make sure that you are legally protected. Your lawyer should review the terms of the will with you and explain its implications. Unless your husband's lawyer was named as personal representative, you need not use him or her to settle the estate. If no one is specified in the will, you are free to choose another lawyer should you decide to do so.

YOUR FIRST MEETING

The lawyer is usually the first advisor you see. It is preferable to take a friend or family member with you to help you remember the substance of your discussion. For this same reason, ask the lawyer to send you a letter summarizing this meeting, reviewing what was covered and what action you need to take.

At this first meeting, ask how long he or she estimates it will take to settle the estate and when you can expect interim distributions. Ask what the lawyer's fee schedule is and what he or she estimates the total fee will be. It is usually an hourly rate or a percentage of assets involved and is paid out of the estate assets. Request a *letter of engagement* spelling out the services he or she will provide. Find out whom you should call if you have a question. Most probate lawyers have very knowledgeable assistants and paralegals who are more readily available than the lawyer and can answer most questions you might have.

You should also establish what records you should keep and what the lawyer will keep. *When in doubt, ask—and don't throw anything away.* If you are inexperienced in dealing with financial matters, the lawyer can arrange, for a fee, to have a member of his or her staff come to your home and sort through things with you or you can gather it all up and bring it to his or her office.

COMMENT

Some widows—particularly older widows—tend to make the lawyer a surrogate husband. Resist this impulse. Most estate planning lawyers have chosen this area of specialization because they care about people. As much as they would like to drop everything to talk with you every time you call, recognize the fact that they do have other clients who also need their attention.

The Accountant's Role

You and your husband may have used an accountant in the past to prepare your tax return. If so, we would recommend you continue to use him or her at least for this first very important year. After the first year, you can assess the work done, the attitude toward you and responsiveness to your concerns. Then you can decide whether or not you want to keep working with this lawyer when life is less stressful.

There are several tax returns to be prepared: federal estate tax returns, state inheritance tax returns, federal/state estate income tax returns and your personal federal/state income tax returns.

A federal estate tax return will have to be filed if the value of your spouse's gross estate (including both probate and non-probate assets), plus the amount of taxable gifts made by your spouse, exceeds $600,000. Even if there are no estate taxes due, a return must be filed so that the Internal Revenue Service (IRS) won't come back to you later with a claim. This return also establishes a cost basis for assets you may sell in the future. In addition, sometimes you owe a state inheritance tax even if you don't owe a federal estate tax.

Federal and state income tax returns will have to be filed not only for the year your spouse died, but also for the year before if your spouse died before filing a return for that year. For example, if your spouse died in March, you will have to file income tax returns for the year he died and for the previous year (assuming he had not done that prior to his death).

The calendar year in which your spouse dies you will file a joint personal return. Thereafter, you file as a single person unless you have dependent children. If you have dependents, then you file as "qualifying widow with dependent children" for the first two years after your husband dies and then as "head of household."

Your accountant will coordinate with your lawyer in preparing your estate tax returns. One of the first things that the accountant will do, if your lawyer has not already done so, is to file for a tax identification number for the estate. Make sure he or she knows who your lawyer is so they can work cooperatively and don't do the same work.

You and your husband might have put most of your assets in joint name. This means that although your husband might have had a will, those assets go to you automatically as the survivor. If this is so, you will probably be using the accountant's services more than the lawyer's to compile a list of your assets and to determine their current market value.

YOUR FIRST MEETING

At this first meeting, your accountant will help you determine what records he or she needs in order to prepare your returns and in what time sequence. Ask the accountant what his or her fees will be and what a reasonable time frame might be for this aspect of your affairs to be settled. Obviously, he or she can only give you an estimate, but note the time frame given you in your financial diary. Also put down the name of the key assistant who will be available to answer your questions.

The estate tax return must be filed nine months after the date of death. You have a choice of valuing the assets on the date of death or six months later. The lawyer and financial planner will help you choose which date is most favorable to you. This is important because the value given the estate assets becomes your tax basis if you sell the asset after the estate is settled.

Some widows fail to have their major assets appraised because the total value of the estate is under $600,000 and, thus, no federal estate tax is due. You still should have all assets valued because this information helps determine the amount of taxable gain on the sale of an asset. In the case of your house, it is advisable to use an independent appraiser rather than a real estate agent. It costs more, but the appraisal will be more reliable. You can find the name of a certified appraiser in your Yellow Pages.

COMMENT

What if you don't have an accountant or really don't like your husband's accountant? Find a new one. If possible, do so in the fall, which is their slowest season, so the accountant can become familiar with your situation before he or she is under the pressures of deadlines. It is wise to meet with this accountant as soon as possible so you can put together the necessary information.

Ask your accountant to give you an estimate of estate and income taxes you will owe so that you can make sure you have sufficient cash to pay them. In addition, if your accountant can estimate what your income taxes will be next year, then you will know how much to have withheld or put aside on a quarterly basis in the future. This is important for all future financial planning.

The Financial Planner's Role

In this initial stage, your financial planner will help you determine what your financial condition is. Your financial planner will help you put together a list of your assets and liabilities as well as your current income and expenses. If you do not have a financial planner, your accountant or lawyer can help you figure out your current situation.

Once these numbers are put together, your financial planner will help you determine what action to take now and in the future to help you become financially secure. However, it is important to first figure out exactly where you are before making any radical changes in your investments. Right now, your major concern is to determine whether you have sufficient income to pay your current expenses. Later, when you are more emotionally able to concentrate on financial matters, your planner will help you look at your longer term goals, such as college education (for a child or yourself), aid for your elderly parents and your own retirement.

YOUR FIRST MEETING

Prior to or at the initial meeting, the financial planner will give you a questionnaire to complete. This will be true even if you are currently a client. On this form, you will list your assets and liabilities and indicate ownership. (Was the asset in your name, your husband's name or jointly held?) You will also be asked to indicate your sources of income now that you are a widow and to estimate your current expenses. With this information, your planner can put together a preliminary budget for you and help you make some initial investment decisions.

At this initial meeting, ask how you will be charged for this current financial evaluation. Usually, you will be charged an hourly fee for this advice. If you and your husband worked with this planner before, this process is a lot easier because all of the information about your jointly held investments will be available.

Ask your financial planner to provide this analysis in writing. This way, you will have something to refer back to in the future and numbers to revise when appropriate.

COMMENT

In the old days, the solution to a widow's need for more income was to find a rich man to marry. Today, statistics indicate that the chances for remarriage are slim—and even if you do remarry, it may not be to a wealthy man. Therefore, it is important to plan for your own financial security.

How To Select These Advisors

Each of these key advisors must be knowledgeable, ethical, empathetic and experienced in working with widows. Following are guidelines for selecting these professionals.

1. Ask your other professional advisors (accountant, financial advisor, banker) to recommend someone. Your widowed friends might also

suggest someone they have worked with effectively. If all else fails, try the Yellow Pages.

2. Call the office of at least two individuals in the profession and ask for an appointment. Explain that you are looking for someone to help you, and you want to meet for an initial consultation before making a decision. There should be no charge for this informational meeting. Ask the secretary what information you should bring to this meeting to make it productive.

3. When you meet, ask the professional if he or she will be handling your case personally or delegating it to an assistant or another person in the office. It is not unusual for a professional to delegate part of the work. This often means that some of the work will be charged at lower rates. What is of importance is that your advisor take primary responsibility for supervising your situation. If that is not so, ask to meet the person who will handle your affairs.

4. Ask for the hourly rate you will be charged. Request a written estimate of what it will cost to take you through the estate settlement process as well as a copy of any agreement you will have to sign prior to working together. Many state bar rules require you to receive a "letter of engagement," which includes this information. The more information you give your professional advisor in an organized fashion, the fewer hours he or she will have to spend finding the information and the lower the fee will be. However, you should not necessarily pick the person who quotes the lowest rate. The person who quotes a higher hourly rate may be more efficient and may take fewer hours to settle the estate due to his or her experience.

5. Ask if itemized bills are sent on a regular basis so you can keep track of what your fees may total. In this way, you can avoid receiving an unexpectedly high bill for several months' work.

6. Tell the professional that you will have questions to ask occasionally. Although it is not your intent to call unnecessarily, you do expect someone knowledgeable to respond to your phone calls in a timely fashion (within 24 hours).

7. Make it clear that you want the work prepared without unnecessary delays.

8. Consider hiring someone younger than yourself so that person can be your advisor for your lifetime.

Credentials

Each profession has its own credentials. Familiarize yourself with the various professional designations before selecting your advisors.

SELECTING YOUR LAWYER

Your lawyer should be an estate and trust specialist. There is a directory of lawyers called *Martindale-Hubbell*. Check to see if the lawyer you select is described in this book as having extensive experience working with estates and trusts. If you are unable to obtain personal referrals, call your local bar association.

For complex situations you may need a more experienced lawyer. If so, there is a professional organization called the American College of Trust and Estate Counsel (ACTEC) composed of lawyers who concentrate on these cases. The members must have a minimum of ten years' experience. However, there may not be a member in your town, or you may not need this high level of expertise. In any case, make sure the lawyer you select has had considerable experience settling estates. Drafting a will is easier than settling an estate.

SELECTING YOUR ACCOUNTANT

The principal credential in the field of accounting is the Certified Public Accountant (CPA). However, some accountants are not CPAs but are enrolled agents who specialize in preparing individual returns and can represent you with the IRS if necessary. To contact one in your area, call the National Association of Enrolled Agents (800-424-4339). Your primary concern is that the accountant you select is experienced preparing individual and estate tax returns (rather than corporate returns). If yours is a very simple situation, a tax preparer at an H & R Block-type firm might be helpful. But be aware that the first year you file a return after your husband's death everything is more complicated, so be careful in your selection.

SELECTING YOUR FINANCIAL PLANNER

The best known credentials in the financial planning profession are Certified Financial Planner (CFP) and Chartered Financial Consultant (ChFC). To qualify for these certifications, the planner must take a correspondence course in all aspects of financial planning. To retain certification, the planner must earn a certain number of continuing education credits each year and abide by a professional code of ethics.

A list of Certified Financial Planners can be obtained by calling the Institute of Certified Financial Planners at 303-751-7600. To receive a list of Certified Financial Consultants, call 215-526-2500. There is also a group called the Registry of Financial Planning Practitioners whose members are required to have practiced financial planning as their vocation for a minimum of three years, agree to take 30 hours of continuing education credits annually and abide by a code of professional ethics. To obtain a list of these individuals in your area, call the International Association for Financial Planning at 1-800-945-IAFP.

There is also a group of CPAs who specialize in providing financial planning advice. They have their own designation: Personal Financial Specialists (PFS). You can obtain a list of these advisors in your state by calling 1-800-862-4272.

Before you get totally confused by this alphabet soup of designations, the easiest approach is to ask if the financial planner is a registered investment advisor (RIA) with the Securities and Exchange Commission (SEC). If the advisor is a RIA, he or she has filed a form with the SEC that is called a "FORM ADV." Ask to see Part II of this form as it will give you a lot of valuable information about the advisor.

Financial planners are compensated in one of three ways: commission only, fee only or fee plus commission. Commission-only planners are compensated by the commissions generated by products you buy through them. Fee-only planners are paid for their hourly advice. Fee-plus-commission planners are paid an hourly fee for financial planning advice. If you decide to invest with them and the investment involves a commission, they also receive a commission. For the initial financial planning services you require, we recommend a planner who charges an hourly fee just like your other professionals.

Estate Planning Councils

As you interview these three key advisors, ask if they belong to an Estate Planning Council. Members of this organization come from the legal, accounting, insurance, banking and financial planning professions. They are proposed by their peers and must have at least five years' experience in estate planning. Membership is a good indicator of whether your advisor specializes in this area. There are many good advisors who might not belong to this organization, but members of this group will be experienced in this field and have a strong interest in it. Be aware that these councils may not be available in smaller communities.

To locate an estate planning lawyer in your area, contact:

The State Bar Association located in your state capital and ask for a list of estate planning lawyers.

American College of Trust and Estate Counsel (ACTEC)
3415 South Sepulveda Blvd.
Suite 460
Los Angeles, CA 90034
(310-398-1888)

To locate a tax advisor in your area, contact:

American Institute of Certified Public Accountants
1211 Avenue of the Americas
New York, NY 10036-8755
(212-596-6200)
   OR
Harborside Financial Center
201 Plaza III
Jersey City, NJ 07311-3881
(201-938-3000)

National Association of Enrolled Agents
6000 Executive Blvd.
Suite 205
Rockville, MD 20852
(1-800-424-4339)

To locate a financial planner in your area, contact:

Registry of Financial Planning Practitioners
c/o International Association for Financial Planning
2 Concourse Parkway
Suite 800
Atlanta, GA 30328
(1-800-945-IAFP)

Institute of Certified Financial Planners (CFP)
7600 East Eastman Avenue
Suite 301
Denver, CO 80231-4397
(303-751-7600)

American Society of Chartered Financial Consultants (ChFC)
Chartered Life Underwriters (CLU)
270 Bryn Mawr Avenue
Bryn Mawr, PA 19010
(215-526-2500)

Personal Financial Specialists (PFS)
Harborside Financial Center
201 Plaza III
Jersey City, NJ 07311-3881
(1-800-862-4272)

Conclusion

These three advisors are your primary helpers in the first stage of dealing with your husband's death from a financial point of view. By this time, you should have a sheet in your financial diary that lists the name, address and phone number of each of these advisors as well as their assistants' names. In the next chapter, we will discuss other professionals whom you need to contact to organize your financial affairs.

Diane: Reactions to Meeting with Key Advisors

In her feeling way, Diane knew what she wanted for her children. She anticipated that her family and close friends would reject her desire to keep the children in their private schools. They would encourage her instead to be realistic and practical and transfer them to public schools.

Upon reflection, Diane realized that Larry and the others at Mark's law firm were doing what they could to be helpful, but they really only succeeded in confusing her. She decided she needed an objective advisor who was not a family member or friend to help her reach the right decision about the children's schools. If at all possible, she wanted to keep them there. Mark had signed contracts with the schools before he died and the first payments were due soon, so she had better get organized.

Again, she decided to call Jennifer Greenberg, Nicole's mother, and see if she had used someone in this capacity. She was pleased to learn from Jennifer that in fact she had and enthusiastically recommended a financial planner, Dorothy Trumbull. Diane contacted her office and made an appointment to meet with her. She asked what kind of information Dorothy needed in order to help her make the right decision. She was tired of hearing from everyone what she should and should not do. In her present state she wasn't up to dealing on this level with her father, her brother or even Larry and his wife, Gail, as well meaning as they all were.

She was frightened at the thought of meeting Dorothy. This was the first time she had ever initiated anything related to finances. She knew she wanted and needed the help of an independent person, but she was afraid of the consequences of revealing her financial ignorance to this expert. She assumed Dorothy would ask her a great many questions she would be unable to answer. She begged one of her closest friends to accompany her to this initial meeting because she didn't want to involve her family. Diane was greatly relieved when she agreed to do so. It hadn't been that long since Mark had died, and she was having a hard time facing the reality of his death.

The meeting turned out to be much less difficult and painful than Diane imagined it would be. Although she didn't have a lot of information, Dorothy didn't laugh at her or tell her she was foolish to even consider continuing her children in their private schools. Dorothy did tell her that she would need more information in order to help her make this decision.

When Dorothy discovered Mark had no will, she had difficulty concealing her dismay. She explained that, without a will, one-third of the assets would go to Diane and the balance to the children. Diane would be appointed by the court to manage the assets for the children, but two-thirds of the assets actually belonged to them! Diane now understood why her father had been so upset. Dorothy went on to explain that if most of the assets were jointly held, the assets would go to her and would not be taxed until she died. Diane knew that the house and their checking account were in both of their names, but she didn't know about the other assets. Obviously, she needed to do some homework.

Dorothy's questions caused Diane to realize that she knew nothing about Mark's life insurance. She remembered that the firm provided Mark with life insurance coverage. Her dad had told her what she needed to do about Mark's insurance, but, like everything else, she ignored his instructions, incapable of action. Now that she realized that obtaining the information about the insurance might impact her ability to keep the children in their schools, she was motivated to learn more. It felt right and necessary to explore this further.

Dorothy asked about the family's health insurance. She told Diane that the firm's insurance would cover them for 18 months, but she would have to pay the premiums that were formerly paid by the firm. Diane wondered if she was supposed to have done something about this sooner. She would have to ask Larry, although she was beginning to feel he was tiring of her lassitude and spaced-out state.

Dorothy gave her a questionnaire to complete and made an appointment for her to come back and review it all with her. Diane found the questionnaire to be a little intimidating because she was not used to financial matters. However, Dorothy reassured her about her ability to provide her with the information she needed. She checked the items she particularly needed to know in order to help Diane decide what to do about the children's education. She explained that basically she needed to know what the family's assets, liabilities and estimated sources of income were. Knowing that she had a professional advisor who was nonjudgmental about her ignorance or Mark's failure to prepare a will made her feel better.

These thoughts were unfamiliar ones for Diane. Just contemplating gathering all the necessary information was overwhelming for her. However, her desire to reach a particular goal (that of keeping the children in private schools) propelled her to overcome her resistance to addressing financial matters. The time had come for her to stop feeling sorry for herself and start doing something for the children.

Susan: Reactions to Meeting with Key Advisors

At this point, Susan found functioning at work and dealing with the many aspects of her mother's situation almost more than she could handle. However, she knew she had to come to grips with her own financial status, particularly in view of her responsibilities for her mother.

The first step was to see Lance's partner and friend, Harry. He was very supportive when she met with him, telling her again how shocked and saddened everyone at the office was about Lance's sudden death. He introduced her to Sarah Stone, Lance's assistant, who was familiar with Lance's personal finance computer program. At the same time, Harry gave Susan information about a user-friendly recordkeeping software program as she had requested.

Sarah would help her with the estate and income tax returns required. In fact, she had already applied for the estate tax identification number. Harry told Susan a return had to be filed for the estate within nine months of Lance's death. Sarah would prepare these returns, and the firm would bear the expense for this work.

Harry was aware of the insurance trust Lance had created, which would provide Susan with lifetime income. When she died, the principal would go to the stepchildren. They discussed the fact that the stepchildren would not be happy that they were not receiving much money now. She wasn't ready to deal with them yet.

Harry recommended she call the trust department of the bank Lance had named to act as the trustee for the insurance trust to go over the details. He volunteered to accompany her to the bank if she would like him to do so. Susan thanked him. She said she thought she could handle that meeting by herself, but she could use some help with the stepchildren. She felt the news about their small inheritance might be better received from someone other than herself since she was the immediate beneficiary. Harry agreed to do so. Lance had discussed with him the reasons he had created the trust, and he thought that he could explain it to Lance's children. They might not like the terms of the trust, but he was sure it was a valid document.

He also told her his wife, Emily, wanted to have her over to dinner and would be in touch with her shortly. Susan, normally a social person, hoped she would be able to deal with this kind gesture. Everything seemed to take so much effort these days, and she wasn't sure she was up to making dinner conversation. At the conclusion of her meeting with Harry, she felt somewhat relieved because at least she had put things in motion and was ready for the next round of appointments—with her banker, Lance's broker and the firm's benefit person.

The following week, Harry and Susan met with Timothy Longwood, Lance's attorney. He went over the terms of the will and the trust with them. He assured Susan that there was nothing the stepchildren could do to get additional money. The two houses were in both their names and, thus, went directly to Susan. The insurance policy proceeds were payable to the trust at the bank. Lance had his pension fund, where Susan was clearly the beneficiary. The only assets registered in his name only were his stocks.

It did appear that Susan was going to have to sell some of these stocks to raise the $40,000 due the stepchildren. Mr. Longwood advised her to do this as soon as possible to reduce tension. He would be glad to talk with the stepchildren for her if that would be helpful.

Audrey: Reactions to Meeting with Key Advisors

Audrey made an appointment to meet with Mr. Humphrey, the attorney. She anticipated that he would provide the guidance she needed in the near future. Undoubtedly, he would also want her to meet with John's accountant, Mr. Lewis. Following her initial meeting with Mr. Humphrey, she would involve her daughter, Joanne. She wanted to make sure she had more information before discussing anything with John Jr.

She was enjoying getting her facts together and keeping her notebook. It allowed her to feel she was not only useful but had the right to begin to make financial decisions for herself. She wondered whether or not she would have been able to get in touch with these emotions as quickly if John had not been ill for such an extended period of time.

Audrey felt good about her first meeting with Mr. Humphrey. He encouraged her to ask questions and acknowledged that this was a painful and difficult process. He emphasized that he didn't want her to feel foolish about posing any questions any number of times. He also introduced her to Sally, his assistant, and told her she would be working with him settling John's estate. If he wasn't available, Sally would be and she was very familiar with the process of settling estates. If for any reason Audrey wanted to speak to him personally, she needed to make that clear to the receptionist or Sally. He would contact her as soon as possible even if he couldn't do so the day she called.

He recommended that she make an appointment to meet separately with Sally to make sure she was setting up the estate files correctly. He was pleased to learn she was already well organized in this area. He also told her to contact the Social Security Administration to determine what income she would receive from them in the future.

Mr. Humphrey asked her if she had a financial advisor. She said no but remembered attending a series of retirement lectures sponsored by her husband's corporation. She had been impressed by one of the speakers, a financial planner, and felt she would be comfortable calling him. Mr. Humphrey encouraged her to do so as he felt she needed someone to help her evaluate her total financial picture.

Audrey left Mr. Humphrey's office feeling better about the future. At least she had a list of instructions to follow and felt Mr. Humphrey would be helpful to her as she moved through the process of settling John's estate. She would ask Joanne to join her on her visit to the financial planner.

When she got home, there was a message on her answering machine to call Dr. PaPadisio's office, but that it was not an emergency. She appreciated his sensitivity to her built-in anxieties regarding calls from his office. When she returned the call, his pleasant receptionist told her Dr. PaPadisio wanted her to set up an appointment to go over her lab work and review the progress she was making with her exercise and eating programs. Audrey made an appointment for the following week. She had tried to do better with her eating but really hadn't focused on it. She hadn't made any arrangements to meet friends or Joanne for lunch on a regular basis yet and was hoping Dr. PaPadisio wouldn't ask her about it. The appointment with Dr. PaPadisio would force her to look at this aspect of her life much the same way she was looking at the financial aspects of her life.

Dr. PaPadisio actually wanted only a consultation with her. He had his nurse weigh her, but other than that, he just wanted to talk. He shared the results of her lab work with her, insisting that basically she was in good health, but had neglected herself while caring for John. He wanted her to focus on nutrition and exercise in a serious way. He suggested she might find a class in nutrition or cooking that focused on cooking for oneself. Other patients had told him about courses they had taken through the local community college. If she wasn't interested in such a class, he would refer her to a nutritionist with whom he had a working relationship. Some of his patients found her both informative and constructive. He thought a class might be a better approach for Audrey because she would be with people in a similar situation. This often led to new contacts, which he thought might be enjoyable for her. She promised him she would investigate a class and get back to him on it as he had requested.

Dr. PaPadisio surprised Audrey by next inquiring about her golf game. He wondered if she had given up playing when John became ill. She hadn't thought about golf in a long time. She and John had both been avid golfers, but both had given it up when John became ill. She realized she did miss it. She had played regularly with her women friends on Tuesday and Thursday mornings, and she and John had had a couples game on the weekends. At this point, she knew her women friends had replaced her, and even if her game wasn't so rusty, she would be uncomfortable asking them if she could rejoin the group. However, she thought it might be a good idea to schedule some lessons with the golf pro. Although she hadn't given it any considera-tion before Dr. PaPadisio began asking her about her exercise program, she decided to take it up again. At least she was able to tell him that she had taken his advice and had begun to walk Achilles on a daily basis. She thought she was up to about three-quarters of a mile a day but wasn't positive. He was pleased with that and encouraged her to investigate other activities in the fitness area.

Before she left the office, he asked her to schedule another appointment for the following month. He wanted to check her weight and possibly repeat some of the blood work. He emphasized that a preventive health plan was often the best medicine he could provide.

Elizabeth: Reactions to Meeting with Key Advisors

When Elizabeth received the letter from the law firm with whom Ben dealt asking her to make an appointment with a Mr. Carroll as soon as she felt up to it, she panicked. Even the name was unfamiliar. She knew she couldn't face any of this alone. She wished the idea of meeting with Ben's attorney and matters of this type didn't intimidate her so.

Elizabeth didn't agonize for any length of time about whether or not she should call the Weatherlys. She located the phone number and dialed quickly before she allowed herself to have second thoughts. Sam answered the phone, and after some pleasantries, she read him the letter she had received from Ben's attorney. He reassured her he had been sincere about his willingness to accompany her when she went for her initial meeting with Ben's attorney. He was somewhat surprised she had no recollection of Ben mentioning Mr. Carroll's name to her, but said it would be best to go ahead and schedule an appointment. He gave her some dates he would be available and asked her to call after she had made the appointment.

Elizabeth scheduled the appointment with the attorney for Wednesday of the same week. Sam and Sarah Weatherly picked her up, and they all drove to the attorney's office. Sarah was going to do some shopping while they had their meeting.

The law firm reception area was very formal and intimidating to Elizabeth. When they were ushered into Mr. Carroll's office by the receptionist, she was shocked. Mr. Carroll could not have been more than 28 years old. Ben couldn't possibly have worked with this young man. He introduced himself and quickly explained that Ben's attorney had died about six months ago and he had been given Ben's account. So that explained her lack of familiarity with the name! He perfunctorily expressed regret about her husband's death and began at once to get into the details. Sam slowed him down by introducing himself and stressing that all of this was new to Elizabeth.

Mr. Carroll seemed annoyed with her because she had not contacted the Social Security Administration. Sam assured her she hadn't done anything wrong and said he would explain what she needed to do. Sam asked Mr. Carroll a number of questions, and as a result, Elizabeth learned for the first time that Ben had a $500,000 portfolio managed by an investment advisor. Mr. Carroll seemed to be indicating she would also need to meet with this individual. She did not like Mr. Carroll at all. He was young and brash, and he talked to Sam as though she were not there. He was patronizing toward her and he made her feel stupid. She didn't know how she was going to work with this ill-mannered man. Tears came to her eyes, but she worked at not letting him know how distressed she was. Now that she had met Mr. Carroll, she was especially pleased that such a kind man as Sam had accompanied her. She would speak with him on the way home about whether she was required to work with this lawyer to settle Ben's estate. If she had a choice, she wanted another lawyer.

As soon as Elizabeth was back in the car, she asked Sam if she had to work with that arrogant Mr. Carroll. He told her she didn't. Before he could elaborate on what she could do, Elizabeth asked him if he would take her on as a client. Sam, in his considerate manner, told her he would be more than willing to do so if he were still in practice, but he wouldn't feel comfortable assuming so much responsibility for her knowing that he no longer kept up with the latest information on estate planning law. The way he said it made Elizabeth feel he was sincere and she wasn't a burden for whom he didn't want to assume any responsibility. Elizabeth apologized for asking him.

Sam was quick to offer further help in the selection of a more appropriate lawyer—one with whom he thought Elizabeth would feel comfortable. He even offered to go with her to meet the various advisors she would need to contact to sort out her financial affairs. They agreed to start with the new attorney whom Sam would contact on her behalf.

When Sam and Sarah Weatherly dropped her off, they asked her if she felt up to joining them at their home for lunch after Sunday services that week. She said yes without even thinking. When she was changing her clothes, she wondered if she had agreed too quickly. Ben hadn't been dead that long and here she was accepting social invitations. Ben would say she was "out gallivanting." She felt guilty but was also looking forward to spending some time with this friendly and thoughtful couple. She decided to bake her special angel food cake for the occasion.

Lunch was nice, and to her surprise, when they were ready for dessert, Sam told her he had asked one of the partners in his former law firm to unofficially drop over to meet Elizabeth. If she felt comfortable with him, she could make an appointment to see him on a professional basis the following week. Mr. Grossfeldt was so easy to relate to while they had coffee and cake that she knew she could talk to him about her financial affairs.

Sam and Sarah had another pleasant surprise for Elizabeth. They had invited Pastor Appletorn to stop over for coffee and dessert. She was pleased when he appeared. It made her realize how supportive the pastor and other members of the church had been to her. She decided she would like to give something to the church. Maybe she could give them Ben's car. It was almost brand new and certainly had not been driven much. She did not feel comfortable driving anymore—it was easier to take cabs. She would ask Mr. Grossfeldt if this was a good idea when she met with him in his office.

CHAPTER 6

Contacting Agencies and Resource People

"Unanswered whys are a part of life."
EARL A. GROLLMAN

Introduction

Now that you have seen your primary advisors, there are other people and agencies you need to notify of your husband's death almost immediately. These people will give you a better idea of what your assets are and what sources of income you can expect to receive. These include your bank, insurance and mortgage companies. You also need to talk with the Social Security Administration, the Department of Veterans Affairs and your husband's employer. If you had an account with a stockbroker or an investment advisor, these people need to be consulted as well.

Bank

Call your bank and ask for an appointment to talk with the manager. Explain the situation and ask him to help you make any changes necessary. If your husband had an account in his name, this should be changed to an account reading "estate of." The joint account with you should be moved to an account in your name. If you have no account in your own name, you will need to establish one.

To transfer the bank accounts, you will need the recently dated power of appointment of the personal representative and a certified copy of the death certificate. You will also need an inheritance tax waiver from the bank. As for any outstanding checks on the existing accounts, you can arrange to have these honored or not as you wish. The bank should not automatically make payments out of your husband's account. However, if they don't know of your husband's death, they will honor the check.

In any event, a bank account should be opened in the name of the estate. To establish this account, you would initially use your spouse's Social Security number and then substitute the estate's tax ID number when it is received. Any income received from assets listed in his name should be deposited in this account.

All expenses associated with the administration of the estate should be paid from the estate account. These include all expenses related to the funeral as well as medical bills. If you have already advanced payments from your own funds to cover these expenses, you should keep the receipts and reimburse yourself from the estate account once there are sufficient funds in it to do so. The receipts will be needed if a court accounting is required.

Ask to see a list of all accounts you and/or your husband has at the bank. These may include retirement assets (such as IRA accounts) as well as your checking accounts and certificates of deposit. If you had any loans with the bank, they may have to be renegotiated.

You may also have a safety-deposit box. The regulations that determine whether you have access to this box vary from state to state. In some states, you must have a tax assessor and a state registrar accompany you to the box to make sure you don't remove something before the estate assets are valued.

The manager should explain what services the bank offers, just as he or she would to any new depositor. You may need different services than your husband did. Keep in mind that the banker wants to retain your account. Just as you did with your other advisors, ask for a contact person to call with questions about your account.

You and your husband may have had accounts in more than one bank, which complicates the situation. Call each bank and then follow up your inquiry with a letter. Most banks have someone who reads the obituaries each day, but if the account is not local or they missed it, you should notify them of your husband's death.

COMMENT

Bankers are accustomed to helping widows, but be cautious about initially investing your money at the bank. Certainly putting money in savings accounts is fine because you can withdraw it at any time, but don't make any longer term investments. The manager may discuss with you the services offered by the trust department. You may want to learn more about that later, but right now, your goal is to gather information about the assets available to you. *Don't make any long-term commitments until you have had time to look at your total picture.*

Mortgage Holder

If you had mortgage insurance, the insurance company will pay off the mortgage on your home upon notification of your husband's death. If your husband had life insurance, you could use the proceeds to pay off the mortgage. However, this might not be the best use for that money. Wait until you can ask your financial planner about it. In any case, you want to advise your mortgage company that you will be making the payments henceforth. If you want these payments to be paid automatically from your checking account, make sure that they have the bank account number of your new account.

Real Estate Title

As part of settling the estate, you will want your joint properties retitled. This involves preparing a new deed and submitting it to the Recorder of Deeds in your jurisdiction. This should be done now to facilitate a sale at a later date. Your lawyer can take care of this for you.

Credit Cards

Many of the credit cards in your husband's name were issued because of his earning ability and credit. If you do not have the same earning power, the credit card companies may be reluctant to provide you with the same lines of credit until you demonstrate your creditworthiness. Some widows solve this by neglecting to notify the credit card companies of their husband's death. However, then you never establish your own credit history. Eventually, you should notify all credit card companies of your husband's death, but there is no urgency to do so.

Life Insurance Agent

If your husband had an insurance advisor, this individual will have information on all the life insurance policies in force and will provide you with the necessary claim forms and instructions to obtain the proceeds of these policies. If your husband bought from various agents over the years, you need to notify each insurance company of his death. A brief letter such as the one shown in figure 6-1 will suffice. They will require a certified copy of the death certificate and a completed statement of claim. Some companies also require that the policy be submitted.

FIGURE 6-1

SAMPLE LETTER TO INSURANCE COMPANY

Your home address
Date
Dear Sir or Madam:

This letter is to advise you that my husband (*full name*) died on (*date*). His policy number was _____ . Please send me whatever documents I need to claim the proceeds. Would you search your files to determine if he had any other coverage with your company?

Sincerely yours,

Your signature

If you can't find the actual policy, you need to ask for a lost policy form. If you don't know the address of the insurance company, look in your phone book for a local office, call them and they will tell you where to write.

If you are not sure whether or not your spouse owned life insurance and you can't find the policy or remember the name of any life insurance agent he might have been working with, look through your spouse's checkbook and canceled checks for payments made to an insurance company. If you send a stamped, self-addressed envelope to Policy Search, American Council of Life Insurance, 1001 Pennsylvania Avenue NW, Washington DC 20004, that organization will ask its members to search their files. The search is free.

If your husband made the insurance proceeds payable to a trust, then the trustee is the person to complete the claimant's statement and submit the documents to the insurance company.

As the beneficiary of life insurance policies, you will be asked how you want to receive the proceeds. You can choose to receive this money in a lump sum, in installments over your lifetime or for a fixed number of years, or in installments of a specified amount until the proceeds run out. This is another decision you should defer until your advisor has looked at your total picture. In the meantime, you can leave the money with the insurance company and have them accumulate interest on the principal for you.

The insurance agent may have some suggestions as to how you should invest the money. Once again, avoid the temptation to rush into an investment you can't change later. Ask the agent to put these recommendations in writing so that you can consider these ideas seriously when you are ready to make your investment decisions. Also ask for a review of your own life insurance policies. If your husband was the beneficiary, you will have to change this designation.

Social Security Administration

The toll-free number for Social Security is 800-772-1213, and you can call this number weekdays 7:00 A.M. to 7:00 P.M. They will be able to answer most of your questions and can refer you to the local office if you want to make an appointment to see a representative. Claims may be expedited if you go in person to the nearest office to sign a claim for survivor benefits. To file your claim, you will need your husband's Social Security number and birth certificate, your Social Security number and birth certificate, a death certificate and your marriage certificate. If dependent children are involved, you need their birth certificates and their Social Security numbers.

Under present regulations, if you are age 60 but under age 65, you may claim benefits. However, the amount you will receive will be significantly lower than that which you would receive if the payments start after the age of 65. The Social Security office will explain this to you in greater detail. If you are under age 60 and have dependent children under the age of 16, you are eligible for benefits. If you are under age 60 but have no dependent children, you are not eligible for any payments, but you should still register your husband's death with the Social Security Administration and apply for the funeral expense payment (currently $255). If your husband was previously married for longer than ten years, his former wife (if she is unmarried) is able to collect Social Security benefits as well. In other words, you will share his benefits with her.

You are eligible for Medicare if you are age 65 or older. Medicare has two parts—hospital insurance and medical insurance. Hospital insurance (Part A) helps pay for inpatient hospital care and certain follow-up care. Medical insurance (Part B) pays for physicians' services and some other services not covered by hospital insurance. Part B medical insurance is optional and you are charged monthly for it. You should opt for this coverage if you are eligible. Even if you plan to keep working, when you turn 65, you should sign up for Medicare.

Veterans Administration

If your husband was a veteran, contact the Department of Veterans Affairs. A toll-free telephone service is available in all states. Some states have their own veterans benefits. Both federal and state governments will want the same information you furnished the Social Security Administration. If you are eligible, they will reimburse you for some of the burial and funeral expenses as long as you file a claim within two years after your husband's burial or cremation. You may also be eligible for a pension for yourself or your children.

Your Husband's Company

Whether your husband was still working or was retired when he died, you need to contact the company benefits person to determine what benefits you should be receiving in the form of pension income, life insurance proceeds or health insurance coverage (see figure 6-2). If your husband was still working when he died, you are entitled to receive group health insurance rates for you and your family for 18 months after his death.

You may have to decide how you will receive pension benefits from your husband's employer. Usually, you can choose to receive the full amount in a lump sum or lifetime payments. If you do have a choice as to how you can receive this money, ask for time to consult your financial planner prior to making this important decision. Your money will earn interest until you make the decision.

Your husband may have worked for more than one company and qualified for more than one retirement plan, so it is important to contact all previous employers just in case you might be eligible for pension benefits from more than one company.

FIGURE 6-2

SAMPLE LETTER TO EMPLOYEE BENEFITS DEPARTMENT

Your home address
Date
Dear Sir or Madam:

My husband (give full name and Social Security #) died on (date). Please provide me with information about any employee benefits I am eligible for as his widow. Please let me know if I have a choice of settlement options if applicable. I can be reached at (phone number). I look forward to hearing from you soon.

Sincerely yours,

Your signature

Other Retirement Plans

Your husband may have had his own IRA and Keogh plans invested at his bank with his stockbroker, financial planner or insurance agent. Try to locate these accounts. All these plans are held by a custodian trust company. When the plans were established, the custodian required a beneficiary to be named. You need to notify the custodian of your husband's death. The custodian will notify the beneficiary.

Again, if you are named the beneficiary, these assets can be invested in your own IRA account, but you need to consult with your financial advisor to make sure this is a good decision. What you are trying to establish now is which retirement accounts he had and who is the beneficiary. At the same time, if you have IRAs, Keoghs or any other retirement plans in your own name, you will want to change the beneficiary on these as well (assuming your husband was the named beneficiary).

Deferred Annuities

A *deferred annuity* is an investment made with an insurance company where your money earns interest sheltered from current taxation. Your husband may have purchased a deferred annuity through his stockbroker, financial planner, insurance agent or bank. This investment is usually intended as a supplementary retirement investment since there are penalties for withdrawing the money in most cases before age $59^{1}/_{2}$. When the annuity was purchased, someone was named the beneficiary. In your husband's papers, you may see some documentation for ownership.

You need to inform the annuity company of your husband's death. They will require you to send them the death certificate and will notify the beneficiary as to what options are available. Even if the beneficiary is not yourself, the proceeds of this annuity are still part of your husband's taxable estate.

State Office for Inheritance Tax

If you live in an urban area, this office will be listed in the phone book under the state. If you do not, your funeral director can provide the proper address. In many states, you must have a release from the state office for inheritance tax before company or insurance benefits can be paid.

Stockbroker

You or your husband may have worked with a stockbroker prior to his death. You should also inform him of your husband's death. He will tell you what paperwork his company requires to change the name on the account either to an estate account or to your name if it was a joint account.

If the assets were in his name alone, then they will go into an estate account and eventually to the heirs once the estate is settled. You or the personal representative can transact business in this account before the estate is settled, but you need the estate tax ID number to do so. The account will be retitled "Estate of John Doe, Mary Doe, Personal Representative."

To transfer his stock and bond positions, you need a notarized "affidavit of domicile" (provided by the stockbroker), the court appointment of the personal representative (dated within the last 60 days), the tax ID number for the estate as well as a letter of instruction signed by the personal representative. A sample letter of instruction is provided in figure 6-3. With some assets, you may need a bank or a brokerage firm to guarantee the signature of the personal representative. Whatever is needed, your stock-broker or his or her assistant will help you with the process.

FIGURE 6-3
SAMPLE LETTER OF INSTRUCTION FOR ASSETS HELD IN YOUR HUSBAND'S NAME

Your home address
Date
Dear Sir or Madam:

This letter is to notify you that (full name of your spouse) died on (date of death), and I have been appointed as his personal representative.

Please change your records of ownership to "Estate of (name of your spouse), (name of personal representative), Personal Representative." Please report to the IRS all dividends and interest received after that date under the estate tax ID number _____ .

Enclosed is a copy of the death certificate, an affidavit of domicile as well as my recently dated appointment as personal representative.

(Add the following paragraph if applicable):

In addition, he was listed as custodian for accounts held in the names of (children's names). Please change the custodian to my name. The Social Security number will remain the same since it is my child's Social Security number.

Sincerely yours,

Your signature

Transferring joint assets is usually easier. To transfer these, you need a certified copy of the death certificate and an "affidavit of domicile" together with a letter requesting transfer to your name (see figure 6-4). The letter of request should include your Social Security number. If you hold the stock certificates yourself, you need one set of papers for each company, and the stockbroker can help you process the transfer.

Ask the stockbroker to value the assets in your husband's as well as your joint accounts as of the date of death if you have not been provided with this information. Do this right away while the information is easy to obtain. As we mentioned before, this information is important because the tax on the estate assets is based on this value or the value of the estate assets six months later. Further, the value of the assets in the estate used to determine the estate tax bill becomes your cost basis should you sell anything at a later date.

FIGURE 6-4

LETTER OF INSTRUCTION IF THE STOCKS WERE HELD JOINTLY

Your home address

Date

Dear Sir or Madam:

This letter is to notify you that (name of your spouse) died on (date of death), and I was the joint tenant of this account (specify account number if appropriate).

Enclosed is a copy of the death certificate as well as an affidavit of domicile. My Social Security number is _____. Please transfer the assets in this account to my name.

Thank you for taking care of this matter for me.

Sincerely yours,

Your signature

Your husband may have bought limited partnerships from your stockbroker or financial planner. If so, you need to notify them in writing of your husband's death, request an estate valuation as of the date of his death and request that the units be transferred to your name. They will write you back asking for the information they require to effect the transfer. This process varies from company to company, and there may be a charge for this transfer.

Tell the stockbroker you don't want to make any radical moves before you and your financial advisors have looked at the total picture. However, if he or she thinks something should be sold based on your current situation, follow his advice. Tell him or her to put the proceeds in a money market fund earning interest for the time being until you contact him or her again.

Investment Advisors/Money Managers

Investment advisors are paid a fee based on a percentage of money managed, as opposed to stockbrokers, who are paid a commission on transactions. Some financial planners act as investment advisors on this basis as well. Your husband may have had this person manage your personal portfolios or his retirement assets.

You need to notify your investment advisor of your husband's death and ask for an evaluation of the account as of the date of death. In view of your new circumstances, also request written recommendations for any changes in the portfolio he or she manages. Again, this account should be retitled to read "estate of" if the assets were in your husband's name and the account should show the new tax ID number for the estate.

Ask for a copy of the contract your husband signed with this money manager. Most have a 30-day "notification of termination" clause in their contracts. Have your lawyer review the document. Since the contract was with your husband, and he is no longer alive, *you* do not have a current contract. Nevertheless, you will probably want to maintain this relationship until you have looked at your total picture.

Trust Officer

Your husband may have been the beneficiary of a trust created by his family. Now that he is deceased, the assets of his trust may go to his children. The trust document will indicate the beneficiaries. If he did have a trust, notify the trust officer of his death and ask for instructions as to what to do next.

Your husband may have set up a trust for your benefit and named a bank as trustee. You want to make an appointment to meet with the trust officer so that you can discuss your situation. You will want to know what investment options are available to you, how often you will receive reports and what the bank's management fees will be. Usually, the bank charges a percentage of the assets to manage the trust and also takes a percentage of the income generated. There is usually a minimum annual fee. Ask for a written schedule of fees for your files.

Unless the trust is worth over $500,000, most banks will invest the trust assets in their version of a mutual fund, which is called a *commingled fund*. This means that your money is invested with other trust accounts with a similar investment objective. You should ask them to give you a written record of how the commingled funds they manage have performed over the past year, five years and ten years. You should show this information to your financial advisor so he or she can interpret for you how good the performance has been. Have the trust officer explain how often income will be paid to you from the trust account.

State Department of Motor Vehicles

If any of the cars you have were registered in your husband's name, you need to notify your local department of motor vehicles so that the registration can be changed. You need a clear title before you can sell, trade in or give away the car.

Property and Auto Insurance Companies

The insurance on your house, car and valuables is usually with a different insurance company than the one which provided your husband's life insurance coverage. In addition, you may have insurance with more than one company. At a future date, you may want to make some changes here, using one company for both types of coverage, but now you need to change the name on the existing policies to you. Presumably, you will need the same coverage on your house, but if you sell a car, it will be necessary to adjust the coverage.

Utility and Telephone Bills

You eventually will want to change these accounts to your name, but this isn't an urgent matter. You may want to change your listing in the telephone book as well. Many widows choose to keep the listing under their husband's name to avoid annoying calls. Others opt for an unlisted number.

Your Children's School

From an emotional as well as a financial point of view, you need to notify the principal of your children's schools of your husband's death. If your children attend a private school, you may not be able to afford to keep them there. If the principal knows your circumstances, he or she will be able to help you by discussing your financial options. The principal will also keep you informed of any behavioral or academic changes the children may display as a result of your husband's death.

Clubs, Fraternal Organizations and Colleges

You should notify all social and business clubs, fraternal organizations, and alumnae groups of your husband's death. In the case of the social clubs, you may want to stay a member. Some offer reduced dues for widows.

Conclusion

By this time, you have set up a work area with a file cabinet. You have a financial diary partially filled with notes and a monthly calendar of tasks partially completed. You have contacted those people who need to know about your husband's death. Now it is time to organize the information you have gathered so far in order to plan your financial future.

Begin by making a list of people and organizations to notify:

· banker
· mortgage holder
· real estate title
· credit cards
· life insurance agent
· Social Security Administration

- your husband's company
- other retirement plans
- deferred annuities
- stockbroker
- investment advisor
- trust officer
- state department of motor vehicles
- property and auto insurance companies
- utility and telephone companies
- children's schools
- clubs, fraternal organizations, colleges

Now that you have identified your key advisors, start a list of important names and numbers, and make sure your family knows where to locate the list.

Employer:_____

Address:_____

_____

Phone:_____ Fax:_____

Assistant's name:_____

Attorney:_____

Address:_____

_____

Phone:_____ Fax:_____

Assistant's name:_____

Accountant:_____

Address:_____

_____

Phone:_____ Fax:_____

Assistant's name:_____

Financial planner:_____

Address:_____

_____

Phone:_____ Fax:_____

Assistant's name:_____

Insurance agent (life):_____

Address:_____

_____

Phone:_____ Fax:_____

Assistant's name:_____

Insurance agent (house):_____

Address:_____

_____

Phone:_____ Fax:_____

Assistant's name:_____

Insurance agent (auto):_____

Address:_____

_____

Phone:_____ Fax:_____

Assistant's name:_____

Stockbroker:_____

Address:_____

_____

Phone:_____ Fax:_____

Assistant's name:_____

Trust officer:_____

Address:_____

_____

Phone:_____ Fax:_____

Assistant's name:_____

Money manager:_____

Address:_____

_____

Phone:_____ Fax:_____

Assistant's name:_____

Doctor:_____

Address:_____

_____

Phone:_____ Fax:_____

Assistant's name:_____

Psychologist:_____

Address:_____

_____

Phone:_____ Fax:_____

Assistant's name:_____

Diane: Reactions to Contacting Agencies and Resource People

When Diane returned from her meeting with Dorothy Trumbull (her financial planner), she called Mark's office and asked for the person who handled the firm's insurance plans. She was advised that Karen Hutchinson handled these matters, so she made an appointment to meet with her toward the end of the week.

It took a great deal of determination and courage for Diane to cross the threshold of Mark's office. It had so many memories for her. She didn't think she could bear to hear the ongoing expressions of condolence and concern from Mark's partners and the murmuring of the secretaries and other support staff to one another, which she was sure identified her as Mark's widow, with some comment on her appearance or demeanor.

Diane was relieved that few people she knew were around when she arrived for her meeting with Karen Hutchinson. Karen was ready for her, and after appropriate but brief condolences, she was all business. She explained that Mark had an insurance policy with the firm that was worth $600,000. Diane had some options as to how she could receive this money, which the insurance agent handling the firm's account would explain to her.

Karen gave Diane his name and phone number. She confirmed that Diane would be able to maintain health insurance for herself and her children through the firm at their group rates for 36 months. Thereafter, she would have to make other arrangements.

In addition, Mark had a retirement account (Keogh plan) worth about $250,000, which he had managed himself and was invested in stocks. Karen gave Diane the name and phone number of the stockbroker with whom Mark had worked.

Finally, Mark had something called a capital account, which represented his investment in the firm. This account was worth $100,000 and would be available to her in the near future on a tax-free basis.

As Diane sat there and listened to Karen speaking in her dry, matter-of-fact voice, she allowed herself to be encouraged. By her rough calculations, she had $950,000 coming to her from the firm as well as the $100,000 from Mark's other insurance policies. Surely this would be enough to allow her to keep the children in their present schools. She thanked Karen for her time and the information and prepared to contact both the firm's insurance person, Jack Blafford, and Mark's stockbroker, Scott Truitt.

As she left Mark's office after speaking with Karen, Diane made a mental note to share her feelings about going into Mark's office at her next widow support group meeting. As she walked toward her car in the parking lot, a familiar route for Diane in the past, she found herself thinking that the woman now crossing the street to the parking lot was not quite the same woman who was married to Mark, the successful lawyer. Tears welled up in her eyes and rolled slowly down her cheeks. Mark didn't even know the women in the widow support group with whom she now shared her feelings and anxieties. Robyn, the school teacher, somewhat older than herself, had discovered that her financial situation was abysmal following her husband's illness. However, she was ever ready with a warm smile and words of encouragement for Diane. Marcy, in her late fifties, was eager to do whatever small thing she could to help Diane. Diane had come to rely on these new friends because they understood what she was experiencing. In some ways, she mourned the loss of the old Diane, yet was finding herself to have strengths she never dreamed she had.

In her impatience to move ahead in acquiring the financial information necessary to decide about the children's schools, Diane resolved to call both the firm's insurance agent and Mark's stockbroker as soon as she got home. She reached Jack first and scheduled an appointment with him for the early part of next week. Her appointment with Scott was for Friday of the same week.

Although she had considerable anxiety about going by herself to discuss money matters, Diane decided to believe what the women in her support group said about her strengths and "bite the bullet." She would try to see the insurance agent by herself. Jack turned out to be a very pleasant, well-dressed man about her age. He explained that she had some choices to make about the insurance money due her. She could receive it in a lump sum and invest it, or she could buy an annuity that would provide her with $3,015 in monthly income for the rest of her life. In fact, she had several choices as to how to receive the income.

Diane's initial reaction was one of relief. This nice man could handle this for her, and she would not have to worry about managing this large sum of money herself. She thought investing in the annuity was a good solution, but to appear more adult told him she wanted to think about it for a few days. However, what he had told her made a lot of sense. He was so sympathetic to her situation. After she left, she reminded herself that she had promised Dorothy she wouldn't do anything without at least discussing it with her first. Diane was sure she would agree with the idea of receiving monthly income from the fixed annuity, but would run it by her anyway.

Diane felt less secure about dealing with a stockbroker than an insurance agent. She considered asking one of the members of her support group to accompany her on this visit but decided instead to ask the mother of one of Jeremy's friends, Nancy Martin. Nancy was divorced, and Diane knew she was more knowledgeable when it came to finances. (Almost anyone would be more knowledgeable than she was, she thought to herself wryly!)

Her appointment with the stockbroker, Scott, to discuss Mark's Keogh plan was not as successful as her meeting with Jack. Scott was a man in his mid-thirties who spoke very rapidly about the investments Mark had made. As nearly as she could determine, Mark had invested in stocks that didn't pay any income. As she looked at the list of stocks Scott gave her, the page blurred before her. There were about 40 different companies

listed, and she had never heard of any of them. Where were the household names like American Telephone and General Motors which she
expected to see?

He told her the Keogh account should be rolled over into an IRA
account—whatever that meant—and that she could not start receiving
income from this account without paying penalties until she was age $59^1/_2$.
He explained if she did take money out of this account before that age, then
she would be taxed on the income received, and there would be an
additional surtax charged on any money she received.

Diane's spirits sank—The $1,050,000 she thought she had available last
week to provide her with income had shrunk to $800,000. However, this
still seemed like a lot of money. Instinctively, she didn't think Mark's
retirement plan was invested as safely as it should be for her and the
children. Also, she didn't think Scott and she could work together effectively. She needed someone who would take the time to explain things to
her, and Scott did not seem to be that person. She took the papers he gave
her to complete and decided that she had better see Dorothy sooner rather
than later about what action she should take next. Diane thought about how
much more complicated her life was these days as she drove to pick up her
carpool and drop Nancy off at her office.

Susan: Reactions to Contacting Agencies and Resource People

As promised, Harry's wife, Emily, invited Susan to dinner. She accepted
because intellectually she knew she should begin to force herself to have
some social activity. Dinner was an emotional struggle for Susan, but she
was pleased with herself for having made the effort, and the food was
delicious. Susan realized this was the first time since Lance had died that
she was aware of what she was eating and its taste. During dinner, Susan
told them she had set up an appointment with the trust officer at the bank to
discuss the $400,000 insurance trust.

Susan asked if Harry had had a chance to discuss this trust with her
two stepchildren since she was very anxious about their reactions. Having
no children of her own, she was unsure of the appropriateness of her

feelings. Susan knew that Lance's daughter would be particularly upset because she was entering her senior year of college. The $20,000 cash left to her would just about cover Leslie's college costs for the year. Eventually, she would receive the money from the insurance trust but not until Susan died.

Harry had met with the two stepchildren, and she had anticipated correctly that they were not pleased with the small amount of money they were to receive in the foreseeable future. They couldn't believe that Lance had not left them more. However, Harry told them that Lance had discussed this with him before making these arrangements. Lance felt very strongly that it was not good for children to have too much money at an early age. He believed they should make their own way in the world as he had done. Lance thought that by the time the children received money from the trust they would be mature enough to handle it. Unfortunately, Lance had not had the chance to tell them this himself.

Susan decided to ask Harry about her mother's situation. Her feelings about her mother's financial needs were representative of those of many adult children, widowed or not. As the elderly population has grown, so too have their economic needs and the likelihood that there may not be sufficient resources to meet these financial needs. Susan was concerned about her mother and felt it was her responsibility to obtain the best care possible for her. Susan was inclined to utilize whatever financial resources were available to her to provide for her mother as opposed to allowing her stepson to take on yet more graduate school education. It was at times like these that she felt overwhelmed by the tasks ahead of her. She was glad she had Dr. Coleman with whom to discuss these feelings.

Susan hoped that when she talked to the bank trust officer she would understand more about the $400,000 insurance trust Lance had established. She was most anxious to know the terms of the trust and what the income from the trust would be.

John Stepstone, the trust officer, explained that she would receive income from this trust for life. At her death, her stepchildren would receive whatever principal remained. He said that the trust department would manage the portfolio so that she would receive a reasonable amount of income—5 percent annually. The trust could be managed to pay her more income, but in view of her relatively young age, they wanted to invest so that the trust would grow in value over the years. Susan wasn't sure she wanted the trust to grow—after all it only meant her stepchildren would inherit more money. Mr. Stepstone explained that in order to increase the annual income he needed to invest so that the principal would also grow. If the assets in the trust paid a higher income, then the growth potential would be limited. If, on the other hand, the principal increased in value and continued to pay 5 percent, then the income she received would increase annually.

For example, at 5 percent the $400,000 would provide her with about $20,000 annual income. In addition, since they were investing for growth, they would hope to obtain a 7 percent increase in principal for an annual total return of 12 percent over the next ten years. If they were able to do this, the $400,000 would grow to $800,000 during this period of time. If the portfolio continued to pay 5 percent, then ten years hence, the income would double to $40,000 ($800,000 × 5%).

This approach was reassuring to Susan because she was concerned about her mother's costs in the retirement home increasing annually. With the current level of income obtained from the trust, it looked as if she could cover most of her mother's expenses. Mr. Stepstone explained that she would receive monthly statements from the bank. The trust department would arrange to deposit the monthly trust income to her checking account. The management fees for this service would be deducted from the income generated by the trust account. When he had estimated a 5 percent return to her, he had already deducted these fees. He mentioned that because Susan was providing the majority of her mother's support, she could declare her as her dependent on her tax return.

Mr. Stepstone introduced her to Ms. Peabody, who would be assigned to manage her account. He explained that he was the head of the trust department and supervised all the accounts, but Ms. Peabody would be her personal trust officer. Susan could call her with any questions she might have.

Susan resolved to talk with Lance's stockbroker, Bob O'Brien. Following Harry's instructions, she called Bob and asked him to supply her with a current list of their stocks. She asked him to value the portfolio as of the date of death. Harry had explained that since the assets were in Lance's name, these stocks would be valued in the estate as of the date of death or six months later, whichever date she and her lawyer selected as most desirable to her from a tax point of view. Harry had told her that the date they chose for valuing the estate assets had to be the same for all estate assets.

Next, Susan asked Bob which stocks he would recommend she sell to raise the $40,000 for her stepchildren. She intended to go over the portfolio in greater detail with him at a later date, but she wanted to make these sales now so she could resolve the situation with them as soon as possible. Bob said he would be back to her with his recommendations as soon as possible. Susan felt she was making some progress. She had a lot of issues to sort through all at once, and she had to be careful not to neglect her job—after all, she couldn't afford to lose that income. Dr. Coleman had impressed upon her her primary responsibility was to herself, and maintaining her mental health was an important part of that.

Audrey: Reactions to Contacting Agencies and Resource People

John Jr. had asked his mother when she would be ready to sit down with him to review her financial situation, and so far, she had been able to postpone this meeting. She found it odd that it never occurred to him that she was capable of dealing with financial matters on her own. As long as she assured him that she didn't need any money, he assumed she hadn't done anything. Fortunately, he hadn't pushed her about it. She realized that he was only trying to help, and she shouldn't be so reluctant to accept his assistance. On the other hand, he was inclined to be domineering, and she wanted to sort things out for herself.

She called Social Security as Mr. Humphrey had told her to and found that as John's widow she would start receiving $674 per month. They told her she could instruct Social Security to deposit the money in her bank account directly, and she decided to do so. That was one less check to worry about losing!

Mr. Humphrey told her to contact the bank where their mortgage was held. They informed her that the current amount due them was $20,000 and that she had eight years left to pay on their 30-year mortgage. The interest rate was $8\frac{1}{2}$ percent, and the monthly payments were $263. Audrey wondered if she should pay off the mortgage so she would not have to worry about the payments anymore.

Mr. Humphrey had told her that she should have the house appraised for the estate valuation. If she decided to sell the house, for tax purposes, one-half of the cost of the house would be based on this valuation, and one-half would be based on their original cost. Since their original cost was $50,000 and the house was now worth $200,000, there would be a $75,000 gain if she sold it. (Half the original cost plus half the current market value equals $125,000.) However, he explained that she did have a $125,000 one-time allowance that she would probably want to use when she sold the house to avoid paying a capital gains tax. He emphasized that it was important to get an independent appraisal to establish the current market value.

It didn't take Audrey long to locate her file with her notes from the retirement lectures given by Mr. Silver (the financial planner). She called his office and told the receptionist she wanted to meet with him. This person said it might be helpful for Audrey to complete a financial questionnaire prior to their meeting. Audrey asked if it were mandatory for her to do this before seeing Mr. Silver. The woman assured her that it was not a requirement, but it would make their first meeting more productive. Audrey explained that she had recently been widowed and at this point just wanted to have an initial interview. The receptionist said there would be no problem with that and made an appointment for the following week.

Before Audrey had an opportunity to meet with Mr. Silver, she was contacted by a Mr. Postman. This man called her on the phone and said that he worked for a local stock brokerage firm and was sorry to learn of her husband's death. Audrey found this comment a little odd since she had never heard of this man—perhaps he was one of John's friends from the office. However, she soon realized that this man did not know her or John—he just read the obituary notices as a way to identify potential clients. She told him firmly but politely that she did not intend to deal with a stranger. She was grateful for the support of the professionals with whom she was working. She was also very pleased with her decision to add what she hoped would be an additional support person by making an appointment to meet with Mr. Silver, the financial planner. She wondered what other widows did who didn't have anyone to trust.

When she met with Mr. Silver, his first question was: "How can I help you?" She told him about John's pension income and her Social Security income. She mentioned the stock in the company John used to work for as well as the $40,000 insurance money she had received. She told him of her concerns about Joanne and her resentment of John Jr. trying to tell her what to do. She wondered if she should sell her house or keep it. Audrey was amazed at all the questions she asked this man whom she had just met, but somehow she really felt at ease with him.

He suggested that she take no immediate action, but fill out the financial questionnaire he used, which would give him a better idea of what her income and expenses might be. At that point, they could determine if she had sufficient income and, ultimately, how best to invest her money. He asked her to fill in as much of the form as she could. If she had trouble, he or his assistant would be glad to help her.

He next asked her how much investment experience she had, and she confessed very little. Mr. Silver said that he wanted her to understand what she was doing and assured her that there was no rush to do anything. He recommended that she leave the insurance money with the insurance company, where it would continue to earn interest. Since the company John used to work for was such a good one, he encouraged her to hold that stock for the time being.

Mr. Silver said that with the information she provided he could estimate what her taxable income and cash flow would be this year and next. He would also prepare a balance sheet listing her assets and liabilities. In order to do this, he also needed to see their last year's federal and state tax returns. Audrey gave him the name and phone number of their accountant, Mr. Lewis. She said she would call him and tell him to send copies of the tax returns to Mr. Silver. Once he had reviewed these calculations, then they could decide what action they should take to make sure she had adequate income. There would be a fee to prepare these computations and to advise her about these decisions. This fee would be based on the hours needed to put her plan together. The bill would be payable after the work had been completed.

Mr. Silver gave her a contract to take home, read, sign and return to him. The estimated fee he quoted seemed reasonable, but Audrey thought she should discuss this with Mr. Humphrey before signing anything.

It was just about noon when she left Mr. Silver's office. Dr. PaPadisio's words echoed in her mind, and she thought she should do something about lunch. But what? Should she call Joanne? What about the children? It was too late to call one of her friends with whom she used to have lunch on a regular basis. She stood on the corner watching people hurry by as the lunch hour began. She roused herself out of her reverie and determined to call Joanne and ask if she and the younger two children had eaten yet. If not, she thought she'd treat them to a picnic at home. She really hadn't had an opportunity to spend much time with her grandchildren this past year, and it would be fun to see them and have some time to talk to Joanne. Joanne was more than pleased with her mother's suggestion since she was just about to make the children their usual peanut butter and jelly sandwich, which was their current food kick. It would be great to have lunch taken care of by her mother. It had been so long since they had done something like that.

Audrey retrieved her car from the parking lot and drove to her favorite delicatessen en route to Joanne's house. She got all kinds of things and toted the bag to the car with anticipation of surprising the children and her daughter. She felt somewhat lighthearted and allowed herself to enjoy the feeling.

The children were so excited to see her. They jumped up and down and tugged at her skirt. Joanne had to peel them off her leg so that she could deposit her food bag in the kitchen. Little Noah had changed so much since she had really looked at him. He seemed to have jumped from an infant to a toddler. Heidi, at almost four, looked different, too. Both of them wanted to drag her off to look at some treasure in their rooms. Joanne allowed "Gran Gran" to be monopolized by the children for a short while before insisting that they all come to the kitchen to eat. The deli sandwiches smelled delicious, and clearly Joanne appreciated the change in daily routine. It turned out to be quite a festive occasion. The children were thrilled with the giant cookies "Gran Gran" had brought for them.

After lunch, Audrey agreed to read them a story before they went down for their naps. She told them how much she had missed them and promised to visit again very soon. She thought she would not be there when they awakened from their naps and didn't want them to be disappointed. She couldn't get over how much little Heidi resembled Joanne, who in turn resembled her dad.

Joanne settled the children on their beds for their naps and returned to the kitchen to have tea with her mother. Audrey seemed to be noticing things with new eyes. She had been so preoccupied with John's care, followed by the funeral and the sorting out of her financial situation, that she had been oblivious to everything else. Joanne looked a little weary, and Audrey wondered just how long she had been looking peaked. When she asked Joanne if she was all right, her daughter burst into tears and said she was fine, but it was so difficult caring for the three children and simultaneously worrying about how they would manage on Keith's current salary. Also, she had apparently had a problem dealing with her father's death. They had always been very close.

Audrey put her arms around her daughter and shed some tears of her own. She hadn't thought sufficiently about what Joanne might be going through. As they wiped the tears from their eyes, Audrey shared with Joanne an idea she had just formulated. She told her about Dr. PaPadisio's recommendations about her nutrition. She thought it would be good for them to spend one day a week enjoying lunch and some shopping or whatever. She wanted Joanne to find a baby-sitter one day a week for about five hours, for whom Audrey would assume the financial obligation. It would be good for both of them. They really hadn't had time for much mother-daughter togetherness since Joanne had married seven years ago.

Audrey also wanted to have the opportunity to get to know her grandchildren better and proposed to Joanne that she plan on spending one-half day a week with the grandchildren. She had always enjoyed the various activities and projects one undertook with children, and in this way, Joanne could have some time for herself and Audrey would have an opportunity to do some of the things she had missed doing since her own children were young.

Joanne was taken aback by her mother's generosity and thought she couldn't allow her mother to do so much for her at this time of stress in her life. Audrey overcame Joanne's reluctance by telling her daughter that what she was proposing would be beneficial to both of them. This persuaded Joanne to agree. She said she would try to find a sitter so they could get started on the "women's day out" as soon as possible. They hugged each other extra hard when Audrey left to return to her home and walk her dog. While en route, Audrey considered some of the other things she had been neglecting and determined to make more of an effort to contact some of the women with whom she had formerly been friendly. She knew they had tried to stay in touch, but she just hadn't been ready.

Elizabeth: Reactions to Contacting Agencies and Resource People

Sam accompanied Elizabeth the following Tuesday for her appointment with Mr. Grossfeldt. The atmosphere of the office was leathery but warm. Mr. Grossfeldt explained to her that presently Ben's account was being managed by an investment advisor, but she should consider using the services of a bank trust department in the future. He said that banks tend to be conservative, and their approach might be more appropriate at this stage of her life—especially since she had no dependents. He would be glad to introduce her to someone at the bank he used for many of his clients.

Elizabeth told him about her idea of giving Ben's automobile to the church, and he thought this might be a good idea. He suggested she talk it over with Pastor Appletorn. He might want to sell it and use the proceeds for current church projects. However, before she could do anything, she would have to change the car registration from Ben's name to her name. Elizabeth had a moment of panic—where did Ben keep the registration?

Mr. Grossfeldt also suggested that she consider doing some estate planning of her own. However, he thought she should put together the necessary information about her expenses, her income and her current net worth before they did any estate planning.

Elizabeth left Mr. Grossfeldt's office greatly relieved and thanked Sam profusely for introducing her. She thought that having a bank handle her money might be a good idea—certainly she didn't know anything about investments. She would follow Mr. Grossfeldt's suggestion and meet with the bank trust officer he recommended. Elizabeth needed to get better organized herself before changing advisors. She was most grateful to Sam. What would she have done without his help?

Before going any further, Elizabeth decided to visit her bank and check the contents of the safety-deposit box. Fortunately, prior to Ben's death, he had moved everything into a safety-deposit box in her name. She had no trouble gaining access to it, but the assistant manager at the bank, Ms. Riley, said that the state of Massachusetts would have required sealing the safety-deposit box if it had been held in joint name with Ben. Elizabeth found little in the box when she opened it other than a few pieces of Ben's mother's jewelry.

With Ms. Riley's help, she set up an account for the income from Ben's estate assets and changed their joint checking account to her name as Mr. Grossfeldt had told her to do. Ms. Riley was very helpful and urged her to call her if she had any questions. Elizabeth was pretty tired by now. She had spent more time with other people than she had in quite some time and had a lot of information to digest. She thought she needed to go home and rest.

CHAPTER 7

Developing a Meaningful Budget

We couldn't possibly know where it would lead, but we knew it had to be done.

BETTY FRIEDAN

Introduction

You have accumulated information about your financial situation from the various people you have visited. Now you want to use this information to estimate what income you can expect to receive and what you think your expenses will be. Once you have these numbers, then you will know if you have sufficient income on which to live comfortably.

To put together a meaningful budget, first you need to list your projected income sources. Then review your checkbook for the past year to determine what your expenses have been in the past. With this information, you should be able to project future income and expense items.

In the next chapter, we will review your assets and liabilities to determine if any of them could or should be repositioned to provide you with additional income should you discover you need more income than you are currently receiving.

126

Projected Income Sources

We suggest that you start a new notebook for this purpose so the new information does not get mixed in with the estate settlement issues.*

When you contacted Social Security, Veterans Administration and your husband's former employers, they told you how much income you could expect from each source and when it would start. List these sources, the amount and the frequency of payment in a notebook (see figure 7-1).

Under this "income" category, list everything you are sure you will receive. If you work, include your employment income. If you are self-employed, list your net income (the gross amount earned less expenses needed to generate the income). If you have other sources of income, list them as well. Also list how often the income is paid: monthly (M), quarterly (Q) or annually (A).

There may be a time lag before the income from your husband's assets and pension plans starts coming in, so for a short period, you may have to live on cash reserves. Be very careful to keep a record of any cash you

FIGURE 7-1
SOURCES OF INCOME

	Amount $	When Paid (M) (Q) (A)
Salary	——————	——————
Net Self-Employed Income	——————	——————
Social Security	——————	——————
Pension	——————	——————
Investments	——————	——————
Other	——————	——————
Total	——————	——————

* In these next two chapters, we will provide you with sample forms to enable you to put together the information you will need to make present and future financial decisions.

receive during this period and its source. With money coming in from various places, you may inadvertently spend principal—which you may need later.*

It is a good idea to establish a separate bank or money market account for any payments you receive as the result of your husband's death, such as insurance proceeds, to make sure the money is segregated for investment purposes.

Current Bills

Before estimating what your current expenses are, you need to list your current outstanding bills. As we discussed before, divide them into your bills, your husband's bills and joint bills. Your husband's outstanding medical and hospital bills should be paid from the estate asset account.

If you are uncertain which bills need to be paid now and which later, ask your primary financial advisor for help. Keep records of what you paid and when. In order to estimate your future expenses, you first need to list your past fixed expenses and then your discretionary expenses.

Current Expenses

FIXED EXPENSES

In order to project future expenses, you need to first review what they are currently. The easiest place to start is with your fixed expenses—those you are committed to pay at regular intervals. Some of them are due monthly, and others, such as household and auto insurance payments, are due annually or quarterly.

Typical monthly bills include the mortgage, car payments and utilities. These expenses are fixed because you must pay them each month, but the amount may vary each month. If you want to regularize some of these

---

* If you are concerned whether you will have enough money to pay all your bills, ask your attorney what to do. Paying the wrong bills may be a problem later.

payments, call the utility companies and ask if they have a monthly payment schedule. They will review your past bills and put you on a billing schedule that will require equal monthly payments. In this way, you can avoid receiving a very high bill in one month that you had not anticipated.

You may also need to make quarterly federal and state tax payments, which your accountant will estimate for you. Mark in your notebook and on your monthly calendar when these bills should be paid. Later, when you pay them, mark the amount paid and the date.

Use a notebook to set up an inventory of your fixed expenses, as shown in figure 7-2.

DISCRETIONARY EXPENSES

Discretionary expenses vary from month to month. These would include: groceries, meals eaten out, clothing, dry-cleaning, entertainment, vacations, personal care (health club, hairdresser and drugstore), dues and subscriptions, housekeeper. Look at your checkbook to see what these have been in the past, and list them in your notebook. You may want to use one page in your notebook for each category. These expenses will probably change in your current situation, but to estimate future expenses, it is helpful to look at past expenses first (see figure 7-3).

Projected Fixed Expenses

Now that you have an idea of what your previous expenses were, it should be easier to estimate what your expenses will be in the future, starting with the fixed expenses.

MORTGAGE PAYMENTS AND REAL ESTATE TAXES

When you notify your mortgage holder of your husband's death, ask him to explain what your current payment includes. Real estate taxes are often included in the payment. In that case, the bank estimates what your real estate taxes will be and incorporates them into your monthly mortgage payments. Once a year, the bank looks at the actual real estate taxes you

FIGURE 7-2

INVENTORY OF FIXED EXPENSES

	Amount Due $	Date Next Due	How Often Due (M) (Q) (A)
Mortgage	_____	_____	_____
Utilities			
Gas	_____	_____	_____
Electric	_____	_____	_____
Water	_____	_____	_____
Telephone	_____	_____	_____
Co-op/Condo Fee	_____	_____	_____
Rent	_____	_____	_____
Loan Payments	_____	_____	_____
Car Payments	_____	_____	_____
Insurance Premiums			
Medical	_____	_____	_____
Life	_____	_____	_____
Homeowner	_____	_____	_____
Auto	_____	_____	_____
Personal Liability	_____	_____	_____
Taxes			
Real Estate	_____	_____	_____
Personal Property	_____	_____	_____
Federal	_____	_____	_____
State	_____	_____	_____
Self-Employed	_____	_____	_____

FIGURE 7-3
INVENTORY OF DISCRETIONARY EXPENSES

	Total Last 12 Months $	*Monthly $*
Groceries		
Clothing		
Home Maintenance		
Home Improvement		
Auto Maintenance		
Entertainment		
Dues (club/professional)		
Subscriptions/Books		
Vacation Trips		
Domestic Help		
Household Purchases		
Gifts/Birthdays		
Dry-Cleaning		
Drugstore		
Hairdresser		
Transportation		
Yard/Pool Maintenance		
Education (indicate whose)		
Unreimbursed Medical Expenses		
Child Care		
Charitable Contributions		
Tax Preparation Fee		
Unreimbursed Business Expenses		
Legal Fees		
Accounting Fees		

owed versus the estimated amount. If taxes due were in excess of the amount paid, then your monthly mortgage payment will increase. Actually, real estate taxes are due semiannually, and some people prefer to pay them on this basis. If your husband chose this method of payment, you need to be aware of it in order to avoid the shock of receiving an unexpectedly large tax bill. If this is uncomfortable for you, arrange to pay on a monthly basis.

You need to know the terms of your mortgage loan. At the end of each year, your mortgage holder sends you a statement of how much principal you still owe, how many years are left on the mortgage note and what your current interest rate is. Interest rates on some mortgage loans change periodically. You need to know if this might happen to you and if so, when. If you don't understand the terms of the mortgage (nowadays they are not always easy to figure out), have your accountant or financial planner interpret them for you and put them in writing.

To develop a meaningful budget for the future, you need to know if your mortgage payment will increase or decrease. Many widows panic about the size of the payments and want to pay the mortgage off right away. This is not usually a good idea. These payments provide you with tax deductions that you may well need. This is another major decision that should be made only after looking at the total picture. Right now you're trying to determine what you owe on a monthly basis.

HOME EQUITY LOANS

Home equity loans (HELs) have become very popular in recent years. However, these loans are difficult to understand. Basically, a home equity loan is a line of credit against your house. It is secondary to the mortgage on the house and often monthly payments are for the interest on the loan only and no principal is being repaid. This loan is usually from a different bank than the one that holds your mortgage.

If you have a home equity loan, ask the lender to spell out its terms and conditions. Have your financial advisor look at this loan right away because it might be one you want to pay off or change. The rate is often higher than what you are paying on your primary mortgage.

Projected Discretionary Expenses

Look at the expenses that seem necessary now but may not be in the future. For instance, it may not be essential to maintain two cars, to keep a second home or to remain a member of a club. Again, these are decisions to make after you have gathered all the facts.

Spending money on groceries is not discretionary, but the amount you spend is. Your costs should be lower now because you are feeding one less person. On the other hand, other expenses may increase. If your husband was an avid gardener, but you don't know the difference between a rake and a trowel, you may have to hire a gardener, which will be an increased expense.

A word of caution: We recommend strongly that you postpone major purchases until you know your total financial picture. The money you spend now on luxuries you might need later for necessities.

When you estimate your future discretionary expenses, we would suggest you put down two budget figures—the minimum amount you could live with and the amount you would like to spend, but you can do without if necessary (see figure 7-4). For instance, you might have been accustomed to going to the hairdresser once a week, but maybe you could go once a month instead. On the other hand, belonging to a health club might seem to be a luxury, but it might be a necessity at this time to maintain your mental health!

Checking Your Estimated Expenses

Once you have estimated your expenses, keep a record of how you actually spend your money. We would suggest you make a page in your notebook for each expense category and then, as you pay the bill or spend cash, note it in your book. Ask for receipts for everything to make this recordkeeping easier. Mark an envelope for each expense category, and put the receipts in these envelopes.

Total each expense category once a month, and see how close you came

FIGURE 7-4

ESTIMATED MONTHLY DISCRETIONARY EXPENSES

	Minimum $	*Preferred $*	*Actual $*
Groceries			
Clothing			
Home Maintenance			
Home Improvement			
Auto Maintenance			
Entertainment			
Dues (club/professional)			
Subscriptions/Books			
Vacation Trips			
Domestic Help			
Household Purchases			
Gifts/Birthdays			
Dry-Cleaning			
Drugstore			
Hairdresser			
Transportation			
Yard/Pool Maintenance			
Education (indicate whose)			
Unreimbursed Medical Expenses			
Child Care			
Charitable Contributions (cash)			
Tax Preparation Fee			
Unreimbursed Business Expenses			
Legal Fees			
Finance Charges Credit Cards			
Accounting Fees			

to your initial estimate. There is no right or wrong here. Most widows find they have overestimated in some categories and underestimated in others. Initially, your grocery bills may be low because friends bring you food or you don't feel like cooking. After a while, this expense will return to something more normal for your new circumstances.

At the end of six months, review your initial estimates, compare them to the actual expenditures and develop a new budget, which should be more accurate. Then check this "new" budget after six months. After a while, you won't need to keep such close tabs on your expenditures. However, don't lose sight of the fact that it is essential to your financial security to know how you spend your money.

Cash Flow Statement

Now that you have calculated your income and expenses, you want to total both categories and find out if you have more than enough income (positive cash flow) or insufficient income (negative cash flow) (see figure 7-5).

This initial estimate of income and expenses will give you a better idea of your current financial situation. However, do not panic if you have a negative cash flow. Your advisor can help rectify this situation. You are still in the fact-gathering stage.

Conversely, if after putting this statement together, you may find that you have sufficient income to cover your expenses currently. Although this information is comforting, you must keep in mind your long-term situation. What is sufficient income today may not be ten years from now.

When planning, make sure your income keeps pace with increasing expenses. If inflation increases at 5 percent annually, you have to double your after-tax income every 14 years just to stay even with inflation. In other words, if $30,000 is sufficient annual income today, you will need $60,000 14 years from now and $120,000 28 years hence. Taxes (federal, state, property and sales) are increasing annually, and you need to budget for these as well.

FIGURE 7-5

CASH FLOW STATEMENT SUMMARY AS OF _____

For: _____

Estimated Income

    Salary $_____

    Net Self-Employed Income   _____

    Social Security   _____

    Pension   _____

    Investments   _____

    Other   _____

      Total $_____

Estimated Expenses

    Fixed Expenses $_____

    Discretionary Expenses   _____

      Total $_____

Excess Income (Expense) $_____

Conclusion

In this chapter, you first itemized your current outstanding bills and determined which ones to pay and which to defer. Then you estimated what your future monthly income would be. Finally, you determined what your monthly expenses have been and what you estimate they will be in the future. These estimates will indicate if you have sufficient income to maintain your current life-style or if you have to make some adjustments.

Diane: Reactions to the Budgeting Process

Diane had a difficult time with her budget. She had never had to keep track of expenses. She just spent money on items needed for the house and the children, and Mark paid the bills. There always seemed to be enough, so she didn't worry about money. She had taken for granted the children needed a private school education because she and Mark had decided it was preferable to the education provided by the public schools. Whether or not the children went to private schools was unrelated to cost for Diane—that had always been Mark's department. She was beginning to recognize that it was that way about everything related to finances.

A part of Diane wished she could return to her former mode of functioning, but another part of her resented the fact that she had been treated like a child when it came to anything financial. She could still see Mark seated at his desk in the den paying the bills and telling the children, if they interrupted him, he couldn't talk to them right then because he had bills to pay. As disloyal as she felt, Diane realized she was sometimes angry at Mark for leaving her in this mess. At first she couldn't tolerate anyone saying anything the slightest bit negative about Mark, but here she was finding herself angry with him for the financial mess with which she needed to deal. When she first heard the women in her widow support group talk about the anger they sometimes felt toward their husbands for abandoning them and leaving them to deal with all of life's problems, she initially couldn't relate to what they were experiencing. She thought they hadn't been fortunate enough to be married to someone like Mark. They told her she'd have similar feelings at some point in the grieving process, but she had rejected what they said as just being something they were feeling because of their particular husbands.

Here she was several months later having the very response she had defended herself against with her group. Actually, she didn't know how she would have managed without this group, and particularly Robyn, these past months. They had become such good friends. Robyn was so understanding. She could talk to her about anything. Jennifer Greenberg had also become a friend. She, too, always made the time to be helpful and available.

Diane couldn't believe the majority of her social contacts were with people Mark didn't even know. She'd have to think about this further, but right now she had to look at private school education on a dollars-and-cents basis. Everything seemed to be so expensive.

At the urging of her financial planner, Diane had gone to the Social Security office and asked them exactly what she could expect to receive from them. It was difficult to understand because the amount of money she and the children would receive seemed to keep changing. However, she realized she needed to understand how it worked, so she wrote it down carefully in her notebook.

The bottom line was Social Security was going to provide her and the children with a monthly income (about $2,000) for the present. However, as each child (assuming he or she was a full-time student) turned 19, the amount they as a family received would decrease. When the youngest turned 16, Diane's payments would stop entirely. This meant Diane would receive no Social Security benefits of her own from age 51 until she turned 60, at which time she would receive a widow's benefit. The idea of having no income from Social Security for nine years was scary—what would she do? She couldn't think that far ahead. Even worse, Diane discovered she could lose her portion of the benefits if she worked and earned too much. The amount she could earn without losing benefits would increase annually to reflect cost-of-living increases.

Diane's head began to swim. How could something as simple as Social Security be so complex? She really didn't know how she could handle all of this. She knew she had to understand it for the sake of the children, so she would continue to review the information she had obtained to date.

Diane knew she had $600,000 insurance from the firm, which the insurance agent had told her could provide her with a lifetime income of $3,015 per month. Since her mortgage payments were just about $2,633 per month, it looked like the family would have to live on the difference ($382) plus the Social Security payments ($2,000 per month).

The three children's private school bills totaled $15,000 per year, and then there was camp and piano lessons and swimming. She had just received a real estate tax bill for $1,600 for six months. How would she ever work this all out? Diane wasn't a financial genius, but she didn't think they could live on $2,400 per month—especially with the tuition payments. The only other money she had was the $100,000 capital account from the firm and the $100,000 from the insurance policies. She made an appointment with Dorothy right away to see how she could cover her expenses.

They had put a deposit on a beach house for a couple of weeks this summer (cost $2,000). This would be an opportunity for the family to be together, so this seemed to her to be a necessary expense. She dreaded the thought of going through Christmas without Mark; it was his favorite holiday. They had planned to take the family skiing. She was tempted to do it anyway so they wouldn't be haunted by the memories of Christmases past. Enough. She had to focus on her financial situation.

Based on the information Diane had provided her, Dorothy prepared an expense statement for Diane and the children which showed their total expenses were $118,460 annually.

Dorothy gave Diane a second statement called a *cash flow statement*, which she emphasized was very preliminary. Under "income," Dorothy had factored in the Social Security payments ($24,000) and the proposed annuity ($36,186). These totaled $60,186. Then she took the $200,000 Diane would receive from the capital account and insurance money and assumed that $160,000 earned 6 percent, and $40,000 earned 4 percent. She also assumed that the $10,000 Diane had in savings would earn 4 percent. She explained she used a lower rate of interest for $50,000 of the money because she wanted Diane to have an adequate emergency cash reserve invested in a money market fund even though this would provide a lower level of income than long-term investments.

The good news was that since part of the projected annuity payment was not taxed (39 percent), and her mortgage payments were relatively high, she would not have to pay any taxes. The bad news was that according to Diane's estimate, her expenses would exceed her income by $46,673 in 1993, $51,785 in 1994 and $55,461 in 1995. Needless to say, Diane was really upset when she saw this, as she thought the expense estimates she had given Dorothy were very low. They certainly were less than the family had spent when Mark was alive.

Her situation was obviously a lot worse than she thought. Diane tried not to panic. Perhaps she should consider selling her house or putting the children in public school. Maybe her father could help out, although she certainly didn't want to admit to him that Mark had not provided adequately for her and the family (even though it was beginning to look that way).

Dorothy suggested that Diane review her expense estimates to see if she couldn't reduce them. Dorothy had some ideas about selecting other investments that might provide more income than the annuity. She would work on increasing the income side of the cash flow statement while Diane worked on decreasing her expense estimates.

Dorothy said that she hated to be the bearer of such bad news, but if they both worked hard trying to solve this cash flow problem, she knew that they would be successful. It was difficult for Diane not to be disheartened as she left the office, but she resolved to review the budget once again. Although she didn't want to worry them too much, she thought the time had come to discuss the situation with the children.

DIANE'S PRELIMINARY ANNUAL BUDGET

Annual Income		
Social Security	$24,000	
Proposed Annuity	36,186	
Investment Income	11,600	
Total		$ 71,786
Annual Expenses		
Mortgage	$31,592	
Auto Loan	5,478	
Credit Card Interest	1,800	
Tuition	15,000	
Other	64,590	
Total		118,460
Annual Negative Cash Flow		$(46,674)

Susan: Reactions to the Budgeting Process

Susan handled her own finances before marrying Lance, but since that was 12 years ago, she realized those figures would be vastly different from her present ones. She needed to locate the records of their expenses as a couple so she could determine what her new budget would be. She knew that

Lance had put all that information on the computer, and she had asked Sarah's help to access these expense figures.

Sarah had located the information on Lance's computer, but as she explained to Susan, Lance's system appeared incredibly complicated. After discussing it further, Sarah helped Susan transfer the relevant information to a more basic program that Harry had given her. It would be much simpler to understand and maintain.

Susan was still worried about her mother. She knew her mother's retirement home would cost $1,500 per month. These costs would increase annually. Mr. Stepstone told her that the trust would provide about $1,700 income per month. This would cover her mother's costs at least initially. Susan realized this trust income would be taxed, so her budget would be tight.

Her mother did receive some Social Security income, so if she kept her personal expenses down, maybe they would have enough. Sarah confirmed that Susan could take her mother as a dependent on her tax return since she was providing over half of her mother's support. At least that was some help! However, Sarah explained that there was a technical tax issue involved if she intended to give her mother $20,000 a year to pay for the retirement home. Under current law, if you give anyone more than $10,000 a year, then the amount in excess of $10,000 is taxable to the recipient, and the donor has to pay a gift tax. However, if part of the $20,000 was spent on medical expenses, as seemed likely in this case, then this part would not be considered a taxable gift.

Susan couldn't believe that paying her mother's expenses might mean she owed additional taxes. That didn't seem fair, especially since she would have to pay income tax on this trust income before she gave it away! Sarah told her that one solution would be to give her brother, Ron, $10,000, which he could turn around and give to their mother. Then Susan could still give $10,000 to her mother. This complicated approach seemed cumbersome to Susan, but if it avoided gift taxes, then she would do it. She needed to explain this to Ron.

In her sessions with Dr. Coleman, Susan was beginning to identify the various ways she dealt with stress and life in general. She had become aware of her tendency to assume full responsibility for things when there was no need to do so. Her mother's financial support was a good case in point. Why had she assumed all of the responsibility for her mother? Her brother, Ron, was single and had no financial obligations other than his personal maintenance, yet she never considered discussing with him either the selection of a retirement facility or its cost. She didn't mind investigating the options related to their mother's care, but with her increasing self-knowledge, she decided she would no longer assume the entire financial burden for her. Although Ron had never taken responsibility for their mother on any level, she thought it was time to make him aware of their mother's monetary needs. She would ask him to help her financially, as his contributing even a small amount would be helpful.

Susan had not been particularly effective in her job recently, but they were very understanding. She found herself working longer hours, but accomplishing less. In this area, too, it had been helpful to discuss her feelings with Dr. Coleman. In the past, if she was not working to capacity at all times, she felt guilty. Dr. Coleman was helping her realize she placed unreasonable demands on herself. She had used the analogy of a machine with Susan, reminding her that only machines worked at the same pace, completing the same process without variation. She stressed to Susan that she was not a machine, but a human. There was no need to feel guilty about her decreased functioning on the job. She had suffered a major loss with no warning. It came as a shock to Susan that Dr. Coleman felt her employer and coworkers would anticipate Susan's performance on the job to be not quite what it normally was this soon after Lance's death. Dr. Coleman assured her that this was not a permanent condition and she would return to her normal functioning as time passed. Susan was beginning to accept the fact that she had always been exceptionally demanding of herself, and she wondered what factors in her life had led her to act this way throughout her life. She would have to explore this issue further, but for now, she needed to address her financial situation.

When she put together her present budget, she had a negative cash flow of about $16,000. It looked as if she could not afford to keep the lake cottage she and Lance had bought. Emotionally, she did not want to sell it because it held so many memories of the happy times she had there with Lance, but cottage costs (mortgage, real estate taxes, maintenance, insurance, utilities) totaled $8,500. She might have to sell their condo as well, but she really loved their apartment. She had become attached to the beautiful view and to the space of two bedrooms. It certainly was much more comfortable than the efficiency she lived in before marrying Lance.

But facts were facts. It appeared she did not have enough income to support her current life-style. Maybe she could find a smaller apartment in the same building—or maybe she should look for a better paying job—a thought that had not previously crossed her mind. In any case, Susan resolved to keep careful records of how she spent her money.

Thank goodness the association paid her insurance premiums (medical, disability and life). It also matched her contributions to her 401(k) pension plan 25 cents on the dollar for the first $4,000 she contributed.

As far as her personal income, Susan thought her salary was pretty secure at $55,000. She had been at the association for ten years and had received regular raises.

SUSAN'S PRELIMINARY ANNUAL BUDGET

Annual Income		
Salary	$55,000	
Trust Income	20,000	
Stock Income	1,280	
Total		$76,280
Annual Expenses		
Mortgage Condo	$15,796	
Mortgage Cottage	5,265	
Mother's Retirement Home	18,000	
Taxes, FICA	14,592	
Other	35,000	
401(k)	4,000	
Total		92,653
Annual Negative Cash Flow		$(16,373)

Audrey: Reactions to the Budgeting Process

Audrey looked at her sources of income, and it seemed as if she had enough to pay her expenses. John's pension provided her with $3,500 per month. However, these payments would remain constant for the rest of her life. She also would receive his Social Security payment of $674 per month. The Social Security people told her this payment would increase the beginning of each year in accordance with the cost of living adjustment (COLA).

Audrey reviewed her checkbook for the past year and put together her expenses for Mr. Silver. It was obvious to her that they would be higher in the future. She had done little else besides care for John over the past couple of years. She had not spent much on clothes, they had done no entertaining, she had not had the time or inclination to go to their club, and they had taken no vacations. These were all expenses she expected to increase in the coming year.

Thinking about life-style reminded her of the invitation she had reluctantly accepted to attend a small dinner party given by one of their closest friends. It had felt very different going to a dinner party by herself. She realized not being part of a couple was an adjustment. She didn't really feel terrible—it was just a new role and one to which she would need to become accustomed. Everyone had been very nice, almost too solicitous. As always, Peg had prepared a great dinner. The only really awkward note was the undue attention paid to her by Walter and his wife Jane's very negative response to it. Audrey thought Jane acted as though Audrey was going to take her husband from her. However, she did have to admit that Walter almost made a fool of himself being attentive to her. Their other friends treated her as they had in the past, but she knew she wasn't the same person. She was sure this type of social activity would feel better to her as time went on and she was more comfortable with herself.

She was also pleased with herself for deciding to do volunteer work for the symphony. She was working on membership. One of her close friends, Claudia, had always worked to raise money for the symphony and had encouraged Audrey to volunteer some time to this group. She had enjoyed meeting the women and getting out one day a week to work with them. She became friendly with another widow with whom she worked, Heather.

Often they went out to lunch following their work, or she and Claudia would plan to do something.

She was feeling better about the way she was spending her time. Her next step was to call the "Reading Is Fundamental" people. She had seen a small piece about this group on TV and the concept really appealed to her. However, none of her friends or acquaintances did any work with them, so she would be going into it cold—on her own. It felt as though it was a big step. She would be trying something totally new. She knew she was almost ready to contact them.

On the activity side, she had been pleased to learn from Mr. Silver she would have no problem maintaining her country club membership. The dues were not high, and she could easily manage the expense. She had gotten back into playing golf, which she had been forced to give up during John's illness. She had forgotten how much she enjoyed it. The women in her foursome now were talking about taking a golf clinic at some place like Hilton Head. She liked the idea; it would be great to get away for awhile. She hadn't been anywhere in at least a year and a half. She didn't think it would be difficult for her because she had been friendly with these women for most of her adult life. They had raised their children together and shared the joy as well as the trials and tribulations of daily life as wives and mothers. They all knew each other very well and usually had a lot of fun. She remembered a time about two years ago when a group of them had gone off for a sports weekend and spent most of the time laughing.

Since it appeared that she had more than enough income to live on comfortably, Audrey wondered about helping to educate Joanne's children. John Jr. could more than provide for himself and his family, but Joanne's husband, Keith, didn't make much money, and his prospects for promotions didn't look good. Joanne would like to send both the younger children to preschool. Earlier, before John had become so ill, Joanne asked if her parents could help out with the payments for Heidi. Audrey knew things must be bad for Joanne to admit she needed assistance. She decided to ask her to be more specific about how much preschool would cost. Audrey wanted to help Joanne, but she also wanted to be fair to John Jr. She thought she could afford to give them both some money each year without sacrificing her life-style, but wasn't sure of the best way to go about this. She decided to ask Mr. Silver for his advice in this regard.

When Audrey met with Mr. Silver, she gave him her expense figures for the past two years and told him she anticipated spending more in the future on food, clothes, entertainment and vacations. Audrey also told Mr. Silver she wanted to become more involved in charitable work and wanted to give more to charities if she could afford to do so.

Audrey asked Mr. Silver about the best way to help educate Joanne's children. He said he wanted to look at Audrey's estimated income and expenses more closely, but it looked as if she could give $6,000 to both Joanne and John Jr. Mr. Silver felt gifting money was a sensitive subject. Even if John Jr. didn't need the money, it had been his experience in cases like this that it was important to treat both children equally. It avoided family arguments later.

Keith might be sensitive about Audrey giving them money, so it might work best if Audrey paid the tuition and child care bills directly instead of handing them a check for $6,000. In John Jr.'s case, they could discuss the best way for her to give him the money. For instance, he might want to use it to add to his children's college fund.

Mr. Silver pointed out that legally she could give as much as $10,000 each to John Jr. and Joanne annually. Audrey would not have a deduction for giving it, but John Jr. and Joanne would not have to pay taxes on receiving it. However, he thought the lower amount of $6,000 seemed more appropriate for her budget. He also suggested that when Audrey spoke to her children about her desire to gift to them annually, she should tell them that she was able to do this now because she had more than enough income. However, since the major source of her income was John's pension money and the payments would not increase from current levels, there might come a time in the future when she could not be as generous.

Audrey decided to talk this over with Joanne and John Jr. and made another appointment to meet with Mr. Silver. He wanted to discuss a more realistic budget for her once she provided him with better expense estimates.

AUDREY'S PRELIMINARY ANNUAL BUDGET

Annual Income		
Pension	$42,000	
Social Security	8,100	
Stock Dividends	4,000	
Savings/Insurance Money	2,400	
Total		$56,500
Annual Expenses		
Mortgage	$ 3,160	
Other	18,075	
Taxes	11,685	
Total		32,920
Annual Excess Cash Flow		$23,580

Elizabeth: Reactions to the Budgeting Process

It appeared to Elizabeth her situation was pretty simple. She had two primary sources of income: Social Security and income from Ben's stock portfolio. The nice woman at Social Security had told her she would receive Social Security income of $878 per month. The portfolio manager told her that Ben's stocks were paying about $15,000 per year, or $1,250 per month. Ben had never set up a retirement fund at his company, so there was no income from that source.

Mr. Grossfeldt gave her a form to complete so he could help her estimate what her expenses might be in the future. She took out their checkbook and reviewed their past expenses. She knew that future expenses would be different. When Ben was sick, they rarely went out and never entertained, so they spent very little money. She couldn't remember when she had last spent time with the "girls." She had let all her friendships lapse over the past few years because watching out for Ben had taken up all of her time. She had really enjoyed her sewing circle and now realized how much she had missed those get-togethers.

She had tried to keep her church activities up but had not been very successful in doing so. Ben didn't like her to be away from him for any longer than an hour, and it was easier to comply than to argue.

There was no mortgage on the house, so she didn't have that expense. On the other hand, she would need to hire a gardener. A neighborhood boy who had been taking care of their small garden was going off to college in the fall. All in all, it appeared she could afford to continue living in her home, but she wondered if she wanted to do so. She felt she was rattling around in all those rooms.

Her older sister, Abigail, enjoyed living in her retirement community in Florida and was urging Elizabeth to visit her. The idea of warm weather after the bitter New England winters appealed to Elizabeth. Ben had refused to visit Abigail, to the point where the effort of convincing him to take the trip outweighed the pleasure of visiting with her sister.

In the past few years, due to the deterioration of Ben's health, the couple had spent most of their time at home. Although she was basically a homebody, Elizabeth secretly yearned to take a cruise. She had watched "Loveboat" often on television and wondered if it were foolish of her to consider taking such a trip. She didn't think she had the courage to take one alone, but maybe she could talk Abigail into joining her. When she was married, Ben and she never took trips—he always said he couldn't be away from work that long—but she thought he really didn't like the idea of being someplace unfamiliar.

When Elizabeth added up her income, it totaled $25,736. Her expenses were $18,675. This left $7,061. Mr. Grossfeldt gave her the name of an accountant he used, Mrs. Greenfield, to see her about her taxes. Mrs. Greenfield determined that her total federal and state taxes would be $3,090 annually. She also told her she would be in the 15 percent tax bracket—whatever that meant! Subtracting the taxes, Elizabeth had $3,971 left over to spend on herself.

Abigail had continued to press her about a visit to Florida. Now that it appeared she could afford to do so, she decided she was ready to travel.

Elizabeth had had more meetings and discussions with people related to money matters since Ben died than she had had in her entire life. Elizabeth appreciated the fact that none of these people made her feel stupid. They all treated her considerately and took the time to explain things to her. She felt she had learned so much in these past few months. For the first time since Ben's death, she started thinking positively about her future. Visiting her sister in Florida, taking a cruise, possibly moving to a warmer climate—all of that sounded pretty good to her. She was so fortunate that she could afford it!

ELIZABETH'S PRELIMINARY ANNUAL BUDGET

Annual Income		
Social Security	$10,536	
Portfolio	15,000	
Savings Account	200	
Total		$25,736
Annual Expenses		
General	$18,675	
Taxes	3,101	
Total		21,776
Annual Excess Cash Flow		$3,960

CHAPTER 8

Calculating Your Net Worth

The moving finger writes; and, having writ, Moves on: nor all thy Piety nor Wit Shall lure it back to cancel half a line, Nor all thy tears wash out a Word of it.

OMAR KHAYYAM

Introduction

When you calculated your expenses and income, you might have discovered (as Diane and Susan did) that there did not seem to be enough income to cover your expenses. If so, the next step is to list your assets and liabilities. Some of these might be estate assets (versus your own), but if you can get an idea of the total value of the assets that will be available to you, this will help you determine potential sources of additional income. Your financial planner, accountant or an informed friend could help you assemble this information.

Eventually, your advisor will need to know the original cost of your investments and the date you bought them, but don't spend a lot of time looking for that information now if it isn't easily obtained. You can research that later. Right now we are trying to put together an accurate list of what you own.

When you list your assets, it is a good idea to indicate ownership as well—that is, what are your assets (P:Personal), your husband's assets (E:Estate) and your joint assets (J:Joint).

Personal Assets

YOUR HOME

When listing your assets, we would start with your personal assets. Under this category, we would include your home, car(s), furnishings and other assets such as art and jewelry.

Starting with your home, you want to indicate:

- ownership
- approximate market value
- original cost
- any major improvements you have made

If the house was held in your spouse's name, then the cost will be increased to the valuation given it in the estate. As we previously indicated, if it were held jointly, one-half the cost is the original cost plus improvements, and one-half is the value in the estate. Taking advantage of this so-called "stepped-up" basis for the cost of your house can be helpful in reducing the capital gains tax when and if you decide to sell it.

Home address:_____

_____

Ownership:_____

Market value:_____

Original cost:_____

Improvements:_____

Once you have estimated the value of your home, it is important to determine how much the debt is against the house. Your mortgage holder(s) will be glad to provide you with the following information:

Amount of current mortgage:_____

Years remaining on the mortgage:_____

Current interest rate:_____

Monthly payment (principal and interest):_____

Amount of second mortgage:_____

Current interest rate:_____

Monthly payment (principal and interest):_____

Years left on second mortgage:_____

HOME EQUITY LOAN (HEL)

A home equity loan is a line of credit against your home. The bank will lend all or part of the approved amount to you as you wish. Repayment schedules vary. You may have agreed to pay certain amounts each month for five or ten years, or you may be paying interest only on the debt. The interest rate you pay can be fixed or variable. This is the information you need regarding your home equity loan:

Amount home equity loan approved:_____

Amount current loan:_____

Current interest rate:_____

Repayment terms:_____

SECOND HOME

If you have a second home that is primarily for personal use and/or own time shares in a vacation home, you need to list similar information for that here. If it is primarily a rental property, you would list it later, under "investment real estate."

Location:_____

Ownership:_____

Cost:_____

Current market value:_____

Current mortgage:_____

Current interest rate:_____

Monthly payment (principal and interest):_____

Timeshares:_____

Timeshares should also be listed under personal assets.

Location:_____

Ownership:_____

Cost:_____

Current market value:_____

Current mortgage:_____

Current interest rate:_____

Monthly payment (principal and interest):_____

PERSONAL PROPERTY

Personal property includes your cars, home furnishings, jewelry, furs, antiques, rugs and art in your home. At a later date, you might decide you don't need as many cars as you may currently have, but for now you are listing what you currently own. A rough estimate of your furnishings will do. The estate appraiser may give you a valuation which is usually lower than the real market value. Under "other," we are including jewelry, furs, antiques, oriental rugs or art you may have in your home.

Description	*Owner*	*Value $*
Car #1 _____	_____	_____
Car #2 _____	_____	_____
Car #3 _____	_____	_____
Furnishings _____	_____	_____
Other _____	_____	_____
Other _____	_____	_____

Personal Investments

CASH

Here you would list your checking accounts, savings accounts, money market funds, certificates of deposit, Treasury bills or notes and any money due to be paid you in the next 12 months. This would include the proceeds of any insurance policies payable to you, to a trust or to the estate.

Place Held	*Owner*	*Balance $*	*Rate %*
Checking Account			
_____	_____	_____	_____
_____	_____	_____	_____
_____	_____	_____	_____
_____	_____	_____	_____
Savings Account			
_____	_____	_____	_____
_____	_____	_____	_____
_____	_____	_____	_____
_____	_____	_____	_____
Money Market Funds			
_____	_____	_____	_____
_____	_____	_____	_____
_____	_____	_____	_____
_____	_____	_____	_____
Notes Receivable			
_____	_____	_____	_____
_____	_____	_____	_____

---　　　---　　　---　　　---

---　　　---　　　---　　　---

Life Insurance Policies

---　　　---　　　---　　　---

---　　　---　　　---　　　---

---　　　---　　　---　　　---

---　　　---　　　---　　　---

BONDS

Here you want to indicate what kind of bonds you own: United States government bonds, tax-free municipal bonds or corporate bonds. Basically, a bond is an IOU to you from the U.S. government, a municipality or a corporation. The certificate states who is loaning you the money, when you will be repaid and the rate of interest you will receive from the borrower. The way you can determine who is loaning you the money is to look on your statement from a bank or brokerage firm or at the actual certificate itself.

For instance, if the statement or certificate reads "$10,000 IBM Corporation 8% 5/1/100," this means IBM is the corporation borrowing the money from you, so it is a corporate bond. The $10,000 is the amount IBM has borrowed from you. IBM has agreed to pay you back the money on the date it comes due—the maturity date. In this case, the corporation will pay you $10,000 on May 1, 2000 (5/1/00). The 8 percent is the amount of interest IBM will pay. In this example, you will receive $800 a year (8% × $10,000). IBM will pay you one-half this amount every six months—on May 1 and November 1 in this case.

If the lender was the U.S. government, then it is a Treasury bond; if the lender was a municipality like the City of New York, then it is a municipal bond. We will discuss bonds in greater detail in chapter 13, but in the meantime, you want to list what you own, indicating for each one the lending agent, the amount of the bond, the interest rate it pays, the date it is due and the ownership.

Bonds Leading Agent	Face Amount $	Interest Rate %	Due Date	Owner

NOTES RECEIVABLE

These would include any personal notes due you or your husband. List the amount owed, by whom, when the note is due, the interest rate being paid and how often the interest is paid. You might also indicate the likelihood of repayment. For instance, if your husband loaned a friend some money and the friend has failed to repay the money in the past, you don't want to count on this as an asset.

Amount Owed $	By Whom	Interest Rate %	Due Date	Repayment $

DEFERRED ANNUITIES

These are investments made with insurance companies. The interest accumulates in a deferred annuity for you on a tax-deferred basis. In other words, you don't pay tax on what your money earns. The end of each year, the insurance company provides you with a statement of the value of the annuity.

Assuming you are the beneficiary, when you write the company informing them of your husband's death, they will let you know what the current value is and how you can access this money. If someone else is the beneficiary, the insurance company will notify him or her accordingly. Right now all we are concerned with is the current value of the annuity, the name of the insurance company and the interest rate it is currently paying.

Current Value $	Company Name	Interest Rate %
_____	_____	_____
_____	_____	_____

STOCKS

List the name of the company held, number of shares, cost if you know it, date purchased if you have it and ownership.

Company	# Shares	Cost $	Date Bought	Owner
_____	_____	_____	_____	_____
_____	_____	_____	_____	_____

If your husband had some unexercised stock options, these would be listed here, with the terms of how they should be exercised (this would be provided to you by his company).

Value of outstanding stock options _____

MUTUAL FUNDS

You usually don't have certificates for your mutual fund shares. They are held by the mutual fund company or by your stockbroker. The most recent statement from the mutual fund company will list the number of shares you own, the name of the fund and the ownership for each fund. If you have been reinvesting dividends and capital gains generated by the mutual funds, the cost is difficult to calculate. We will discuss this in greater detail later.

Fund Name	# Shares	Cost $	Date Bought	Owner
_____	_____	_____	_____	_____
_____	_____	_____	_____	_____

LIMITED PARTNERSHIPS

This is where life gets more complicated. If you own any limited partnerships, you list the name of the partnerships. Hopefully, you have a file on the partnership that contains the name and address of the general partner. If you know the date the partnership was originally purchased and the cost, this is helpful, but not essential.

Name of Partnership	*Name/Address Contact Person*	*# Units*	*Cost $*	*Owner*
_____	_____	_____	_____	_____
_____	_____	_____	_____	_____
_____	_____	_____	_____	_____
_____	_____	_____	_____	_____

INVESTMENT REAL ESTATE

List any real estate investments you own. Include rental properties as well as raw land. These should be appraised to establish a tax basis. Your most recent tax return will provide your advisor with information needed to help you decide if you want to keep these properties or sell them.

Property	*#1*	*#2*	*#3*
Address	_____	_____	_____
	_____	_____	_____
	_____	_____	_____
	_____	_____	_____
Owner	_____	_____	_____
Market Value	_____	_____	_____
Amount Mortgage	_____	_____	_____
Terms Mortgage	_____	_____	_____

BUSINESS INTERESTS

Business interests would include your ownership in any privately held business. This might have been your husband's business or an investment made in someone else's business. The valuation will be complex, but your professional advisors will help with this process. For your purposes, you need to know an approximate value of these business interests and how much cash you may receive from them.

Value of business interests _____

OTHER

This category would cover anything we haven't covered heretofore—like stamp and coin collections, precious metals or commodities. These are often worth less than you may think but should be listed in the asset statement.

Description	Ownership	Market Value $
_____	_____	_____
_____	_____	_____

Retirement Assets

RETIREMENT ACCOUNTS

By now you have been told what retirement income you will receive from your husband's previous employer(s). In addition, he may have other retirement accounts, such as IRA, Keogh, TIAA/CREF, 401(k), 403(b) and SEP/IRA accounts.

If you are the beneficiary of these accounts, you can "roll over" these accounts into a retirement account in your own name. If you choose to receive the cash instead, then any amount you remove from a retirement account is taxable to you, and there are additional taxes due if you take out the money prior to age 59½. Taking money out of retirement accounts is a complex decision, so be sure to get professional advice before you do so. If you don't, you may create adverse tax consequences that are irreversible.

	Current Value $	Where Invested	Interest Rate %
IRA			
Keogh			
SEP/IRA			
401(k)			
403(b)			
TIAA/CREF			
Other			

Liabilities

Now that you have a list of your assets and their approximate value, you can begin listing the money you owe other people. These debts are your liabilities.

OUTSTANDING DEBTS

List here any debts you owe to anyone—the amount you owe, the interest rate you are paying, how often you make payments and to whom. Include your mortgage loan, overdrafts, credit card debts, auto loans, etc.

Kind of Debt	#1	#2	#3
Owed To Whom?			
Current Amount Outstanding			
Payment Amount			
Due Date			
Interest Rate			

OTHER (MORAL) OBLIGATIONS

Prior to your husband's death, you both may have said that you would pay for the education of your grandchild. After looking at the total picture, you may find that you are unable to do so. List any such promises with the idea that you may have to amend them.

_____

_____

Conclusion

You now have a comprehensive list of your assets and liabilities. With this information, your financial advisor will prepare a statement of your current financial condition, also called a net worth statement, as outlined in figure 8-1. In the previous chapter, you estimated your income and expenses. Now you are ready to review all this information with your financial planner. Your goal is to make sure that you have sufficient income both now and in the future. This may involve changing some of these assets. Finally, you are ready to do some longer-term planning.

FIGURE 8-1

NET WORTH STATEMENT AS OF _____

For: _____

I. Personal Assets
    Home Value $ _____
    Less Mortgages/HEL   _____
    Equity in Home   _____
    Equity in Second Homes _____
    Equity in Time Shares   _____
    Personal Property   _____
    Cars   _____
        Total $ _____
II. Cash   _____
III. Personal Investments
    Bonds $ _____
    Notes Receivable   _____
    Deferred Annuities   _____
    Stocks   _____
    Mutual Funds   _____
    Limited Partnerships   _____
    Business Interests   _____
    Real Estate   _____
    Other   _____
        Total   _____
IV. Retirement Investments
    IRA $ _____
    Keogh   _____
    SEP/IRA   _____
    401(k)   _____
    403(b)   _____
    TIAA/CREF   _____
    Other   _____
        Total   _____
V. Liabilities
    Mortgage Loan $ _____
    Auto Loan   _____
    Other Debts   _____
    Other Obligations   _____
        Total   _____

Net Worth
  (I + II + III + IV − V) $ _____

Diane: Reactions to Calculating Her Net Worth

Diane had checked their bank accounts and found that they totaled about $10,000 in cash. She had also made a list of outstanding balances on their credit cards. They seemed to also total about $10,000. How had they gotten so high?

She had not had the house appraised yet but knew it was worth about $500,000. Her neighbor across the street had recently sold her home, which was similar to theirs, so she knew her estimate was about right. The mortgage officer had told her that their mortgage was $288,156 and that they still had 25 years of mortgage payments. By the time she paid it off, she would be 67 years old! For the first time, Diane actually considered that she might have to sell the beautiful home she loved so much.

The firm's insurance policy on Mark was $600,000, and she had the quote for the income she could receive from the annuity. She needed to make that decision soon, as she needed some money to pay their current bills. The other insurance policies totaled $100,000. Diane was beginning to get panicky about the number of unpaid bills she had on hand. Her inclination was to cash in these insurance policies so she would have some money to pay the mounting bills.

Mark's retirement account (Keogh) was worth $250,000, but the stock-broker, her dad and Larry all told her she shouldn't touch this because she would need it for her retirement. At this point, she felt she couldn't worry about retirement. There were too many other immediate needs to worry about. She needed to find money now to educate her children.

Karen, at the firm, had told her she would receive $100,000 from the capital account. She needed to find out how soon this money would be available to her. Perhaps she could use this money to solve her immediate financial problems.

It was obvious she had better get back together with Dorothy right away to see what she should do. Even to Diane's nonfinancial brain, things looked pretty grim!

DIANE'S FINANCIAL STATEMENT

Assets		
Cash	$ 10,000	
Home	500,000	
Insurance (firm)	600,000	
Insurance (other)	100,000	
Capital Account	100,000	
Retirement Account	250,000	
Van	15,000	
Total		$1,575,000
Liabilities		
Mortgage	$288,156	
Auto Loan	15,000	
Charge Accounts	10,000	
Total		313,156
Net Worth		$1,261,844

Susan: Reactions to Calculating Her Net Worth

After reviewing her income and expenses, Susan realized that she did have a cash flow problem, so it was important she review her assets and liabilities more carefully to see if they could produce more income.

Lance and Susan had a small money market account with $2,000 in it. Their condo had appreciated greatly in recent years. It was now worth about $300,000, and the mortgage was $150,000. The cottage was worth $105,000, and the mortgage was $50,000. The more she looked at the situation, the more obvious it was that the cottage was a luxury she could not afford. She decided to put it up for sale.

Bob O'Brien, Lance's stockbroker, sent Susan the list of Lance's stocks, together with his recommendation of which ones to sell to raise the $40,000 she needed for Lance's children. She met with Bob to finalize these sales and to figure out a strategy for the future. The stocks Lance owned paid no income because they were growth stocks. She discussed with Bob the advisability of changing these stocks to ones that would produce more income. He informed her that Lance had invested $50,000 five years ago, and now the account was worth $100,000. He was reluctant to trade growth stocks for income stocks that did not offer the same growth potential. He suggested she look for other ways to increase her current income before they made that change.

Susan asked her brother, Ron, about helping out, but he was not reassuring. He told her that his salary was not high and he had his own financial problems. At best, he would be able to contribute $100 per month toward their mother's expenses. However, he realized that it wasn't right for Susan to take on all the responsibility. If he could not help much financially, at least he could help personally. He told Susan he would be glad to cooperate on the gifting issue so she would avoid paying unnecessary taxes, and he would try to visit Mom weekly in the future.

If she really had financial problems, Susan could withdraw money from Lance's pension fund (worth $300,000). However, since any income she withdrew would be taxable to her, Susan wanted to avoid doing that. Further, since she didn't have a very large retirement fund of her own, taking money from this fund was really her last resort. This pension plan was invested in mutual funds at Lance's firm. Harry told her she could leave these assets with the firm's pension manager for the time being. Eventually, she would have to make a decision about managing this money but not now.

Her own retirement fund at the association was invested in a bond fund managed by an insurance company. It had seemed to be a safe place for Susan to invest her money, and she had never paid much attention to it. Susan thought to herself, now that she was dealing with larger amounts of money, it would be a good idea to learn more about investments.

Upon reviewing her situation, Susan considered seriously the thought she might have to look for a better paying job. Maybe she should talk to her boss at the association about raising her salary. They had been so good to her during these recent painful months that she hated to make a change. However, she had to be realistic about her situation. It was clear she needed more income than she currently had if she was going to keep the apartment.

She wanted to discuss these feelings and options in her next session with Dr. Coleman. She realized she was truly benefiting from these sessions with her.

SUSAN'S FINANCIAL STATEMENT

Assets*

Cash	$ 2,000	
Condo	300,000	
Lake Cottage	105,000	
Stocks	100,000	
Lance's Pension Plan	300,000	
Susan's Pension Plan	25,000	
Car	10,000	
Total		$842,000
Liabilities		
Mortgage Condo	$150,000	
Mortgage Cottage	50,000	
Due Stepchildren	40,000	
Car Loan	8,000	
Total		248,000
Net Worth		$594,000

* Trust assets do not appear as Susan's assets because she is entitled to receive income only from the trust.

Audrey: Reactions to Calculating Her Net Worth

Audrey reviewed her assets. She had about $20,000 in a savings account. The house was worth $200,000, and it was really too big for her. It was the house she had lived in most of her married life; now she wanted something newer and easier to take care of than her present home. On the other hand, she wasn't in any rush to move. She liked the location, particularly since it was close to Joanne. She wanted to help Joanne as much as possible and didn't want to miss the opportunity of seeing her grandchildren grow up.

In addition to the $20,000 in their savings account, Audrey had received $40,000 in insurance money. She didn't know where to put it, so she added it to her savings account at her local bank. The manager certainly had been nice to her when she made the deposit.

Shortly before John was diagnosed as having cancer, they had decided to redo the kitchen and had applied for a home equity loan of $20,000. Fortunately, they hadn't started the work, although they had made all the plans with the contractor. She wondered if she should go ahead with this project. She decided to ask Mr. Silver if she should use the home equity loan or some of the insurance money to finance this expense if she did decide to fix up the kitchen.

The thought of dealing with all the workmen and the mess involved in redoing the kitchen was not appealing, especially if she might move sooner rather than later. The idea of spending money on a much-needed vacation was much more appealing. The prospect of going to a golf clinic at Hilton Head was becoming increasingly attractive. It would also be a good way to brush up on her skills. She knew Dr. PaPadisio would think it was a good idea. She needed to give more time and thought to how she wanted to spend her time and money.

Then there was the question of the company stock held in John's name, which was worth about $200,000. It paid her $4,000 per year in income, which wasn't much (2 percent), but John never wanted to sell it because he loved the company so much. Besides, he said, the taxes on the gain would have been prohibitive because his cost for the shares was so low. The lawyer had mentioned something about the fact that because the shares were part of John's estate, the cost basis would be increased to reflect current market values. That meant she could sell some of them without worrying about paying tax on the gain. But she knew John would not have approved! This was something else she needed to ask Mr. Silver.

By the time Audrey had completed her assets and liabilities statement, it was time to get ready for her lunch with Joanne. They had begun to meet for lunch regularly on Wednesdays, and both women looked forward to it.

When she had last seen Dr. PaPadisio, he was very pleased with her because she had gained five pounds. She attributed this gain in part to the efforts she had been making to include a lunch out with friends in conjunction with her volunteer work as well as her regularly scheduled lunches with Joanne. Today she was looking forward to discussing the preschool issue with her daughter.

Audrey was also pleased with the results of her conversation with John Jr. He called when he was about to leave the office a few days ago and asked if he could drop by to see her. He said they hadn't had much time to talk, and he didn't want her to feel neglected by him. She assured him she wasn't feeling neglected and encouraged him to stop by on his way home.

She thought this would provide her with a wonderful opportunity to discuss her financial situation with him. When he arrived, he looked somewhat more tired and older than she remembered. She guessed she'd been so preoccupied with John's care and then her financial situation that she hadn't really seen her children, even though she had spent the usual amount of time with them. Somehow, this older look made him appear less formidable to her.

She offered him a glass of wine, and they sat at the kitchen table in the comfortable, well-worn kitchen. After telling him about her decision to become involved with the "Reading Is Fundamental" organization, Audrey told him she was really pleased he had decided to stop over because she had been meaning to talk with him about her financial situation. She could see him imperceptibly stiffen. She immediately went on to say that his father had provided very nicely for her, and she anticipated no financial problems. She laid out the various sheets she had been working on—her assets and liabilities sheet and a summary of her monthly financial needs. She told him about her work with her lawyer, Mr. Humphrey, and with Mr. Silver, the financial planner. She explained that after reviewing her total financial status with these men, she found that she was in a position to give some money to each of her children and wanted to do so on an annual basis.

He was somewhat taken aback by both her understanding of her financial situation and her generosity. She could tell that he was also relieved that he wouldn't have to help support her. She could see him visibly relax. He was generous with his praise of all she had accomplished, and he seemed to view her with greater respect. She went on to tell him that she had decided on $6,000 per year per family. He worked hard to dissuade her from making that sum available to him in view of the disparity in income between his family and Joanne's. She assured him she had taken all that into consideration but had decided on giving each of her children the same amount. If he wanted the money to go directly to his children, that was all right with her. She told him she would discuss with Mr. Silver the best way to accomplish this.

Audrey also asked John Jr. if he would be willing to meet with her and Mr. Silver to review her financial plans for the future. He was most agreeable to doing that and told his mother to make an appointment for them in the next two or three weeks.

Both mother and son realized they had gotten beyond the barrier that had existed between them for such a long time now, although neither one verbally acknowledged it. He invited her over for dinner the next week, and they hugged each other extra hard when they parted. Audrey thought she might make more of an effort to see John Jr. than she had done in the recent past. She realized he really wasn't pompous; it was just that he didn't know how to express his concern for her.

She hoped things would go as well with Joanne. She was running late and called Joanne to take the table she had reserved for them at a new restaurant about which she had heard a great many good things recently. She was really excited about sharing with Joanne what she had discussed with Mr. Silver. As soon as they ordered, Audrey elaborated on her discussion with Mr. Silver regarding the $6,000 a year to each of her children. Audrey could see that Joanne was taken aback and somewhat defensive. She apologized to her mother for being a burden and told her she felt like a charity case, which made her very uncomfortable. However, not wanting to hurt her mother's feelings, she went on to tell her how very grateful she was for making the money available. Audrey reassured her and was pleased she could tell her she was doing the same thing for John Jr. and had already discussed it with him. Joanne appeared greatly relieved and perked up considerably.

AUDREY'S FINANCIAL STATEMENT

Assets		
Savings Account	$ 60,000	
Home	200,000	
Stock	200,000	
Car	20,000	
Total		$480,000
Liabilities		
Mortgage	$ 20,000	
Total		20,000
Net Worth		$460,000

Elizabeth: Reactions to Calculating
Her Net Worth

Elizabeth had $5,000 in a savings account, and she thought that should tide her over until she worked out the rest of her financial situation. Her home was worth $150,000, and Ben was proud they had paid off their mortgage several years ago. She had received a $10,000 check from a small life insurance policy and used that money to pay for the funeral and some outstanding bills. She also had some land in Vermont that Ben bought years ago with the idea they might build a house on it. Somehow they never got around to it. The appraiser said it was worth $25,000.

Elizabeth was having trouble dealing with the portfolio Ben owned. She was torn between leaving it with the money manager Ben had worked with all these years and taking it to a trust department of a bank to be managed, as Mr. Grossfeldt had suggested. She really didn't know enough to make an intelligent decision in this regard. She hated to impose on Sam Weatherly once again to help her, but she didn't know where else to turn. Her friend, Mabel, told her that municipal bonds were wonderful. They paid tax-free income and were safe. Perhaps she should sell everything and buy them— certainly life would be simpler that way.

Making financial decisions wasn't easy for her, but Elizabeth knew she needed to make some decisions. For example, she had to decide where she wanted to live for the remainder of her life. She had never really given much consideration to major decisions during her marriage. Ben would usually come home and say something like, "I've been thinking it's about time we did such and such, Liz. What do you think?" Her predictable response was, "Whatever you think, dear, is fine with me." She had always thought of herself as somewhat timid and had allowed her older sister, Abigail, when she was a child, and later Ben, to make decisions for her. She was grateful to them for not expecting anything of her on this level. Now her new financial advisors expected her to make certain decisions after they provided her with the advantages and disadvantages of each of her options. It was a new and uncomfortable role for her. She would have preferred to do nothing, burying her head in the sand and allowing others to decide for her. Unfortunately, she knew all too well there were no longer appropriate others to do so. There was no one to turn to but herself.

She was frightened by the thought of living any place other than her home, yet the harsh winters in Boston were beginning to bother her. The idea of moving to Florida was becoming more and more appealing. She enjoyed her church work and her friendship with the Weatherlys, but many of her friends had moved away when they retired and some had died. Actually, if she were truthful with herself, she would admit she was lonely. It would be good to be near her sister.

She realized that in order to make a change of this magnitude, she really needed to visit Abigail. Then she could see where she was living and meet her friends. Her sister had been encouraging her to come for a visit for years and was insistent in their recent phone conversations. Elizabeth thought to herself, why was it so hard for her to initiate anything? She had had to deal with so many new people and money matters since Ben's death. She was becoming annoyed with herself over her ambivalence and lack of action.

As she mulled over what to do about a visit for the umpteenth time one gray morning, she became irritated with herself for her own inaction. With resolve that she wasn't feeling, she picked up the phone and dialed a travel agent. She was surprised how simple it was to arrange for a direct flight to Miami. After making the necessary arrangements, she shocked herself when she heard herself asking the travel agent to send her some information on one-week cruises that left from Ft. Lauderdale or Miami for the Caribbean.

As soon as she hung up, she called Abigail to tell her when she would be arriving. She decided not to mention the cruise until she got there. She wasn't sure how serious she was about it for herself just yet. Somehow it seemed too daring—but maybe not.

ELIZABETH'S FINANCIAL STATEMENT

Assets			
Cash	$ 5,000		
Home	150,000		
Land in Vermont	25,000		
Portfolio	500,000		
Total		$680,000	
Liabilities	$ 0		
Total		0	
Net Worth			$680,000

CHAPTER 9

Dealing with Today's Financial Realities

Time is a dressmaker specializing in alterations.
FAITH BALDWIN

Introduction

The time has come to make sense out of all the information you have accumulated and brought to your financial advisor. By now you should have a pretty good idea of whether or not you have enough income to cover your expenses. Whatever your circumstances, your advisor may be able to improve your situation by recommending changes in your investments.

Before making any adjustments, you need to review with your advisor your attitude toward risk, your investment goals and your investment objectives.

Risk Attitude

It has been our experience that most widows say they don't want to take any risk because they are worried about having sufficient income and they don't want to lose any of the money they have. After the first year, the widow usually has a better understanding of her situation and is more willing to take some risk. As the years go by and her financial knowledge increases, she may find she is ready to take even more risk. It is like learning how to ride a bicycle. At first you are unsteady, but as you become more skilled, you gain self-confidence. The more you ride, the more venturesome you become.

There are different kinds of risk. Most people equate risk taking to gambling. However, all life entails taking chances. You can't even cross the street without taking some risk! What you can do is try to limit that risk—in this example, you wait for the light to turn in your favor so you can cross the street safely.

The primary kind of risk you as a widow need to consider is potential loss of principal. If you don't have much money and you can't afford to lose any principal, then you should limit the amount of risk you take. You have read stories about women who lose their inheritances shortly after being widowed. These are sad stories, but when you learn the details, you find that the widows took more risk than they should have, usually by investing in something that they were told paid higher return than most other investments and/or by putting all their money in one investment.

Beware of someone who tells you that their investment can pay you a higher return than any other investment. If the promised return on an investment is higher than the norm, this means you are taking greater risk with your principal. It is understandable that widows who are inexperienced in financial matters might seek higher-than-normal returns because they are worried about having enough income, but by doing so, they may jeopardize receiving a reliable stream of income in the future, or even lose all of the principal.

How much risk are you willing to take? Rank yourself on a scale of one to ten. One indicates that you want to take very little risk, and ten indicates that you are willing to take a high degree of risk. This helps your advisor understand your risk tolerance level.

Circle the number that applies to you. #1 indicates you are a low risk taker. #10 indicates you are willing to take a high degree of risk.

Ultra Conservative	Conservative	Moderately Conservative	Middle of Road	Moderately Aggressive	Aggressive	Ultra Aggressive
1	2	3	4	5	6	7	8	9	10

Investment Goals

You undoubtedly have certain financial goals you want to achieve with your money. Typical goals include: education of children, retirement in comfort, building wealth, reducing income and estate taxes.

For example, a younger widow like Diane is primarily interested in education for her children, and the concept of retirement seems very remote to her. The primary concern of an older widow such as Audrey would be a comfortable retirement and then reducing estate taxes so she can leave her children as much as possible.

We have listed five common goals and left a place to add your own goals under "other," which might be "buying a new house" or something like that. Write down which goals are most important to you, and rank them in order of their importance to you.

#1 would indicate the most important goal for you.

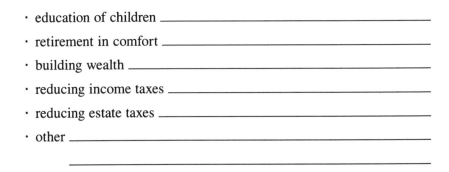

- education of children _____
- retirement in comfort _____
- building wealth _____
- reducing income taxes _____
- reducing estate taxes _____
- other _____

_____

Investment Objectives

After you have determined your risk attitude and listed your investment goals in order of importance, next you want to determine which investment objectives are most important to you.

Ask yourself whether your highest priority is preserving principal, obtaining the highest current income or building your principal. Most of us want to achieve all three objectives in one investment, but it is important to recognize this is not possible. An investment that has more of one advantage—such as safety of principal—will have less of another—such as potential for growth.

You need to decide which investment objective is most important to you and what you have to give up in order to attain it. For instance, if you want high current income, then the investments you select will have limited potential for growth of principal. If growth of principal is your priority, the income you receive from this investment will be lower and you will have to take more risk. Basically, it is an issue of trade-offs. Even if your stated investment objective is high current income, your advisor will probably select different kinds of investments for you so that there is balance between investments with growth potential and those that provide high current income.

For instance, you might feel very comfortable investing in certificates of deposit (CDs) with a bank because they are held by a bank, are fairly liquid and are guaranteed by the Federal Deposit Insurance Corporation FDIC (as long as you invest under $100,000). But let's look at an example that might convince you otherwise:

Let's say you invest $10,000 in a 1-year CD that pays 6 percent. This means you will receive $600 of income during the first year. On this income, you will pay federal and local taxes. If your combined state and federal tax bracket is 30 percent (ask your accountant or financial advisor what your tax bracket is), multiply 30 percent times $600, which means you will owe $180 in taxes on this income. This means your after-tax income from this CD is $420 (you subtract $180 in taxes from $600 income). If the inflation rate is 5 percent this year (as it has averaged in recent years), this means the $10,000 investment you made at the beginning

---

Details of the Explanation

$10,000 earns $600 in a year
          minus   180 taxes
          minus   500 inflation
leaves you with $ 80 net loss on your investment

of the year will lose 5 percent of its value by the end of the year ($500). Subtracting $500 from $420, you have actually lost $80 after taxes and inflation.

This is just one example of an investment which appears to be "safe" but might not be as safe as you think it is. We will discuss different investments and their advantages and disadvantages in greater detail in chapter 11.

Rank the three investment objectives listed here in their order of importance to you. #1 would indicate the most important objective for you.

- preservation of principal _____
- growth of principal _____
- high current income _____

Reviewing Your Financial Statements

At this point, you have told your financial advisor what your risk tolerance is, your investment goals and objectives. Your advisor also knows your various sources of income and estimated expenses as well as your current assets and liabilities. The next step is to review three schedules that will help you plan a secure financial future. These are your taxable income statement, your cash flow statement and your balance sheet.

TAXABLE INCOME STATEMENT

This statement lists your different sources of taxable income and gives you an idea of what your federal and state taxes will be for this year and the next two. At this point, it is still a best guess since the estate is not settled and you are not sure what all your sources of income or actual expenses will be. There might be estate taxes and estate settlement fees due, which will lessen the amount of the assets you inherit. In addition, the income tax laws will probably change during the next couple of years. But this statement will give you an idea of what you will owe in taxes under current law.

The taxable income statement is helpful because your tax status may change over the next few years. For instance, you will file as "married" this year and may file as "surviving spouse" or "single" next year. These three categories involve three different tax tables. This statement is also useful because it identifies your tax bracket. This will help your advisor determine whether you need to select investments that generate taxable or tax-free income. We find many widows are obsessed with reducing their income tax bills, but when we compute what they will owe as a percentage of their total income, they aren't paying that much in taxes. If this is true for you, selecting tax-free investments may not be your best choice.

CASH FLOW STATEMENT

On this statement will be listed all your estimated sources of income and expenses, including state and federal taxes. The bottom line will show you whether you have more income than expenses at the end of each year or vice versa.

If the number is a negative one, then you need to reexamine your expenses to see if you can reduce them. Your advisor can also look at your investments to see if they can be changed to generate more income (without sacrificing too much in the way of future growth potential). For instance, you may increase your income by renting out a room in your home, or you may have to face the fact that your current home is too expensive to keep. After looking at your expenses, it may become apparent to you that you may have to go to work if you are not already working. If you are currently working, you may have to find a better paying job or work at more than one job. If you have children, you may have to talk to them about getting part-time jobs.

The important thing is to look at your income and expense situation for the long term as well as the present. Remember that your income has to exceed your expenses FOR THE REST OF YOUR LIFE.

NET WORTH STATEMENT/BALANCE SHEET

In the last chapter, we showed you a typical net worth statement (sometimes called a balance sheet) for each widow. It is nothing more than a listing of everything you own and everything you owe. The difference between the two numbers is your net worth. In the future, this number should be computed annually to determine whether you are building your net worth or losing ground.

Conclusion

Now you have indicated how much risk you feel comfortable taking with your money. You have prioritized your financial goals and your investment objectives. You have reviewed your taxable income statement so you have a better idea of what your state and federal income tax bill will be as well as your tax bracket. You know whether your current income is sufficient to pay your estimated expenses, and you have a current balance sheet. With this information, your advisor can now help you do some short- and long-term planning for your future.

Diane: Reactions to Dealing with Today's Financial Realities

Diane told Dorothy when they met that *she didn't want to take any risk*. In fact, she circled #1 on the risk table. The security of receiving fixed payments from the annuity for the rest of her life looked very attractive to her.

Her *primary financial goal* was to *educate the children*. She thought she could worry about retirement later—after all, she had 20 years before she was 62—and by that time, her youngest would be 27 years old.

Her *investment objective* was to have *high current income* so she could keep her children in private school and not have to sell the house.

DIANE'S BUDGET

Diane proudly showed Dorothy the revised budget she and the children had worked out together. After her last visit with Dorothy, she sat down with the children and explained the situation to them. She told them that she thought the family should determine as a unit what to do. She had several ideas as to which expenses could be eliminated from the budget but wanted to hear what the children had to say.

When they reviewed the budget, they all agreed that they didn't need to belong to the country club, which eliminated $2,500 in dues. Much as she wanted to go to the beach, she could at least make it one week instead of two ($1,000 savings), and she could forget the Christmas trip ($2,000). She needed a maid once a week to help out with the heavy housework, but the older children could certainly pitch in and baby-sit when necessary ($1,000 savings) and help with the yard work ($1,500 savings). They could cut down on their cleaning and drugstore bills by $2,000. Much as she didn't want to, she would have to reduce the charitable contributions by $500—after all, charity begins at home! Those items together would save $10,500, so she was making progress. She couldn't eliminate Jeremy's orthodontia—after all, he really needed braces.

Diane thought she could make up the remaining negative flow each year with the cash she would receive from the non-firm insurance policies ($100,000) and the firm capital account ($100,000). Dorothy gently told Diane that even though she had lowered her expenses, if she attempted to use the $200,000 due her from these two sources to make up the almost $36,000 negative cash flow each year, that money would last only six years, and that solution would work only if none of her expenses increased— which appeared highly unlikely. She also pointed out that Diane had to consider college education costs for the children.

COLLEGE EDUCATION PROJECTIONS

Dorothy told Diane that college expenses had increased 10 percent annually over the past few years. She projected what it would cost to send her children to college and showed the numbers to Diane. Diane was in a state of shock because she had not even thought of the cost of their college education since she was so concerned about their present educational expenses.

In these projections, Dorothy assumed that college costs would continue to increase 10 percent annually, as they have in recent years. If this were true, she would need the following amounts of money accumulated by their freshman year:

	Public	Private
Alice (7)	$81,805	$203,559
Jeremy (11)	55,874	139,033
Erin (15)	38,163	94,962

In other words, if she was going to send all three to private college, it would cost about $440,000—a mind-boggling figure. If she wanted to put aside sufficient money now to cover this future expense (assuming it earned 8 percent after tax annually), she would need to invest:

	Public	Private
Alice (7)	$31,089	$77,361
Jeremy (11)	28,889	71,886
Erin (15)	26,845	66,799

Now Diane was really depressed. She had known vaguely that college would cost a lot, but Mark made a lot of money, so she had never worried about paying for the children's college education. Now she had something new to be concerned about. The idea of being able to pay for their private school education on a secondary level was becoming more and more remote. Clearly, this was a case of choosing between long-term and short-term economic goals.

DOROTHY'S REVISED CASH FLOW STATEMENT FOR DIANE

Dorothy told Diane that she was not at all comfortable having Diane choose the "immediate annuity" approach with the $600,000 firm insurance money. While she realized that Diane would find the certainty of receiving $3,015 per month comforting, it worked out to only a 6 percent return on $600,000. (To find out the return on an investment, take the annual income [$36,186] and divide it by the principal invested [$600,000]). Further, the payment would be set at $36,186 annually for the rest of her life. If Diane's expenses remained fixed, then it would be all right to receive fixed income. But since they were bound to increase, her income needed to increase.

Dorothy had worked on Diane's net worth statement as she had promised. She suggested that Diane take the cash available in her savings account ($10,000) and use that to pay off the outstanding charge accounts ($10,000). She urged her to try to keep her monthly bills current. Next she recommended that Diane combine the $600,000 firm's insurance, the $100,000 from the personal insurance and the $100,000 from the firm's capital account. From this total cash amount of $800,000, she would pay off the van loan ($15,000). This way, her only debt would be the mortgage, and she wouldn't have the interest costs on the loans to pay.

Dorothy told Diane to put aside $50,000 in a money market fund earning 4 percent. This would be an emergency cash reserve so that Diane would have cash available to pay expenses as they occurred. After six months, they should look at this reserve to see if she needed that much. However, initially, Dorothy thought it would be a good idea to have a large cash reserve. She emphasized this was a cash reserve, to be used *only* for emergencies.

Dorothy recommended the remaining $735,000 should be invested to earn 8.5 percent. She took Diane's revised budget but added one additional expense—the premium for a ten-year level term $1,000,000 life insurance policy. The annual premium would remain the same for ten years at $1,480. She thought this was a necessary expense to provide for Diane's children should something happen to Diane.

Running these revised numbers, the negative cash flow number had been reduced to $20,392. They were making progress, but more had to be made.

Diane was confused. Jack Blafford, the insurance man, seemed so sure when he proposed the annuity to her, and it seemed like the solution to all her problems. Dorothy explained to her that Mr. Blafford had not had an opportunity to look at Diane's total situation and to run these cash flow projections. Receiving an immediate annuity payment might be a very good solution for some people, but in view of her comparative youth and high expenses, it was not a good choice for her. Diane was right to want the highest possible income, but she also needed to invest where there was a chance for her principal to grow. If her principal grew, then the income should increase and would keep pace with inflation. Dorothy pointed out that especially since her Social Security payments would decrease as the children grew older, Diane needed to figure out how to increase her income over the years ahead. She also had to worry about future college costs.

Her two biggest expenses kept staring Diane in the face—the tuition and the mortgage payments. These two items represented almost half of her expenses.

Dorothy told Diane that since she still had a negative cash flow, she had to make some choices to reduce her expenses further. One option was selling their house and buying a less expensive one. Another was to consider sending the children to public schools. She pointed out that the public schools in Diane's area had a good reputation and her children might do very well there. She suggested that Diane visit the local schools and talk to the principals about their curriculum and facilities available to the students.

Although Diane didn't like to hear what Dorothy was telling her, she knew she was right. Changing her children's schools would be disruptive, but so would moving out of their home of many years. Diane decided to call Robyn, her new friend from the widow support group who was a teacher in the county system, and learn more about the schools in her area. If she was going to change their schools, she would like them to start at the new schools in the fall. She also wanted to talk to a real estate agent about what their home was really worth. If they moved to a less expensive home in the Washington area, where would they have to go? Dorothy had told her to consider something in the $250,000 range. Maybe they should rent.

Diane realized that going back to work was no longer optional. She really had to do it—but it had been so long since she worked. What was she qualified to do? She enjoyed her former career as a paralegal. Perhaps she could take a refresher course and go back to working at a law firm. But it would take a while before she would be earning a salary.

Making all these major decisions was overwhelming, and although she had avoided talking with her dad in an effort to be self-sufficient, she thought the time had come to do so. She thanked Dorothy for all her help and said she would be back to her as soon as she gathered more information. There was so much to do that Diane was tempted to give up, but she knew she couldn't, for the sake of the children!

Diane's risk tolerance: very low
Diane's primary financial goal: children's education
Diane's investment objective: high current income

DIANE'S REVISED FINANCIAL STATEMENT

Assets
Cash Reserve	$ 50,000	
Investments	735,000	
Home	500,000	
Retirement Account	250,000	
Van	15,000	
Total		$1,550,000

Liabilities
Mortgage	288,156	
Total		288,156
Net Worth		$1,261,844

DIANE'S REVISED ANNUAL CASH FLOW STATEMENT

Income
Social Security	$24,000	
Investment Income	64,475	
Total		$ 88,475

Expenses
Mortgage	$31,592	
Tuition	15,000	
Life Insurance	1,480	
Other	54,090	
Taxes	6,706	
Total		108,868
Negative Cash Flow		$(20,393)

Susan: Reactions to Dealing with Today's Financial Realities

Susan was comfortable *taking some risk* with her investments. She didn't enjoy betting on the horses, but she and Lance had discussed his investments during their marriage. She had come to realize that you had to take a certain amount of risk to make money. She probably wasn't as venturesome as Lance had been because she was not as knowledgeable, but she was willing to take some risk with professional guidance.

Her primary financial goal was to take care of her mother. It appeared that the trust income would cover most of those costs. A secondary goal was to figure out a way she could stay in their apartment, which she loved so much.

Her investment objective was growth of capital. Although her current income picture did not look that good, she thought she could improve it by rearranging some assets.

Susan knew you were not supposed to make momentous decisions such as selling a house in the first few months of widowhood, but it was painfully obvious she could not afford to keep the lake cottage. At first she had considered renting it, but after reviewing the matter with Lance's assistant, Sarah, she discarded that possibility. She was more interested in keeping her present apartment than maintaining the lake cottage.

Susan called the real estate agent who sold the lake cottage to them and told her of her decision. The agent thought she would receive about $100,000 from the sale of the cottage and that it would sell fairly quickly. Susan realized that if it sold for $100,000, she would net about $94,000 after paying the agent's commissions. Since they had paid close to this amount for it, there would be no capital gains taxes due. After paying off the $50,000 mortgage, she would have $44,000 left. However, it looked as if her expenses would exceed her income by $16,000 this first year. After covering these expenses, she would have $28,000. She wanted to add $3,000 to cash reserve, bringing it up to $5,000. This would leave $25,000 to add to her investments.

However, even if she sold the cottage, she would still have a negative cash flow. Until she found a more permanent solution, she could liquidate some of Lance's stocks to cover her deficit. But she knew she couldn't do this indefinitely.

She didn't like to think about it, but her mother was not going to live forever. She was 74 now, and when eventually she died, Susan would no longer need to use the trust income to pay her expenses. However, the women in her family historically lived long lives. Her mother might live to be 95 or 100, and she needed to plan for that possibility.

Susan knew she had to be realistic about her financial future. She knew she couldn't depend on finding a husband to support her. Although she was attractive enough, she was picky. After all, she hadn't found Lance until she was 37 years old, and she didn't think there were many other Lances available. She had been comparatively happy living on her own before, and she imagined that she would be again.

As long as she and Lance had been married, money was not a problem. He earned more than enough to keep them comfortable, so she never considered looking for another job. It was funny how quickly she had become used to having the comfortable life-style that Lance's income made possible. She decided she better consider the idea of looking for a higher paying job seriously. On the other hand, she already had experienced a lot of change, and a job shift might be more than she could handle right now. Although the thought was appealing, she felt a little guilty leaving her present job, where everyone had been so nice to her.

Right now she had to focus on selling the cottage, settling her mother in the retirement community and making sure the trust was invested to generate sufficient income. Next on her list was to try to learn more about investing since she had Lance's stock portfolio, the proceeds from the cottage sale as well as the pension assets to manage.

Susan's risk tolerance: moderately high
Susan's primary financial goal: mother's retirement expenses
Susan's investment objective: growth of capital

SUSAN'S REVISED FINANCIAL STATEMENT

Assets		
Cash	$ 2,000	
Condo	300,000	
Stocks	60,000	
Equity in Cottage	44,000	
Lance's Pension Plan	300,000	
Susan's Pension Plan	25,000	
Car	10,000	
Total		$741,000
Liabilities		
Mortgage Condo	$150,000	
Car Loan	8,000	
Total		158,000
Net Worth		$583,000

SUSAN'S REVISED ANNUAL CASH FLOW STATEMENT

Income		
Salary	$55,000	
Insurance Trust	20,000	
Investment Income	1,280	
Total		$76,280
Expenses		
Mortgage Condo	$15,796	
Mother's Retirement Home	18,000	
Taxes, FICA	14,592	
Other	31,807	
401(k)	4,000	
Total		84,195
Negative Cash Flow		$(7,915)

Audrey: Reactions to Dealing with Today's Financial Realities

Audrey didn't consider herself much of a risk taker. She had no experience investing, so didn't want to "gamble" her money. *Her investment objective* was *current income.* Although she had ample income, she liked the idea of investing more for income than growth. She told Mr. Silver she also wanted to preserve her principal.

Her primary financial goal was to help educate her grandchildren. Her secondary objective was to be financially independent.

Audrey had assessed her financial situation with Mr. Silver and felt very comfortable with where things were. Her income situation appeared to be fine. Her expenses were not that high, and her income from John's pension plan was secure. Mr. Silver estimated the amount she needed to reserve each month for tax payments.

They discussed the mortgage situation, and he explained that the interest on a mortgage provided a tax deduction. However, because she and John had owned the house for 22 years now, most of the payments were no longer deductible. Since the tax deduction was low and she would prefer to have the mortgage paid off, Mr. Silver recommended she do so. With a sigh of relief, Audrey called the bank and asked for the necessary papers.

Altogether, she had $260,000 in liquid assets if she totaled her savings account ($60,000) and stocks ($200,000). Her home was worth $200,000.

Mr. Humphrey told Audrey that, as things stood now, John's estate was under $600,000, and since all his assets had been left to her, there would be no federal estate taxes due. He further explained, under existing law, if her assets exceeded $600,000 when she died, there would be estate taxes only on the amount over $600,000.

Since the estate was under $600,000, she questioned whether it was worthwhile to have the house appraised. Couldn't she just make an educated guess? Both Mr. Humphrey and Mr. Silver were adamant that she needed to have it appraised. They explained that if she had a professional estate appraisal, the IRS would not be able to question her cost basis when she wanted to sell the house. Since the house had been held in both their names, the cost for half of the house would be based on half of the original cost (plus improvements). The cost for the other half would be based on half of the estate value (the current market value). Audrey knew the original cost was $50,000. She didn't expect to sell the house right away, but she now understood why she needed an appraisal. She would add that to her list of things to do.

John's company stock had always been registered in his name because it was acquired primarily through stock options. Audrey had always been a little annoyed that it was not jointly held. After all, she helped John be the success he was at the company, so she thought her name should be on the stock, too. However, Mr. Silver explained to her that it really was better this way. Since it was part of John's estate, the stock was valued at the date of his death (or six months later). This value would be used to determine the taxes she would owe when she sold any stock.

Audrey quickly realized that this was a big benefit. If she wanted to sell this stock, she would pay a very small capital gains. Apart from the sentimental attachment John had for the company stock, he always told her they couldn't afford to sell it because of the taxes they would pay on the gain. Now that obstacle was removed. Although he thought the stock was a fairly good one, Mr. Silver felt it was unwise to have all her investments in one company. Diversifying her investments was basic to protecting her principal, so he would advise her to sell part of her stock in the not-too-distant future. It was a little too soon for Audrey to take the big step of selling John's stock now, but she thought she would be willing to do so eventually. Mr. Silver recommended she consider selling it gradually, and that made sense to her.

Audrey asked Mr. Silver what she should do with the $40,000 she had left in the savings account after paying off the mortgage. He suggested she maintain $10,000 of this money as a cash reserve. This would leave $30,000, which they could invest at a later date. Until she knew what her expenses were going to be, he suggested she keep this money in the savings account. He told her to use her checking account at the bank to pay her monthly bills and suggested her Social Security and pension checks be deposited in that account automatically. She should use her savings account as her investment account and emergency reserve.

Audrey spoke to Mr. Silver about redoing the kitchen, and he agreed with her that it might be a little too soon to attack such a major renovation. Perhaps six months from now she would be better able to face it.

As for the vacation, he encouraged her to take one. A widow friend of hers had asked her if she was interested in going to London with her on a theater tour four months from now. Audrey thought that might be a very good idea. Due to John's illness, they had not traveled in a long time, and she would welcome the change of scenery. Besides, it would give her something to look forward to doing. Maybe she would even buy some new clothes!

Audrey's risk tolerance: middle of the road
Audrey's primary financial goal: educate Joanne's children
Audrey's investment objective: preservation of principal

AUDREY'S REVISED FINANCIAL STATEMENT

Assets		
Cash	$ 40,000	
Home	200,000	
Stock	200,000	
Car	20,000	
Total		$460,000
Liabilities	$ 0	
Total		0
Net Worth		$460,000

AUDREY'S REVISED ANNUAL CASH FLOW STATEMENT

Income		
Pension	$42,000	
Social Security	8,100	
Stock Dividends	4,000	
Savings/Insurance	1,600	
Total		$55,700
Expenses		
Living Expenses	$30,790	
Gifts to Joanne and John Jr.	12,000	
Taxes	11,443	
Total		54,233
Excess Income		$1,467

Elizabeth: Reactions to Dealing with Today's Financial Realities

Elizabeth was definitely *risk averse*. Although it was said that business owners, such as her husband, Ben, were risk takers, his had been a pretty traditional business—owning and running a hardware store. Neither she nor Ben took chances.

Her primary financial goal was to have sufficient income to provide a comfortable retirement. After reviewing her budget, she decided that, since her home was paid for and her needs were small, she had sufficient income to pay the bills.

Her primary investment objective was to preserve principal—that is, to make her money last as long as she did. Since she and Ben had no children, she didn't have to worry about leaving anyone a lot of money. She had taken care of Ben in his declining years, so she was well aware of the medical expenses involved in long-term care. She wanted to be financially independent and able to take care of herself.

Elizabeth decided the next important thing to do was to meet with Mr. Samuels, the trust officer Mr. Grossfeldt had recommended to her. Sam Weatherly agreed once again to accompany her. Mr. Samuels had reviewed Ben's portfolio report, which Mr. Grossfeldt had sent him prior to their meeting. He explained to her that it contained blue-chip stocks that paid an annual income of about 3 percent. This return didn't seem very high to Elizabeth. She knew banks paid more on certificates of deposit.

Mr. Samuels reviewed the list of stocks Ben owned and told Elizabeth he thought there was no urgent need to make any changes in the portfolio because the stocks were good quality. He said that if he managed the portfolio, he would recommend she be invested in what he called a "balanced" portfolio, partially invested in corporate and government bonds, and partially in good quality stocks paying dividends. He indicated that with this mix she could double her income from its present rate of 3 percent to 6 percent. Her income would increase from $15,000 to $30,000 annually without taking undue risk.

Sam asked Mr. Samuels about the fee the trust department would charge and the services it could provide. He said that it would be 1 percent of assets managed and would be deducted from the income in the account, so Elizabeth would not have to pay a separate bill. She was pleased to hear this, as she wanted her financial life to be as easy as possible.

Mr. Samuels also suggested that she discuss with Mr. Grossfeldt the idea of putting this portfolio into a living revocable trust in her name. If she did this, she could be her own trustee, but the bank could act in her behalf if she wished to travel or became incapacitated. In addition, when she died, the assets would go directly to her heirs without going through the probate process. He said she did not have to make this decision right away, but several of his widow clients had found it to be a good solution.

Elizabeth left the trust department reassured. It appeared Mr. Samuels clearly understood that she didn't want to take much risk and that her investment objectives were to preserve her principal as well as provide sufficient income to take care of herself. The fact that Mr. Grossfeldt had recommended Mr. Samuels was comforting to her. She liked the fact that they were used to working together.

After discussing the meeting with Sam Weatherly, Elizabeth decided she would make the change. The portfolio manager may have done a terrific job for Ben, but she didn't know him at all, and she felt much safer working with a bank trust officer. The next step was to transfer the portfolio to Mr. Samuels.

Mr. Grossfeldt told her all that was necessary was to write a letter to the portfolio manager telling him of her decision. Ben's contract with the manager stipulated that they needed 30 days' notice in order to transfer the account. Mr. Grossfeldt provided her with a letter to send the manager. In it, she asked for a final bill, a statement of the portfolio value on the date of Ben's death and a statement of any purchases or sales that had been made in the account in the calendar year prior to the date of Ben's death. Also needed was a statement of any dividends collected and fees charged during the calendar year. Mr. Grossfeldt explained that her accountant would need all these numbers.

Mr. Grossfeldt suggested Elizabeth call Mr. Samuels telling him of her decision so he could send her the forms she needed to sign and make sure that the transfer occurred. Mr. Grossfeldt made it clear to Elizabeth that this did not have to be an irrevocable decision. If at any time in the future she decided she no longer wanted the bank to manage her money, she could move her assets elsewhere. In addition, he said that he thought setting up this account in an irrevocable trust was a good idea.

Elizabeth was relieved. Since this portfolio was a large part of her inheritance, she wanted to make sure it was well managed. Between Mr. Samuels and Mr. Grossfeldt, she felt everything would be in good hands.

Elizabeth's risk tolerance: low
Elizabeth's primary financial goal: retire in comfort
Elizabeth's investment objective: preserve principal

ELIZABETH'S FINANCIAL STATEMENT

Assets			
Cash	$ 5,000		
Portfolio	500,000		
Vermont Land	25,000		
Home	150,000		
Total		$680,000	
Liabilities	$ 0		
Total		0	
Net Worth			$680,000

ELIZABETH'S REVISED ANNUAL CASH FLOW STATEMENT

Annual Income			
Social Security	$ 10,536		
Portfolio	30,000		
Savings Account	200		
Total		$ 40,736	
Annual Expenses			
General	$ 18,675		
Taxes	5,999		
Total		24,674	
Annual Excess Cash Flow			$ 16,062

CHAPTER 10

Addressing Today's Personal Realities

Above the title of wife and mother, which, although dear, are transitory and accidental, there is the title human being, which precedes and outranks every other.

MARY LIVERMORE

Introduction

Many widows find themselves looking at where they are personally about six months to a year following the occurrence of their loss. Again, there are no exact time frames when this is likely to take place, and there is nothing amiss if you find it takes more or less time. Some widows, out of economic necessity, are forced to deal with these issues in a much shorter time frame, while others take longer and are financially able to do so. The ability to take a new look at where you are in life usually results from the passage of time, a better acceptance of your widowed state and the courage to face a future without your spouse. You had to address certain realities in your financial situation, and now you are ready to look in a comprehensive way at other issues that affect your life both now and in the future.

Depending on your age, physical and mental health, financial resources, responsibilities and education, you need to make certain decisions about your future. Such things as life expectancy, financial security, personal goals, dreams, hopes and fears need to be identified. Whatever your pattern

194

has been in the past, give serious thought to your desire to maintain that type of activity. Surprisingly, upon reflection, a number of widows find themselves drawn to activities other than those they previously thought to be of critical importance.

We suggest it is essential at this juncture of your life to assess both your skills and needs. You want to identify for yourself what you need to do with your life to experience some fulfillment, acknowledging that your husband is no longer there to help you meet your needs or to participate in your realizing any objectives you may have set for yourself. Your life has not ended because you have lost your spouse; it has changed dramatically.

We have not focused at all on the widow who was unhappily married and felt trapped in her marriage for financial, religious or family reasons. Widows comprising this group are those who were physically and/or psychologically abused, those who found themselves in a marriage devoid of emotion or those whose beliefs about duty to husband and family predominate over any other considerations. This widow's reaction to her loss may be complicated by feelings of relief. She may therefore feel guilty because she is unable to experience the feelings of sorrow she believes she is expected to feel.

If this is your situation, accept where you are, and look ahead to what you may realize in the future. You did what you did. It is now over, and you have the opportunity to focus on yourself and the obtaining of personal goals. At long last, you can attempt to meet your personal needs. For some widows, just the termination of the fear, stress and tension will be sufficient. As you heal, think about your needs and where you are in life. This will enable you to move forward. For some, the pace may be rapid, while for others, it is interminably slow. The important thing to remember is regardless of the pace, you are making progress down your personal path to a new you.

If for any reason at this point in the grief process you are unable to move forward, you may want to seek the services of the groups or individuals described in Chapter 3 whether or not you did so at an earlier time.

Who Am I Today?

Regardless of your circumstances, you are emerging from what is likely to have been the most painful experience of your life. You have survived, and you are now ready to move forward personally. To help you identify who and where you are, we developed the Who Am I Today? chart shown in figure 10-1.

In completing your Who Am I Today? chart, consider under "Personal Strengths" characteristics people admire about you or things that come easily to you. Under "Personal Weaknesses," identify those areas with which you have had more difficulty than many others you know. We all have strengths and weaknesses. Personality traits should be viewed on a continuum from least to most. Most people have more or less of a certain characteristic, which leads people to say they are outgoing or shy, overly emotional or stoic, or whatever. It is the combination of these traits in a given individual that results in the image the individual presents to the world.

It is time to clarify your needs. Are you a person who requires a great deal of emotional support in order to feel good about yourself? Do you thrive on social contacts, or do you prefer a quiet life with little intrusion from the outside? Is learning, whether from exposure to cultural events or in an academic environment, important to you? Is travel for recreation or the expansion of horizons important to you? Do you feel best when you are working or volunteering?

FIGURE 10-1 **WHO AM I TODAY?**

	Personal Strengths	Personal Weaknesses	Personal Needs
1			
2			
3			
4			

What you are attempting to do here is define where you are personally at this time in your life. Once you have identified your strengths, weaknesses and needs, you are ready to move forward.

Family Issues

If you live in close geographic proximity to your family, whether parents, children or grandchildren, they probably will encourage you to spend more time with them. If you enjoy your family, you may be willing to do so. You may also feel closer to your children now and want to be surrounded by their families as often as possible.

ELDERLY PARENTS

If you have elderly parents in need of your attention, you may now find yourself more focused on their needs. Many of you were unable to do so for a period of time prior to your husband's death, and perhaps you feel guilty about having neglected them. Elderly parents likewise present financial needs that most children, widowed or not, feel obligated to meet. As the elderly population continues to grow, so do their economic needs. It is not uncommon for elderly parents to have insufficient financial resources. We see this is the case with Susan, who is concerned about her mother's situation. She truly feels the need to help her mother and to provide her with the best care possible. She will be more likely to lean in the direction of providing for her mother than in enabling her stepson to take on yet more graduate education.

DEPENDENT ADULT CHILDREN

Perhaps the most complex emotional issue on a family level with which a widow may deal is that of the dependent adult child. Increasingly, in better educated families, adult children are marrying later, staying at home longer and sometimes seeking parental support of a financial nature as they pursue more and more education. Parents often feel guilty about this turn of events, thinking that in some way the very fact that they have a child who has not found him- or herself by this point in life suggests they have not done a good job of parenting. This tends to increase the likelihood of the mother providing him or her with funds for whatever need is presented to alleviate her guilt. It might be additional education, a business venture or a place to live.

Social Contacts

It is quite usual for recent widows to surround themselves with family members and friends if they are available. While this is helpful on some levels, it is too exclusionary. Despite the fact that you have little or no energy to devote to something or someone unfamiliar, in your daily life, try to do something that will bring new people into your world. Determine your comfort level, and work toward some new contacts. You might start with something as simple as a conversation with someone you've met casually in conjunction with your new responsibilities, such as a salesperson or a member of your congregation. Although we have introduced this concept earlier in the book, you may not have been ready to venture beyond your circle of family and friends. Our goal here is to broaden your existing support group. Looking ahead to new activities makes a positive contribution to one's mental health.

EXISTING FRIENDS AND ACQUAINTANCES

Widowhood sometimes creates serious shifts in existing friendships. You and your husband may have had a few close couple friends with whom you did most of your socializing and vacationing. Now you may find yourself uncomfortable with these coupled activities and therefore relegated to sharing social activities with only the wives during the day. Some widows report they detect a difference in the attitudes of their close women friends. They sometimes feel these women whom they thought of as close friends now act as though they are a threat to their own marriages and are reluctant to include them in activities that may lead to extra exposure to their husbands. Needless to say, if this occurs, the widow is reluctant to continue to socialize with her friends the way she had in the past.

On the other hand, some widows have friends who go out of their way to encourage them to continue their former social life. They deal directly with their concerns about picking up a dinner bill or paying for a ticket. Still other widows had few contacts outside of their home and their husband and find themselves at a loss as to how to occupy their time.

Reflect upon previous patterns in relation to what you would like for yourself now. You may want to maintain your existing patterns, but you may also want to make some changes. There are many groups one may join to develop new social contacts based on age or interest. Consider joining such a group. Joining a new group does not preclude maintaining your previous social activities. It is a way of adding to your existing network of friends. Take this opportunity to expand your contacts and knowledge.

NEW FRIENDS

Perhaps you find yourself sitting in your home or apartment wondering what you are going to do about developing new social contacts. Will you need to find all new friends? Will you or should you think about male social contacts? Will anyone find you attractive again? What if someone did ask you out? How would you respond to the introduction or expectation of some physical relationship between you and this new person? Could you ever have sex with another man?

These questions may seem overwhelming at first, but in time, they will be answered in what is a natural progression for the widow. Now, as in the past, you will make decisions about your life when you are ready. Decide which areas you feel comfortable exploring first and get started. If you decide to investigate widow groups, do so. Again, a friend, spiritual leader, physician or the widowed person service of AARP might be helpful in identifying an appropriate group for you. We have found that there is a difference in the attitudes and needs of the divorced population from that of the widowed population. However, many of these groups feature discussions on various topics dealing with aspects of relationships between men and women following separation and divorce that are applicable to both the widowed population and the divorced population. You can usually contact a given group and find out about its structure and topic to be discussed on a given evening. If you are affiliated with a church or synagogue, it may offer some group meetings for the widowed or single population.

If a group approach does not appeal to you, think about something you might like to do for personal satisfaction. You might enroll in a class at a local community college, taking anything from flower arranging to Chinese. Check out classes offered by universities and museums, as well as adult education classes sponsored by the library, the public school system, the YMCA/YWCA, your church or synagogue, or senior citizen organizations, just to name but a few. Many areas have a variety of singles activities that are advertised in the local newspaper. Some of these may be of interest to you.

If you are going to develop a new you, you need to let go of the past and move into the future. One way to accomplish this goal is to allow yourself to meet new people, acquire new knowledge and broaden your horizons. Adding new dimensions to your life will enable you to find greater satisfaction in the years ahead.

Physical Health

Your physical health is of particular importance at this point in your life. It is crucial both to your recovery and to your future health. Studies show that physical fitness programs are essential to physical and mental well-being. Exercise programs are known to reduce stress and tension, and certainly this has been a time of considerable stress for you.

If you have been involved in an exercise program, make every effort to maintain it in some form. If you have not been involved in an exercise program, try to develop one that is suitable for your age and present physical condition. Your efforts will be rewarded. You will relieve stress and feel better about yourself.

Walking is a great way to begin. In some areas, group walks are sponsored by various agencies or organizations. There are many different facilities that provide advice on exercise in relation to health. Some are free or charge a minimal fee, while other health clubs, country clubs, the YMCA, YWCA, and JCC charge a stated fee for participation in their programs and the use of their equipment and facilities.

You might consider joining a local athletic club, where an instructor will show you how to use the equipment. You might also consider taking aerobic classes on a regular basis, which may be the best way to motivate you to maintain a sustained exercise plan.

If in the past you were an avid or even casual player of a particular sport, your health allows you to remain active in that sport and it still interests you, maintain this activity. It might be that you need to find a new group of people with whom to share your interest. Most municipalities offer group programs in various sports. If you belong to a country club, discuss your situation with the appropriate pro, and he or she will help you find someone to play with on your level.

Groups such as the Sierra Club offer different levels of activities for environmentally oriented hikers and campers. Most areas will have some group focusing on skiing or tennis. Read the papers; ask your friends and relatives about groups with which they have had a successful experience. If you are shy and uncomfortable at the thought of entering some activity on your own, work at overcoming these feelings. These groups are designed to meet your needs, and the members will usually extend a warm welcome to you. You'll find, to your surprise and comfort, others in the group may have had similar feelings to your own.

The most individualized approach is the personal exercise trainer. This person will work with you either in your home, if appropriate, or in a given facility to create an exercise regimen tailored to your needs. Again, information about these programs may be obtained from newspapers, the Yellow Pages or friends.

For those women with sufficient funds desirous of trying to work on a personal health and exercise program, a trip to a spa is a wonderful way to refocus. For one thing, many people go alone. There is no awkwardness in being there without a friend or mate. Some spas have a dining structure designed to promote conversation for those alone. Everyone is friendly, and you are able to do as much or as little as you want on the physical side while

202 On Your Own

being pampered. There are all sorts of beauty treatments available and often classes in meditation, stress reduction and other health-related topics. The focus is on inner and outer recovery, the very process you need.

Sex

Many widows with whom we have worked are most sensitive and awkward about dating and the thought of a sexual relationship with another man. Sentiments such as "I can't go back to dating the way I did when I was younger," "I feel ridiculous" and "I can't imagine myself in bed with another man" are frequently expressed. Keep in mind, any man whom you might meet at this stage of your life has similar anxieties and feelings—perhaps even more so, based on his concerns about sexual performance.

It is often advisable to discuss these feelings with a friend or to meet with others in a group who are in a similar situation. You will be able to articulate your fears and questions, and you will recognize that what you are experiencing is probably not unique to you but shared by others. After a while, you will be ready to envision spending time with a man and to think of him as a person with feelings and a lifetime of experiences, just like yourself. If you should meet a man or be introduced to a man you may be interested in, you will begin this relationship by getting to know each other. This process is much the same as when you were younger, but now with the addition of maturity and a better sense of self. **There are no givens!** If the relationship progresses, there will come a time when both of you are ready for it to become a sexual one. Most women feel embarrassed and uncomfortable at first but relax as time goes by. Frequently, you need to deal with your feelings of guilt toward your deceased spouse or those who are living, such as children or other family members. Many widows experience difficulties with the issue of loyalty. Do not feel awkward if the only man you ever slept with was your husband. This should not prevent you from seeking a new relationship. The new man in your life will not be your husband, but he may very likely provide you with an equally positive sexual experience.

If you have moved successfully through the mourning process, you should now be able to get past these normal feelings of discomfort and move forward with your own life in whatever way feels right for you. Some widows have no desire for any new sexual experiences. Others miss sex a great deal and do not know what to do with their feelings. Sex, in addition to other things, often provides an emotional release for the tension experienced by the widow in her new state. The lessening of tension and stress is something most widows desperately need.

We are all sexual beings, and self-satisfaction is also an option. Some young widows—and some not so young—find themselves seeking sexual encounters early on in their widowhood just to affirm their femininity and sexuality. Others have no interest in pursuing this area. Once again, there are no real guidelines here. Do what is right for you.

In addition to sex itself, an experienced need often more important than sex is the need for the warmth, closeness, tenderness and affection which was provided within the marital relationship. Some women feel a greater loss on this level than they do on the sexual one. The familiar pat on the head, peck on the cheek or hug when needed is gone. The absence of these shared intimacies creates a major void. Some widows would be most grateful to have this need met without any sexual component.

For some women, socializing with other widows or friends is sufficient. They feel no strong need for another man in their life. They feel too old or are uncomfortable trying out new experiences that expose them to new people. If such is the case and you are content with your decision, go ahead with it. If your decision is based on feelings of inadequacy or uncertainty and you are aware of that, seek group or professional help to move forward (see chapter 3).

Conclusion

After you have dealt with the feelings and issues associated with initial loss, you will find yourself at a point where you need to think about your own present and future. It is time to think about yourself in a new light.

Perhaps it is time to explore new horizons. Perhaps being in a position to maintain your existing activities and contacts is sufficient. Perhaps you are still uncertain as to what you would like to do in the future. Whatever you are experiencing, it is essential to allow yourself to think about your own needs, desires and aspirations in a new light. It is time to make the most of what has been for you such a painful experience. As in childbirth, out of pain comes a rewarding new beginning.

Diane: Reactions to Addressing Today's Personal Realities

Diane completed her Who Am I Today? chart as follows:

WHO AM I TODAY? CHART

	Personal Strengths	*Personal Weaknesses*	*Personal Needs*
1	Outgoing	Seeks excessive approval for personal and financial decisions	Affection
2	Better organized	Underestimate my intelligence	Recognition of strengths from others
3	Financially more aware	Tends to spoil children (to compensate for loss of father)	Friends
4	Becoming more self-confident	Places children's needs over my own	Financial security

As she reviewed her responses, she realized how much she had personally changed since Mark's death. She had learned so much. Now, for the first time in her life, she was responsible for herself and—even more scary—for her children.

She reflected upon her general acceptance of what anyone she viewed as an authority in the financial area told her shortly after Mark died. She remembered how willing she was to accept whatever Jack Blafford, the insurance man, said about putting all her money in an annuity. What if she had gone ahead and done that? She now knew that would not have been advisable for her situation. It was now difficult for Diane to relate to the woman she was when she was married to Mark. Why was it that she never questioned him on anything?

In her widow support group, she had identified that she had resisted growing up and Mark had assumed the role of her father, especially in the financial area, probably because he thought it was expected of him. Sometimes when she thought about her ideas about things when Mark was alive, she wondered why she had adopted certain views without any appropriate investigation. In her musings, she thought that she would be a much better marital partner today than when she was married to Mark. She also wondered, when she allowed herself to do so, whether or not Mark would have loved the person she was today. Did he enjoy having her so dependent on him? She'd never know the answer to that question.

She had been so anxious about being unable to maintain the children in their private schools. Diane and Robyn had become such close friends that Diane had no trouble turning to her to discuss her dilemma about the children's education. Robyn told her about the various programs the public schools offered to children depending on their needs. Diane was surprised to learn that they made an effort to identify those children who were particularly bright as well as those with learning difficulties. There were specialized enrichment programs in what were designated as magnet schools; there were schools in which the children were instructed in English plus one of two foreign languages; there were various honors classes, advanced placement classes and so on. Some schools had school counselors and even support groups for children living in a single-parent home.

Diane had no idea the public school system provided its students with so many different options. Robyn encouraged her to make appointments to meet with the principals of the schools the children would attend if they went to public school. She assured Diane these professionals would be very cordial and wouldn't mind discussing their particular school with her. Robyn told Diane it was not uncommon for prospective students to spend a day at the school in advance of their actual enrollment. The school would designate a student in the same grade with whom Diane's children would spend the day. This way they would get an idea of what the school day would be like if they attended that school. Diane followed Robyn's advice and was fairly impressed with her meetings with the principals. If she had to go this route, she could feel satisfied with these schools.

Dorothy Trumbull had been very definitive with Diane about her financial options: She would have to either move out of her house and buy a less expensive house or remove the children from their present private schools and place them in public schools. She might even have to do both. In addition, she would have to work. Diane knew she had resisted dealing with this issue long enough. She knew she needed to discuss this with the children the way she had earlier discussed the budget. Before doing so, she decided to talk with her father. Previously, she had avoided getting him involved with her financial problems, but she knew how much he loved and cared about the children. She could no longer worry about what he thought of Mark. She had to resolve this matter now.

She called her dad and asked him if he would meet her for lunch at a local restaurant because she wanted to go over some things with him. Diane had always talked to her parents in the house in which she had grown up, and she wanted this to be different. She still lacked the personal security she hoped she'd eventually achieve when it came to money matters, and she didn't want to regress to her former dependency.

After they had ordered their lunch, Diane brought out the most recent financial statements she had developed with Dorothy. They clearly indicated her assets and liabilities as well as a negative cash flow. She told her dad about her visits to the schools. She had reconciled herself to the idea of putting the children in the local public schools but wanted his input as to the advisability of selling the house. She really felt the stability provided by staying in the house was exceedingly valuable for the children.

After Diane had laid all of this out for her father, she sat back somewhat nervously to listen to his response. For a few seconds, which seemed much longer, her dad said nothing. She looked up at him expectantly and was shocked to see a tear in his eye. What had she said or done to sadden or upset him? She couldn't think of anything. At about this point, her dad reached across the table and took her hand. "Diane," he said, "I can't believe how much you've changed since Mark died. You'll always be my little girl, but now you are an adult woman, and I am so proud of how much you've grown. I don't know this financial planning woman you've been seeing, but she has certainly given you good advice. I basically agree with the direction in which you are moving and think you should stay in your current home, but am really concerned about Erin. She'll be going into her junior year next year, and I would hate to see her have to adjust to a new school in that critical year in relation to college preparation. I know I don't need to tell you this, but Erin will always have a special place in my heart because she is my first grandchild. In any case, I'd like you to allow me to pick up the financial responsibility for her tuition for the next two years. I'm sure your mother will agree."

Diane smiled to herself, thinking her mother would go along with anything her father suggested, just the way she would have with Mark. She wasn't sure how she felt about this offer. Was it fair to Alice and Jeremy? How would they feel about their sister having the opportunity to remain in her school while they had to go to a public school? On the other hand, she had the same concerns about Erin her dad had expressed. Before she could reply and thank Dad for his generous offer, he went on to say he wanted to do something for the other two children, but it would have to be at a later date. Perhaps he could pay one year of college tuition for each of them. Diane thanked him profusely but said she would have to discuss it with the children.

Seeing his quizzical look, she explained that they functioned differently as a family now and discussed as a unit decisions that involved all of them. Diane realized this was the first time she had eaten a meal with her dad by herself since she graduated from high school. She felt good about it. She recognized from the way he looked at her that he had a new respect for her. He hugged her extra hard when they parted in the restaurant parking lot.

That very evening, Diane resolved to discuss with the children the financial realities that prevented them from continuing in their present schools. She expected a big fuss and lots of tears. She was pleasantly surprised. They all said, given the choice, they would rather stay in the house than attend their present schools. Erin did not feel it was fair for her to continue at her school if Jeremy and Alice had to go to public school. Jeremy told her she was being ridiculous. He could accept what his grandfather proposed and was willing to risk that his grandfather would be willing and able to help him when he entered college. Alice said she was scared, but if Jeremy could deal with public school, she guessed she could too. She wanted to know if she could still see her present school friends. They had a good discussion about the schools. In the end, everyone agreed that Erin should finish her last two years in her present school.

Diane was so proud of her children. She was pleased with their family meetings. When Mark was alive, all of them seemed to function individually although she never looked at it that way at the time. They had all matured. It was hard for Diane to acknowledge that they worked better as a family unit now than they ever had in the past. In addition, she thought it was healthier. Erin asked if she could call her grandfather to thank him and tell him that they had talked it over and she was going to accept his generous offer. Diane thought that was a nice idea.

Diane felt relieved when the discussion about schools was finalized. She had been preoccupied with the question of the private school since she had "come to" following Mark's sudden death. She was now ready to pay attention to her own needs. She decided to investigate whether or not the University of Maryland had a paralegal brush-up program. If they didn't offer one, perhaps they knew of a course that was offered by another school in the area. She wondered how she would feel about working again. It would all be so different now.

Diane wanted to call Robyn and have her be the first to know she had resolved the school issue. She had never had a friend like her before, yet they might never have met and become friends if it weren't for the widow support group. Robyn was so pleased to learn of Diane's decision.

Robyn told Diane she would not accept any more excuses from her about not going to the health club. Robyn knew Diane played tennis when Mark was alive but that she had not been ready to do anything on a physical level since his death. Robyn had often told her how working out at the health club had enabled her to survive after her husband's death. She had been trying to get Diane to go with her almost from the time they met. She would no longer accept no as an answer because of this or that, and she was going to take Diane as her guest this coming weekend.

Diane laughed and said, "O.K., you win. I'll go with you and see what I think. I'm so out of shape I'd be embarrassed to put on exercise clothes." Robyn told her no matter what, in view of her age, she would look better in exercise clothes than Robyn did, and Robyn really benefited from her exercise program. She assured Diane the other people would make her feel welcome and comfortable. As always, Diane felt good about her conversation with Robyn.

Next, Diane called Dorothy with her decision about the schools. She had checked with the University of Maryland, and they did have a brush-up course. The counselor there had been very helpful about what courses she would need to qualify her for a job. It appeared that she could go to school at night and that it would take about two semesters. The current cost was $940 per semester. She and Dorothy agreed that this was a necessary investment in her future. Then Diane somewhat reluctantly told Dorothy that she really wanted to join the health club. The initiation fee was $250, and the monthly cost was $60. This was a special promotional offer, and she wanted to take advantage of it. She realized it was an extravagance, but she thought it was necessary for her mental health. Could she afford it?

Dorothy looked at Diane's budget once again. Needless to say, reducing the tuition costs to $1,500 from $15,000 annually helped a lot. She added the expense of $940 per semester for the paralegal course and $970 for the health club. The result was that Diane had a negative cash flow of $8,443 this first year. This discouraged Diane, but Dorothy reassured her that she could cover the negative cash flow from her emergency reserve this first year. Next year, if she began earning money as a paralegal, she might even have a positive cash flow.

Susan: Reactions to Addressing Today's Personal Realities

Susan completed her Who Am I Today? chart as follows:

WHO AM I TODAY? CHART

	Personal Strengths	*Personal Weaknesses*	*Personal Needs*
1	More self-confident on a personal and professional level	Sometimes insensitive to feelings of others around me	Physical and emotional affection
2	Sense of responsibility for my mother	Reluctant to delegate responsibility both personally and professionally	Regular fitness program
3	Acquisition of investment knowledge	Difficulty establishing friendships	Need to be perceived as a good daughter
4	More in touch with my feelings		

In contemplating her responses to the Who Am I? chart, Susan realized that the death of Lance and her work with Dr. Coleman had had an impact on the way she saw herself. She now saw herself in her personal life as someone capable of being proactive, whereas before, she would have described herself as reactive—in other words, waiting for something to happen and then responding. Today, she was more likely to analyze a situation, giving thought to possible actions she might initiate to resolve the matter as opposed to waiting for she knew not what. Her increasing awareness of her financial situation had made her aware of her need to earn more money. Her sessions with Dr. Coleman had increased her sense of self-worth. They had discussed her functioning at her job. She now realized she was underpaid for the work she was doing in her present job. The association had given her regular salary increases; however, if she was honest with herself, she had to acknowledge that her pay was not commensurate with her job responsibilities. She also realized she was capable of assuming greater responsibility than her current job entailed.

Susan knew she would need to attend the American Society of Association Executives convention in two weeks. She found herself actually looking forward to having the opportunity of talking with her peers about the current job market. As she boarded the plane for the convention two weeks later, she surprised herself with the realization that she was no longer afraid to think about the future without Lance. The time away from home and the demands of daily life would allow her to reflect upon her options in a more leisurely fashion. She noted, as she seemed to do with most events which occurred following Lance's death, that this was the first flight she had taken since Lance died. Before she knew it, she had landed, transported herself to the hotel and checked into her room.

After getting settled in her room, she went downstairs to register for the convention. Susan found herself on a short line in front of a man of about her age who began to chat with her while they waited in line. He asked which association she represented and identified both the city in which he lived and the association with which he was affiliated. The line moved very slowly. Apparently, one of the registrants on their line had misplaced his packet. It took some time to locate it and delayed them. Susan and the gentleman, who had now identified himself as Andrew Neily, commiserated about the interminable pace at which their line was proceeding. By the time Susan reached the head of their line, Andrew had asked her to have a drink with him later on that day. Both of them were attending the convention without coworkers. Susan found herself hesitating. She had never considered the possibility of having this type of social contact at the convention. She had been exclusively focused on her career and business concerns. Her lack of response caused Andrew to inquire if something was wrong. She assured him "no," and without further thought accepted the invitation.

When she returned to her room, she was panicked. What had she done? What would this outwardly friendly guy think of her? How could she socialize with a man other than Lance? She wanted to escape but realized Andrew had caught her so off guard she had neglected to find out which hotel he was staying at, so she could not call him to cancel. Oh well, she guessed one drink couldn't hurt. As the time to meet Andrew approached, Susan found herself thinking about what she would wear. She felt almost girlish, yet simultaneously was ashamed and guilty about her feelings. She put on what she thought was a professional-looking dress, softened somewhat by a scarf. "Well," she thought, "if I'm going to do this, I'm going to put my best foot forward."

Andrew was waiting for her in front of the bar, and she was relieved not to have to wait for him. They found a table and placed their order. Susan was unprepared for how easy it was to talk to Andrew. She told him about Lance, and he told her he was recently separated from his wife and was having a difficult time with it. Drinks led to dinner in the hotel. Andrew insisted on paying for the drinks but was very agreeable to their each paying for their own dinner. The evening seemed to fly by, and Susan realized how much she had missed talking to a man about anything other than Lance's estate, other financial matters or her work. She wondered to herself if she would ever find another man with whom she could have a relationship. This was the most pleasant evening she had had since Lance died. Up until now, she had taken for granted that there would not be another man in her life. She experienced a twinge of guilt when she returned to her room and made a note to herself to discuss these feelings with Dr. Coleman. As she prepared for bed, she returned to her earlier thoughts about taking advantage of this convention to get a better sense of what was going on in the association world both personnel and salary wise.

Over the next several days, she reestablished some former contacts and made some new ones. She was busy and had little opportunity for socializing other than on a work-related basis. She found herself chatting with Andrew again on the evening of the banquet. They exchanged business cards and agreed to keep in touch. He was from Chicago, and Susan doubted there would be much opportunity for them to meet since she lived in Seattle. Perhaps it was just as well. Susan knew that Andrew would have liked to have pursued a relationship with her. Although he had made her realize she was not dead as a woman, she was not yet ready for a relationship with a man. She was glad she had met Andrew but was also grateful for the distance between their homes.

On the job level, Susan was very pleased with what she learned. One of the people she met had actually offered her a job as an executive director with a smaller association based in Seattle. The salary was $70,000—$15,000 more than her current annual income. She felt good about the offer and thought she was ready to take on a job with greater responsibility. However, before making a final decision, she knew she would discuss her options with Dr. Coleman. Her inclination was to move ahead to something new with greater responsibility, but she wondered if Dr. Coleman would think she should first investigate a raise with her present association. Even if she was able to get the raise, she wasn't sure she wanted to maintain her present role. The prospective job was a greater challenge, and she felt ready for it.

On the plane back to Seattle, Susan allowed herself to contemplate where she was in her life in a somewhat new light. Since Lance's death, she had devoted more time to her mother than ever before. Dr. Coleman had suggested to her that she was becoming preoccupied with her mother's situation in order to delay facing more painful personal issues. She knew just how important Susan's mother was to her but emphasized that she could not be all things to her mother. Perhaps if Susan did somewhat less, her mother might become more active on her own behalf. Dr. Coleman did not feel it was healthy for her to assume the role she had in the past to the exclusion of her brother. She pointed out that Ron was capable of taking a more active role. He probably never gave it much thought because Susan had always orchestrated everything where their mother was concerned. If she accepted the new job offer, she most certainly would have to involve her brother more actively with her mother. She was pleased she had already discussed this issue with him.

As the plane brought her back to Seattle, Susan recognized that her psychological need to order her life was causing her to review just about every aspect of her life. Having dinner with a man had caused her to think about her physical being. She and Lance had been fairly active people, but she realized she hadn't done anything in this area since his death. She wondered if she could bear to go bicycling. This was an activity from which she and Lance had derived much pleasure. She knew her memories of their rides together would be too painful if she attempted to ride on any of the bicycle paths they had taken. Once, Lance had investigated a cycling club because they had given some thought to taking a bicycle tour through France. Without warning, tears came to her eyes as she thought about the trip they would never take. However, she thought she might be able to get back into her bicycling if she had the opportunity to do it with others. This was another area she needed to investigate sooner rather than later, and she even thought she had seen the information in Lance's desk.

Thinking about the bicycle trips she and Lance had taken reminded her of the one they attempted with his children. She had not seen or even heard from Leslie and Adam in quite some time. She guessed they would no longer play a role in each other's lives; perhaps they would send each other perfunctory Christmas cards. In some ways, Susan wished things were different with them because they were a part of Lance. Both she and the children had shared a special relationship with him. Unfortunately, Susan knew all too well that wishing didn't accomplish anything. Instead of ruminating about something that would never be, she should pay more attention to something she did have control over—mainly her friends. Dr. Coleman had been stressing to Susan the need for her to reestablish relationships with some of her former friends and to investigate some new contacts. Attending the convention had moved her to the point where she was ready to deal with people. It felt good to talk to people and share common interests. She hadn't been ready before, but now she was, and she planned to do something about her social life upon her return.

Dr. Coleman would be pleased with her response to the convention and her willingness to give serious thought to a new job. Her work with Dr. Coleman had resulted in Susan seeing herself in a new light. She had contacted this person to help her deal with the aftermath of Lance's death but in the process had begun to look at herself in ways she never had before. She hated to admit it even to herself, but her work with Dr. Coleman had gone far beyond the issues surrounding Lance's death.

Audrey: Reactions to Addressing Today's Personal Realities

Audrey completed her Who Am I Today? chart as follows:

WHO AM I TODAY? CHART

	Personal Strengths	*Personal Weaknesses*	*Personal Needs*
1	Willingness to assume personal responsibility	Tend to allow myself to become overly committed	To be my own person
2	Socially conscious	Neglect my health	To be actively involved with my family
3	Willingness to learn	Inclined to procrastinate investment decisions	To contribute to society

Going to the golf clinic at Hilton Head with her friends had been just what the doctor ordered, so to speak. The golf pros had improved her game considerably, but even more important, she enjoyed being away with her friends. They were upbeat and teased her about finding a man. They even came up with elaborate schemes to attract one man they thought was right for her and laughed themselves silly in the process.

In fact, they were all shocked when he approached her on his own about having a drink after having inquired about her marital state and being apprised of the fact that she was a widow. Her friends insisted that she accept, and everyone had something to say about what she should wear. It was like getting ready for a prom. They all laughed so hard she didn't think she'd be able to walk to their designated meeting place. She wasn't sure how she felt about this, but all of her friends encouraged her and told her it would be good for her. She didn't even know what she would say to a man at this point in her life. She felt plain weird but decided to go ahead with the meeting anyway.

Lionel, the gentleman in question, was a recently retired corporate executive who lost his wife two years ago. His wife had also died following a lingering illness, which gave them something in common. In addition, he was charming and witty. He had lived in Atlanta, Georgia, all of his life and had four grown children, busy with their own lives. She found she was quite comfortable with Lionel, and drinks naturally led to dinner. Her friends told her they bet she would end up having dinner with him, but she had said the idea was ridiculous. They'd have a thousand questions for her when she got back to the suite as well as "we told you so's." Before dinner was over, she had agreed to see Lionel again during her stay at Hilton Head. His interest in her was flattering, but she wasn't sure she was ready for a relationship or that she wanted one. She guessed she hadn't expected anyone to be interested in her, so she hadn't focused on such an eventuality at all. She knew she would give the whole area of relationships more thought when she got back home.

So much had taken place since John's death. She was still dealing with all the changes in her life and attempting to make good decisions for herself as to how she spent her time. She was very positive about her current relationships with her children and grandchildren. She was closer to Joanne than she had ever been, and both women had benefited from the opportunity they had created to get to know each other better. The weekly lunches had really been a plus. They now shared things with each other they had never shared before. Audrey tried to be as supportive as she could to her daughter with regard to her marriage. She now knew there was ongoing tension between the couple because of their financial situation.

She adored Joanne's children and they, her. All of them looked forward to her day with them. Since she had more time to spend with Heidi and Noah, she made a point of doing extra things with the oldest child, Jamie, who was usually in school during Audrey's visits. She and "Gran Gran" had had some special sleep-overs. Audrey always got a thrill out of having the chance to personally watch her grandchildren acquire new skills and proudly demonstrate them for her. Children learned so much in such short periods of time.

She was also pleased with where things were with John Jr. In his high school and college years, he had been fairly close to his mother. It was not uncommon for him to come to her with a question about which course might be better for him or more likely a question related to a relationship he had with some girl. Their relationship changed when he entered medical school, as did his overall attitude. Audrey couldn't pinpoint when he developed what she called his superior attitude, but she hadn't found it attractive. It created more distance between them. The conversation she had with him in the kitchen about her financial situation had brought them close again. John Jr. had gone with her to Mr. Silver's. He liked his approach to his mother's situation as well as his mother's understanding of her financial affairs. He realized he had never given much thought to his own financial affairs, and this type of approach would be of value to him. Before he left the office with his mother, he had made an appointment for him and his wife to meet with Mr. Silver and took home with him various forms that Mr. Silver requested be completed in order to give him a full picture of his financial status.

After this, there had been more invitations from her daughter-in-law, of whom she was fond, for dinner or an activity involving her grandchildren. She hadn't seen much of their children prior to this time and felt she had just gotten to know them. J.T., the older boy, was a freshman in high school and all boy. His younger brother, Casey, was more sensitive and serious. He spent all of his spare time poring over computer books and doing scientific experiments. She had both of them over to spend the night and was pleased with the way things turned out. All of them seemed to be discovering each other.

She was basically comfortable with her social life, too. A nucleus of couples from her married days had remained friendly with her. They included her in their dinner get-togethers and other activities. There had been some rocky times in the beginning over money, but it had been resolved. The men didn't know what to do about her when it came to buying a ticket or paying a restaurant bill. They had tried to pick up her share and split it among them, but that made Audrey feel like a charity case. She had told them as firmly as she could that she wanted to join them but couldn't do it if they would not allow her to pay her own way. It was too uncomfortable for her not to do so. They finally got the message and now treated her as an equal on that level. She realized she was the first widow in their circle of friends, so it was like breaking ground. Walter and Jane were still a problem sometimes because of Jane's reaction to her husband's attention to Audrey, but she paid less attention to it, as did everyone else in their group.

Her new friends were more diversified and exciting to her. She had become quite friendly with Heather, the woman she met through her symphony volunteer work. She, too, was a widow, and they had gotten into the habit of getting together about one evening a week now to take in a movie, have something to eat together and just go shopping or whatever else appealed to them. She was probably her closest friend now, mainly because they were both widows. It did make a difference! She could discuss things with Heather that her other friends wouldn't understand.

Audrey was most pleased with the friends she had made through her work with the "Reading Is Fundamental" program. The women who were active with this group were very aware of federal, state and local legislation that impacted children's literacy issues. They did not appear to Audrey to be overly aggressive, but they were knowledgeable and worked zealously to accomplish the organization's goals. They certainly had expanded Audrey's horizons. She realized what a sheltered life she had led as a corporate wife and enthusiastically embraced these new challenges. Although she was initially intimidated by the group, she responded positively to their acceptance of her. They made her feel welcome very quickly, and she was able to realize that her organizational skills were helpful to this involved group of women. They were also very complimentary to her about her contributions to the program. This made her feel good about her decision to become active with this group.

Elizabeth: Reactions to Addressing Today's Personal Realities

Elizabeth completed her Who Am I Today? chart as follows:

WHO AM I TODAY? CHART

	Personal Strengths	*Personal Weaknesses*	*Personal Needs*
1	More outgoing	Lack self-confidence	Companionship
2	Ability to seek and accept professional advice	Depend on the approval of others	Financial security
3	Beginning to make my own decisions (financial and personal)	Slow to change	Physically self-sufficient

Elizabeth had a difficult time completing her Who Am I Today? chart because she wasn't sure she really knew who she was anymore. She wasn't the same person she had been when Ben was alive, but she hadn't changed a great deal either. She had amazed herself on the cruise she had taken with Abigail; she had participated in almost everything. She thought it was the most exciting experience she had ever had. She wished she had been brave enough to insist Ben take her on a cruise after he had retired. She had made comments about cruises, but he never picked up on it as something she really wanted to do. She wondered if he would have gone if he knew it was important to her. Well, she'd never know. She thought about the expression on Abigail's face when one of the crew members asked her to dance and she had accepted. She smiled to herself just thinking about it.

The ports they visited were all interesting, and the heat hadn't bothered her. There were several senior citizens on the ship, and she and Abigail had found themselves with a small circle of friends at the end of the first full day on board. She would never cease being surprised at what close friends they had all become in the course of a week. She had discussed things with these people that she had never discussed with the few people with whom she and Ben had socialized in Boston in all the time they had known them. One of the couples she became friendly with on the ship lived in Florida, as did another widow whose company she particularly enjoyed.

She was giving more and more thought to relocating to Florida. In Boston, she really had only acquaintances, with the exception of Mabel and now the Weatherlys, who were her friends. When she visited Abigail's retirement community, she was taken aback by the number of activities offered to the residents. She sat in on Abigail's Wednesday afternoon bridge group and remembered how much she and Ben used to enjoy their bridge games. Someone even asked her if she would take a hand for a while. She was reluctant to do so because it had been so long since she played, but she agreed after the players assured her they wouldn't get upset with her if she made a mistake. She felt she hadn't done too badly although she knew she was rusty. It would be nice to play bridge again.

Abigail had encouraged her to attend some of the activities with her, and she had done so. She'd always wanted to take a quilting class but never gotten around to it. The class which she visited at the retirement facility seemed perfect—it was neither beyond her sewing level nor too simple. The young woman teaching it seemed to be very pleased to answer any and all questions. When she saw other women about her age participating and asking questions, she felt more comfortable about undertaking such an activity herself. She was beginning to get frustrated with herself for always needing support from someone else. The senior citizens she saw in Florida didn't seem to need the same kind of approval and support she appeared to need. A part of her was tired of being this way, worrying about who she was and what she was going to do. Another part was reluctant to change.

Mabel suggested to her that she visit some retirement communities in the Boston area before she made a decision about moving to Florida. Elizabeth thought this was a good idea. Mabel had a widowed friend living in a nearby retirement community, and she suggested they go over for lunch. Mabel agreed to make the necessary arrangements with her friend, Caroline. Caroline turned out to be very gracious. She made reservations in the dining room for the three of them and insisted on taking them as her guests. She gave them the grand tour of the grounds and shared with them the various programs and lectures offered. The day they were there, there was a lecture scheduled by a well-known antique dealer in Boston. Caroline's apartment was quite nice and tastefully decorated. Her son and daughter apparently lived nearby, and she was able to spend time with her children as well as on her own.

Elizabeth thought such a place would clearly be an option if she stayed in Massachusetts. Although, if she stayed in Boston, she didn't know if she was quite ready to give up her house—all these decisions. There was something about Florida that was more appealing to her, but she wasn't quite sure what it was. She decided to invite Pastor Appletorn to tea. She thought it would be helpful to discuss her dilemma with him. She hadn't had much of an opportunity to talk with him personally since she had returned from her cruise. She faithfully attended church on Sundays, but that wasn't the same as speaking with him personally. She thought about how much more she had gained from his sermons these past few weeks since she had been fitted with her hearing aid. Now that she had adjusted to it, she readily admitted that she had needed one. Funny, she hadn't realized how much her hearing had deteriorated until Abigail had drawn it to her attention.

When she had gone for her physical, Dr. Longworth, her doctor, had said he hadn't seen her in so long he had forgotten what she looked like. He was pleased with her overall health but confirmed that she had a moderate hearing loss in definite need of correction. He was sure the type of loss he suspected would improve markedly once she was appropriately fitted with a hearing aid. He referred her to another doctor to handle the hearing problem. It turned out he was right. The hearing aid made a world of difference!

As she greeted Pastor Appletorn at the door, she was pleased to see his smiling face. He had a way of making all of his parishioners feel special. They had tea with some scones she had baked for the occasion. He complimented her on how good they were. He asked about her cruise and her sister. She told him all about the cruise, her sister and where she lived.

She made a special point of telling him she had attended church with Abigail in Florida and enjoyed the sermon, but assured him it wasn't the same as attending his church. He reminded her that it didn't have to be just the same to be valuable. He was sure the Lord appreciated diversity amongst his flock. He added, as she knew all too well, that nothing stayed the same forever. Toward the end of the tea, he surprised her by saying, "Elizabeth, I've known you for a long time, and I hear something different and new in your voice when you talk about Florida. There is a spark, a greater sense of self-confidence than I have ever heard before. I can't tell you what to do, and if you do move, it will be a loss to our congregation, but I think you should give it some serious thought."

After he left, Elizabeth sat in her familiar, comfortable dining room for some time. What really was keeping her in Boston? She guessed she felt disloyal to Ben because he was buried there and they had always lived there. It was as though what he had decided wasn't good enough for her any more. But Ben was no longer with her, and she was all alone. The winters were really hard, and she would have to increasingly depend on Pastor Appletorn and other members of the congregation for one thing or another when the weather was bad. In Florida, she had been able to be something more than Ben's wife. She was Elizabeth in her own right, and she liked the feeling. She wasn't sure who she was quite yet, but she liked the way she had felt in Florida. Besides, she did want to be close to Abigail. She was getting closer to making a final decision every day.

PART THREE

Building a
Secure and
Rewarding
Future

CHAPTER 11

Developing Your Long-Term Financial Plan

You have to have confidence in your ability, and then be tough enough to follow through.

ROSALYNN CARTER

Introduction

When a woman becomes a widow, she has to understand and manage her own money in order to survive. In general, though, widows have not had the primary responsibility for controlling the family's finances. The recognition and acceptance of the fact that financial decisions now rest in their hands requires a major adjustment in mind-set. It is not that they are incapable of it; it is more likely they were never involved in the process. Since they are accustomed to their husbands assuming responsibility for their finances, the natural tendency is to find someone else to assume that role.

While this is not a bad idea, immediately delegating total responsibility to someone else frequently causes widows to run into financial trouble. It is understandable that you want to trust someone else since you were used to trusting your husband. Many new widows assume the "child widow" role because it is familiar and they resent the fact that they are forced to manage their own money. Others resist dealing with finances because it is symbolic to them of the fact that they are widows—a state they did not choose and

don't like. Perhaps not taking charge of their finances allows them to cling
to the myth that their lives have not really changed.

Regardless of how you felt about money management in the past, as a
widow, you must accept the fact that you and you alone have the ultimate
responsibility for your financial future. To do this, you have to understand
your financial situation from both a short-term (budget) as well as a long-
term (future planning) point of view. Ultimately, you may decide to delegate all or part of the management of your money to someone else, but
before you take that step, you need to understand your situation.

Updating Your Budget

Now that you have been living *On Your Own* for a while, you have a better
idea of what you are actually spending as opposed to what you estimated
you would spend. In chapter 7, we presented a format to help you estimate
the money you needed to maintain your current life-style. The temptation is
to go through this exercise initially and then ignore it. It is essential to keep
monitoring your expenses and income periodically to make sure you are
not spending your principal. This is not easy to do while the estate is being
sorted out. In these early stages, the difference between income and
principal is not always clear.

As has been mentioned many times, the first year of widowhood is one
of transition—one during which many mistakes can be made. We have
tried to demonstrate how to avoid these mistakes. After you have gone
through this initial stage of dealing with crisis—both emotional and
financial—your life becomes more predictable, and new patterns may be
established. Now is the time to look at your budget again. Are all your
expenses necessary? Hopefully, you are past the splurges you might have
indulged in initially—the special vacation, the clothes you bought or the
redecoration of the house—all of which were designed to cheer you and
your family up. Are things costing more than you expected or less? Is your
income sufficient to cover your expenses?

At this point, it is important to do some longer-range planning rather
than the "getting by" approach of the early stages of widowhood. We have

used the time frame of a year, but as we said previously, this settling down period may take a shorter or longer time for you to reach.

After you have reviewed your current financial situation, it is time to meet with your advisors again to discuss your future financial planning.

In the early stages of widowhood, it may have been more convenient to work with your husband's advisors. Now that you hopefully feel more in control of your situation, we recommend you review your relationship with these advisors. Were they helpful to you and responsive to your requests? If not, you may want to change them (see chapter 5). If your experiences were good, make appointments with them to discuss your future financial plans.

Estate Planning with Your Attorney

YOUR WILL

The attorney who handled the settlement of your husband's estate undoubtedly reviewed your own will or created one for you to ensure your estate would be in order. However, you should reexamine the will that you approved when you first were widowed. It may not accurately reflect your intentions now that things have quieted down somewhat and you have more time for reflection.

Questions to consider when drafting a will are:

· Who will inherit which of your assets?
· Who will supervise the distribution of these assets?
· How will they be distributed? Outright gift or trust?
· When will the distribution be made?
· Who will be the guardian for your children if they are minors?
· Do you want the personal and financial guardian to be the same person?

On this last issue, if you don't have a valid will and you have minor children, the proceeds of your estate will be divided equally among them.

The court will appoint a guardian for them as well as an administrator to settle the estate. To avoid this, you need to designate a guardian or personal representative in your will. Make sure the person you select agrees to assume that role. The person you have in mind may not want to take on that responsibility.

It is a common misconception that, if you are single and you don't have children, you have no need for a will. This is not correct. The purpose of a will is to make sure that your assets go where you want them to go (to individuals or institutions). It is recommended that you use percentages rather than dollar amounts in your will. For example, if your will specifies that your estate should be divided $100,000 each to six heirs and your estate totals $500,000, then your personal representative has a problem. If instead you had said each heir was entitled to one-sixth of the estate, it would be easy to divide your assets.

Under current federal estate tax law, when you die, $600,000 of your assets will be excluded from federal estate tax. If your assets exceed that amount, your estate will be taxed according to an established formula. The only way to avoid this tax is to leave all your assets in excess of $600,000 to charity. If your estate looks as if it will exceed $600,000, it is very important to do some estate planning.

Any assets jointly owned are not governed by the terms of the will. To make certain that your assets are received by the people you have designated in your will, you must make sure they are titled in your name. Some people have very good wills but then mistakenly title their stock and bank accounts jointly with some member of the family. For example, your will may specify that your five children share equally in your $600,000 estate. If you have a jointly held bank account of $100,000 with one of your children, this asset will go directly to that child, and the balance of your estate ($500,000) will be divided equally among your five children. This probably was not your intention.

Some assume by titling all their assets in joint name they have done their estate planning and they don't need a will. For smaller estates under $600,000, this may work, but it is always advisable to have a will to make sure your estate is in order.

You should consider changing your will if you remarry, you divorce, there is a tax law change, you have a child or grandchild, someone mentioned in the will dies, you move from one state to another or the size of the estate has changed significantly. In the past, you might have added a codicil to your will to reflect a desired change. Today, making this change to your will and signing a new will costs about the same and will be less subject to challenge.

Once your will is drafted according to your specifications, your lawyer should make sure that it is signed, witnessed by the required number of people, valid in your state of residence and put in a safe place, where the appropriate people can find it.

POWERS OF ATTORNEY AND LIVING WILLS

In addition to a will, you should give someone a power of attorney to act on your behalf should you be traveling or incapacitated. You may want to give two different people your power of attorney—one for health matters and the other for financial matters.

You may also want a living will that specifies who has the ultimate decision about whether you live or die should you be unable to make that decision.

LIVING TRUSTS

Many people use a living trust instead of a will. If you set up this trust and register all your assets in the trust name, then your assets do not go through the expense of probate. When you die, they will go directly to the heirs you have designated in the trust. The living trust is also useful if you become ill and are unable to manage your own affairs. With this type of trust, you can be your own trustee, but you designate someone else as your successor trustee. This person will act on your behalf if you are unable to do so as well as manage the assets and take any other action necessary.

Some advisors recommend that everyone have a living trust instead of a will. They point out the advantages of having a living trust: You avoid the expense of probate, you don't have to use a lawyer to settle the estate and the transition is a smooth and relatively painless one. This is fine in theory. However, some widows set up a living trust but never follow through with the next step of titling all their assets in the trust name. If you do not take this step, then the living trust is ineffective.

A living trust can be a useful device, particularly for a single person with an uncomplicated financial situation. However, it is not a panacea. Other advisors consider having a will essential. Before deciding to establish a living trust or any other legal document, make sure you have the advice of an estate planning lawyer.

THE ROLE OF THE LAWYER

You may be tempted to use the forms available in popular books or computer programs to set up your estate in order to save the lawyer's fees. We recommend using an attorney to make sure that every legal aspect of your situation has been considered. He or she will prepare the appropriate documents required in the state in which you live and will make sure they stay valid if tax, probate or property laws change.

After you have completed your estate planning with your attorney, it is time to consult with your accountant.

Tax Planning with Your Accountant

The best time to do tax planning is in the late fall, when you have a good idea of what your income will be for the year. It is also usually the slowest time of year for accountants, so they have time to spend with clients on planning. At that time of year, you should have enough information so that your accountant can estimate your tax liability for the current year and project it for the next year.

If appropriate, he or she will also make suggestions as to what you can do to reduce your tax bill for the current year. By visiting your accountant in the fall, you will have enough time to implement any recommendations made. This is also the best time of year to find a new accountant should you so desire.

Your accountant will tell you what financial information you need to keep track of during the year and how best to present this information to him or her. As with any other professional advisor, the better prepared you are when you meet with him or her, the lower the fee you will be charged. If you appear with a shoe box full of receipts, you will have to pay for someone else to organize them. If instead you have kept the records in the binder as we suggested earlier and present them in this organized form to your accountant, your fee will be lower.

In the future, you might even get to the point where you feel that you are able to prepare your own tax returns without the services of an accountant. If you do complete your tax returns yourself, you should at least have a professional review them. Tax laws keep changing, and an accountant will be aware of any new action you should be taking in light of these changes. Also, if the IRS audits your return, it is very comforting to know that you have a professional who can represent you.

THE ROLE OF THE ACCOUNTANT

As we previously mentioned, the accountant's role is to prepare your tax return in a timely fashion and give you tax advice. Some accountants may also help you with budgeting and long-term financial planning. Sometimes, because they are asked or are so inclined, they may make investment suggestions, but be careful about taking this advice without consulting your investment advisor. For instance, if you complain to your accountant about the amount of taxes you are paying, he or she might suggest you could reduce your tax bill by investing in municipal bonds. By making this recommendation, he or she is responding to your concern. Municipal bonds do produce tax-free income. However, from an investment point of view, your principal rarely grows when invested in municipal bonds. If your primary investment objective is growth of principal, this recommendation might be shortsighted.

Financial Planning with Your Financial Advisors

After getting your legal and tax situations in order, you should focus on your long-term financial planning. When you were first widowed, your major concern was whether you had sufficient income to cover your expenses. Now that you are past this initial stage, you should review your investments with your advisor to see if they meet your long-term needs. Managing your investments can be a monumental task. Even if you don't have a lot of money (or especially because you have limited resources), you should consult a professional financial advisor.

Most widows realize they need help but don't know where to turn. There are many types of financial advisors—all of whom claim to be the one you should select as your primary, if not only, financial advisor. In chapters 5 and 6, we discussed how financial advisors can help you in the initial stages of widowhood. Now we will describe what long-term services each of these advisors can provide and what they will charge.

Thirty years ago, it was much easier to select a financial advisor. At that time, insurance agents ascertained how much life insurance you and your husband needed. They were paid by the commissions earned on the insurance you bought. If you invested in stocks and bonds, stockbrokers would advise you as to what to buy or sell in your portfolio. They were paid by the commissions made on transactions. The roles of these two professionals were clearly defined. Insurance agents did not sell you stocks and bonds, and stockbrokers did not sell you life insurance. The term "financial planner" was nonexistent.

Today, the lines are blurred. There are many competent, well-educated and experienced people who provide the same services. The question is: Which person should you select to give you advice? The answer depends on what kind of advice you need the most and the quality of advisors available to you in your area. Whomever you select, it is important that the financial advisor has been personally recommended to you, works with a reputable firm and has been advising individuals, including widows like you, for several years. When your financial future is at stake, there is no substitute for experience, expertise and integrity.

Included under the description of financial advisors are: financial planners, stockbrokers, money managers, life insurance agents and trust officers. Although each of these advisors can provide you with financial advice, each has his or her own area of specialization.

THE ROLE OF THE FINANCIAL PLANNER

The financial planner's job is to look at your situation in its totality to ensure that the financial and investment decisions you make enable you to achieve your long-term economic goals. Since planning is a lifetime process, you should expect to meet at least annually with your planner for a checkup, just as you would with your doctor.

In addition to financial planning, you may need some investment advice. This service can be provided by your financial planner. Whereas fees for financial planning are based on an hourly rate, if your planner also takes responsibility for selecting and supervising your investments, he or she usually will charge a percentage of the assets managed.

If you have different financial advisors managing all or part of your assets, such as a trust officer or portfolio manager, you may want your financial planner to coordinate and interpret the reports they produce. In short, your planner acts as your primary financial advisor.

THE ROLE OF THE STOCKBROKER

The stockbroker's job is to help you select investments suitable to your investment objectives and situation. He or she will review your current holdings and advise you on what to keep or sell. As with all your advisors, it is important to sit down at least once a year with your stockbroker to review your portfolio to make sure it is structured to meet your investment objectives.

Initially, we recommend you select a stockbroker who has a reputation for being conservative. Later on, you may want to be more venturesome, but until or unless you are an experienced investor, this is the time to be conservative. The money you have inherited may have to provide for your financial needs the rest of your life. It is important to invest it wisely!

The stockbroker is compensated by the commissions earned on the transactions in the accounts he or she handles. A well-established broker with a number of clients does not have to buy and sell often in your account to earn a living. If your stockbroker fits this description and you are comfortable working with him or her, you may want to make this person your primary financial advisor. Some stockbrokers have taken courses in financial planning. However, this is not their primary focus. They may utilize this knowledge when advising you.

In addition to buying and selling securities, your stockbroker may recommend that you use the services of a money manager. If so, he or she will help you select one. In this situation, you are charged an annual fee by the stock brokerage firm. This *wrap fee*, which is computed quarterly, can run as high as 3 percent of the assets managed. Of this fee, the manager usually receives 1 percent and the stock brokerage firm, the balance. Under this arrangement, you are not charged commissions. Although this approach has some merit, we think the total fee charged should be no higher than 2 percent.

Some of your friends may recommend the services of a discount stock brokerage firm. Here you make your own investment decisions and call the firm with the transaction you want to make. The commissions are lower than you would pay with a full-service stockbroker because you don't have a personal stockbroker familiar with your situation giving you advice. This type of arrangement is best suited to the sophisticated investor, although even the most experienced welcomes the advice of a professional financial advisor.

THE ROLE OF THE MONEY MANAGER (ALSO CALLED AN INVESTMENT ADVISOR OR A PORTFOLIO MANAGER)

A money manager's job is to manage investments for wealthy individuals. He requires a minimum investment of a certain amount ($50,000 or more). You will receive quarterly statements of your account accompanied by a letter reviewing your current situation and making recommended changes or explaining changes that have been made in the last quarter. Usually, you give this manager total discretion to make changes in your account whenever necessary without calling you.

Traditionally, money managers manage individual stock and bond portfolios. There are also managers who put together portfolios of mutual funds. They select these mutual funds the way other managers select stocks and bonds. They diversify the portfolio by selecting different types of funds with different management styles.

Whichever type of money manager you select, you pay an annual fee based on the value of your account. Fees vary, but 1 percent for managing a stock portfolio and ³⁄₄ percent for a bond portfolio are the norm. There is usually a sliding scale for these fees. The larger the amount of money managed, the lower the percentage fee you pay. For instance, a typical annual fee is 1 percent of the first $500,000, ³⁄₄ percent of the next $500,000 and ¹⁄₂ percent above $1,000,000. This amount is computed as an annual amount but is billed quarterly.

For instance, if your account was worth $100,000 on December 31, you would receive a bill for $250 on January 1 to cover management of your portfolio from January 1 to March 31 (1% of $100,000 = $1,000 ÷ four quarters = $250). There are usually no or very low commissions charged on the transactions in your account, and the money manager does not receive any of that revenue. The minimum annual fee is usually $1,000. You will sign a contract spelling out the terms of the arrangement with the money manager. Make sure you get a copy for your files.

This profession is not highly regulated, so you need to be especially careful in your selection of a money manager. In order to call oneself a money manager, the applicant need only submit a form and pay a small fee to the Securities and Exchange Commission. If the SEC does not decline the application in 60 days, then the applicant can call him-or herself a registered investment advisor (RIA). In addition, some states have more rigorous requirements of RIAs.

If you are not sure whether you want to put all your money with a money manager, you can start out investing a portion of your assets. Then, after a year, you can decide if you want to add more to this account.

THE ROLE OF THE LIFE INSURANCE AGENT

The primary role of a life insurance agent is to make sure that you and your family have sufficient life insurance protection. In the past, these agents recommended only life insurance policies—usually whole life. Today they offer several different kinds of life insurance as well as deferred annuities and mutual funds. A life insurance agent usually does not take care of your auto or household insurance. There are other agents who specialize in those areas. Health insurance is usually available from life insurance agents or from agents who exclusively concentrate on health policies.

The more experienced life insurance agents have passed a series of rigorous tests to become a Chartered Life Underwriter (CLU) or Chartered Financial Consultant (ChFC). They are well versed in the various types of insurance as well as estate planning.

Insurance agents are compensated by the commissions earned on the policies you buy. Premiums (the amount you pay for the insurance coverage) vary widely from company to company and by the type of coverage you buy. It pays to comparison shop. Make sure you are working with a well-rated company whenever you buy insurance. (More on buying insurance will appear in chapter 12.)

THE ROLE OF THE TRUST OFFICER

Your husband's will may have named a bank trust department to manage a trust for part or all of the assets he left to you. The trust officer performs the same role as a money manager—that is, he or she manages your investments.

In some cases, the trust department is designated solely as the custodian of your trust assets. In this situation, they hold the assets, and someone outside the bank manages them. The fee for this custodial account is lower than it would be if the trust department were also managing the assets it holds for you. Unless the language in the will or trust specifically allows a change of banks, you must keep these assets in that bank.

If the trust department is managing your assets, a fee will be charged based on the amount of money managed. A second fee will be charged based on the amount of income earned by the trust assets. The bank's fees are usually deducted from the income accumulated in the account.

Like an independent money manager, the bank sends you periodic written reports of your account that show the current market value of your trust assets as well as an itemization of income received and distributed during the period. The bank also provides you with an annual report of capital gains and losses taken in the portfolio during the year. You can arrange to have the income from this account transferred to your checking account on a regular basis.

Trust accounts under $500,000 usually are invested in the bank's own mutual funds selected to meet your stated investment objectives. From their point of view, this is a more efficient way to manage accounts rather than managing individual stocks and bonds for each trust account.

Be aware that the trust department in most cases has two legal obligations in managing your trust: to produce a competitive level of income for you while at the same time preserving the principal for the ultimate heirs of the trust. To achieve these two objectives, they often invest half of the trust assets in bonds and half in stocks. Sometimes the trust terms favor you over the ultimate heirs—sometimes not.

While you can't tell the bank how to manage the assets, it is worthwhile to visit with them annually to discuss the current status of your portfolio. If you have a financial planner, ask the bank to send him or her copies of your trust statements. That way, the bank knows someone else is looking at your portfolio. You may even want your financial planner to accompany you on your visits to the bank.

Trust departments have been criticized for being too conservative as investment managers. However, their mandate is to preserve your principal, so they are prohibited from taking undue risks. This approach has merit. Although you may not make as much money as you might with an independent money manager, you have less chance of losing money.

Trust department officers are trained to be responsive to clients' needs and will often perform services that aren't in their job description. One trust department in our area distributes poinsettias at Christmas to all its clients. That gesture is much appreciated by the lonely widow in the retirement home.

Having the trust department of a bank manage your assets is often a good choice for someone who is disinclined or unable to handle her own investments. It also protects the widow from her children's sometimes unreasonable requests for money. In this case, the trust officer can be the "bad guy" and say that she doesn't have sufficient income to give them the money, or the widow can say that she would like to help but that all her money is tied up in trust.

If you are fortunate enough to have sufficient assets and your husband did not set up a trust for you, you may decide to give part of your inheritance to the trust department of a bank to be conservatively managed. You can give the rest of your assets to your financial advisor to manage to achieve your particular financial objectives.

THE ROLE OF THE REAL ESTATE BROKER

The real estate broker's role is to assist you should you decide to sell your home and/or buy a new one. As in choosing any other professional advisor, select someone from an established, well-regarded firm familiar with the area in question. This is not a time to make a sentimental choice. Don't give the business to a neighbor who has been particularly nice to you but sells one house a year if he or she is lucky. The real estate agent is paid a percentage of the sales price of the house. This amount is seldom negotiable.

If you are selling, your agent should provide you with a list of recent sales of comparable homes in your area. The REALTOR® should market your property through the multiple listing service (MLS), newspaper ads and open houses. He or she should be able to help the potential buyer locate financing. You should avoid helping the buyer finance the transaction. A buyer who is unable to obtain his or her own financing usually is a poor financial risk.

Conclusion

Any or all of these advisors can help you. At first, you may select a money manager to handle your inheritance; later on, you may decide to handle it yourself with the help of a stockbroker or financial planner. Or the opposite may be the case. You may manage your inheritance initially and as you grow older turn it over to be managed by an independent money manager or trust department.

You may conclude that one person is unable to meet all your financial needs and that it is best to work with more than one financial advisor. If you make this decision, you should select one advisor to function as the "quarterback." This advisor may be your lawyer or an accountant or a financial planner, but it is his or her job to supervise your total financial picture in order to make sure all your advisors are working together on your behalf. We think the best advisor to function in this capacity is a financial planner, but this choice must be based on your particular situation and the quality of advisors available in your area.

Diane: Reactions to Working with Advisors

A year had gone by since Mark died. It was hard for Diane to believe. She had completed the first semester of courses at the University of Maryland. She was amazed at the new developments in the paralegal field—particularly in the computer area. She had thought it would be difficult to master the different computer programs, but she found that after a while it all made sense. Best of all, she was enjoying the classes as well as the people she met.

Dorothy had called Diane and suggested they get together to update her budget. Diane had been able to keep fairly reliable records of what they had spent over the past six months using the forms Dorothy had given her. When she totaled her expenses for Dorothy, she realized that, although they had spent more money in some areas than she had estimated, they had spent less in other areas, and it all seemed to equal out. She was proud of the children, who had really pitched in and helped. Adjusting to the new schools had not been easy for Jeremy and Alice, but after an initial period, they seemed to be doing well and making new friends. It looked as if they had made the right decision to stay in the house instead of keeping the children in private schools.

When Dorothy met with Diane, she urged her to review her will. She knew that Diane had put the will together in a hurry after Mark's death and thought it would be advisable for her to look at it again.

Following her advice, Diane met again with Mary Sue Ryan, the partner at Mark's firm who was in charge of estate planning. Mary Sue reviewed the will with Diane. Diane had appointed her father as guardian for the children, and that still seemed to be a good idea. Mary Sue told her that, in addition to the will, she also needed to give her father a power of attorney so he could act on her behalf should anything happen to her. She should also have a health power of attorney and a living will.

Diane vaguely remembered that Mary Sue had mentioned these items to her when they had met shortly after Mark's death. However, at that time, she was in no condition to comprehend the information given to her.

Now, as Mary Sue reviewed these items with Diane, they seemed to make more sense. Diane asked her to draft these documents for her. She would have to check with her father to see if he was willing to be the designated person for these powers, but she was sure he would agree.

Diane had initially resented her father's advice on financial matters, but now she realized how valuable it had been. She felt fortunate she had located such a good financial planner as Dorothy. So far, Dad had agreed with her advice and in fact was considering going to her himself. He didn't think he needed any help with his own financial planning, but Mark's death had made him worry about what Mom would do if she were widowed. He realized that she would be as ill-prepared as Diane had been to handle her finances.

Diane took the opportunity of this meeting with Mary Sue to tell her about the paralegal course she was taking. Mary Sue was very interested and encouraged her to talk with her when she completed the course. They might have a job opening. If they didn't, she might know of someone else who was looking for a paralegal. She herself had found the estate planning area very rewarding. She especially liked it because, unlike some other kinds of law, you could actually see how you helped people.

A few months later, Diane called Dorothy and told her that with Mary Sue's help she had gone on a couple of interviews and had received a job offer to start the end of June with a salary of $25,000. The law firm would pay half her medical insurance premiums and all her disability insurance premiums. It also offered a retirement plan (called a 401[k]), which meant that she could contribute up to 15 percent of her salary to her own retirement plan. She asked Dorothy to see how much her salary would improve their cash flow situation. Maybe the family could afford to take that Christmas vacation this year. She was concerned because her cash reserve was down to $40,000 from $50,000 due to the expenses of the past year.

Dorothy put Diane's new numbers into her computer and was gratified to see that by 1995 she would finally have a positive cash flow of $5,421. She knew how happy that would make Diane. When she showed these numbers to Diane, she warned her not to get too excited because there were always unexpected expenses. She should try to save some excess income for such events rather than spend it all.

Susan: Reactions to Working with Advisors

After considerable thought and discussion with Dr. Coleman, Susan accepted the job as executive director at the new association. The pay was considerably higher ($70,000), and so was the responsibility. Being selected for this challenging job gave her a sense of accomplishment, as there had been many applicants. However, she hoped she had not taken on more than she could handle.

Susan had gone back to the lawyer Lance and she had previously used, Tim Longwood. She realized that her mother would have some real problems paying for the retirement community if anything happened to Susan. If she died, the trust assets would go to her stepchildren, so therefore this income would no longer be available for her mother. Based on estate tax considerations, she decided to make Ron the heir of her assets. She would have to discuss this idea with him because she wanted to make very sure that he would use this money to take care of Mother as long as she lived.

She talked her idea over with Ron, and he agreed to provide for their mother if Susan died. He was somewhat concerned because he really did not have much experience managing investments. She suggested that he might want to use the bank trust department to help him. They both hoped this was a problem he wouldn't have to worry about, but certainly the premature death of Lance had affected all their thinking.

She returned to Bob O'Brien, the stockbroker, to update him on recent developments in her life. She was now clear about her investment objectives. In view of her increased salary, she no longer needed this portfolio to generate income for her but instead wanted to concentrate on growth of principal. She told him that when she settled on the lake cottage, she intended to add $28,000 to this account. Bob was glad to hear of her change of investment objectives and agreed to make recommendations for the portfolio she had inherited as well as the new money.

Susan also showed Bob the statements she was receiving from Ms. Peabody, the trust officer. He reviewed them for her and explained that she really had no control over this account because the bank had been named by Lance to manage the trust. He went on to tell her the bank's obligation as trustee was twofold. It had to provide her with sufficient income but at the same time preserve the principal for the ultimate beneficiaries, her stepchildren. Given these dual objectives, it appeared they were doing a good job—the principal and the income had both increased during the time they had managed it. He suggested she review the account with him at least once a year to make sure the trust objectives were being met.

Audrey: Reactions to Working with Advisors

At Mr. Silver's request, Audrey had reviewed her budget one year after John died. As she had anticipated, her expenses were much greater this past year than they had been when John was sick. However, she had sufficient income to cover her expenses. She felt it was time she enjoyed herself rather than focusing on the care of everyone else.

She did think she should pursue further the idea of moving to a smaller place. Since she had lived in the same house for the past 23 years and John had handled the original purchase, she really wasn't sure where to start in either putting her house up for sale or buying a new one.

One of her friends from the club, Georgia Brown, was an active REAL-TOR® with a leading firm in her area. Audrey decided to call her and talk to her about a potential move. She wanted to ask this friend how much the house would sell for and if she should look for a new place now or concentrate on selling her home first.

Georgia came to her house the following week and was very helpful. A couple of comparable houses had sold in the neighborhood recently—one for $240,000 and the other at $230,000. After looking at the house, Georgia suggested she put an asking price of $250,000 on the house and be happy if she sold it for $225,000. The kitchen did need modernizing. Audrey asked Georgia if she should fix up the kitchen before she put the house up for sale, but Georgia said that it wasn't worth the aggravation she would have to go through. The purchasers would have their own ideas about what they wanted in a kitchen, and it was better to let them deal with it. However, it did mean she would have to accept a somewhat lower price. Georgia thought it would sell quickly. The neighborhood was a good one, the garden looked particularly pretty at this time of year and it was perfect for a young family.

Audrey knew she should talk to more than one REALTOR®, but she really liked and trusted Georgia and felt she would take a personal interest in the sale because they were friends. She had accepted the maxim of not making a major move in the first year of your widowhood and had not done so, but she was ready to do so now. The question was: What type of home should she buy?

One thing she was sure about was that she wanted to stay geographically close to Joanne, her friends and the golf club. She also wanted to have three bedrooms so her grandchildren would have a place to stay when they visited. She asked Georgia to help her find the right place. She had looked at townhouses, smaller single-family dwellings, condominiums and even retirement communities. She had made multiple lists of the pros and cons of each and finally decided on a townhouse that suited her needs. The space was manageable, and it had the requisite numbers of bedrooms. There was minimal yard work required, and she could go outside and barbecue if she wanted to do so. The kitchen was well designed, modern and cheerful. All in all, it suited her needs and the price was right—$175,000.

She consulted with Mr. Silver, and he concurred that the move appeared to be a good one from a financial point of view. Knowing her aversion to debt, he recommended that she pay cash for the house. The seller of the townhouse was willing to wait until she sold her own home. Since a number of people had already expressed an interest in buying her home, she thought it would not take long to sell.

Audrey spent many hours deciding which pieces of furniture to move, which to replace and which to give away. The end result was a tastefully decorated home that combined new purchases with valued pieces from her former home. A few months later, when Audrey moved in, she was immediately comfortable in her new home. It certainly was a lot easier to take care of, and she loved the fact that everything was brand new. She didn't have to worry about maintenance problems the way she did with the old house.

She was pleased the grandchildren liked it as well. She was much more involved in their lives now than when John was alive. She valued these expanded relationships with her grandchildren and always made time for them.

Audrey had called her lawyer, Mr. Humphrey, for the name of a lawyer to handle her real estate transactions, and he had recommended someone to her. In the same conversation, he suggested they get together to review her estate planning.

As soon as Audrey was settled in her new home, she made an appointment to see Mr. Humphrey, as he had suggested. She was concerned about the education of Joanne's children should anything happen to her. She was also a little worried about the stability of Joanne's marriage. Mr. Humphrey pointed out that in her will she could set up a trust for the grandchildren that specified it was to be used for their education. If anything was left in the trust after they were educated, Joanne would receive it. Audrey said that although she had a comfortable income due to the pension and Social Security, she didn't have a lot in assets to leave them. Mr. Humphrey explained that although it might not seem like that much now, hopefully her investments would grow over the years so there would be sufficient funds to take care of the children.

Once again, Audrey expressed her wish to treat John Jr. and Joanne equally in her will, even if John Jr.'s financial condition was much better than Joanne's. Mr. Humphrey suggested Audrey discuss her concerns with John Jr. In fact, he might be a good person for her to name as the Trustee for the Education Trust since he was more financially astute than Joanne. John Jr. might not have as warm a personality as Joanne did, but Joanne was his sister, and if she needed financial help, Mr. Humphrey was sure that John Jr. would take care of her and the children.

Mr. Humphrey also discussed with Audrey to whom she should give her financial power of attorney as well as her health power of attorney. She thought that John Jr. was the best choice for the financial power of attorney, but wanted to give Joanne the health power of attorney since she felt emotionally closer to Joanne. Audrey thought that, as tough as the decision would be, Joanne had seen her father suffer and would do the right thing for Audrey. She also wanted Mr. Humphrey to prepare a living will for her.

Based on the fact that she appeared to be in good shape financially, Audrey decided to approach Joanne about spending a long weekend with her at a spa. She thought it would be good for both of them. Joanne was somewhat overweight. She had never really lost the weight she had put on during her pregnancy with Noah. Audrey thought a trip to a spa would help her get started on a weight loss program and would be a good break from her daily routine. Audrey was doing well with her walking regimen and her golf, but the latter was seasonal, and sometimes they used the golf carts instead of walking the course, which she preferred. She thought she might want to take on some other exercise activity in the winter, and a visit to a spa would help her learn more about all the exercise equipment available to her. Maybe she'd purchase a piece of equipment if she found one she particularly enjoyed.

Audrey was going to suggest that perhaps Keith's parents could take care of the children on the two weekdays involved and Keith could manage them on the weekend. If they couldn't do it, Audrey would offer to pay for a sitter for the weekdays.

Elizabeth: Reactions to Working with Advisors

Elizabeth had spoken to Mr. Grossfeldt about the possibility of moving to Florida. He had given her a list of information to ask for from the director of the Continuing Care Retirement Community (CCRC) in Florida. He also suggested she look at her budget to see whether she could afford to do this. Which expenses would change if she moved?

Elizabeth decided she would probably spend more on clothes since she didn't have much in the way of summer clothes (+$2,000). She wouldn't spend as much on food since one meal a day would be provided for her at the CCRC (−$1,000). She would have no home maintenance costs (−$2,000). Entertainment and travel had become more important items in the past year (+$6,000). She had enjoyed the cruise so much that she wanted to make sure she had sufficient money to travel every year. If she moved to the retirement community, she probably would spend more on gifts (+$700) since she anticipated having a wider group of friends than she did in Boston. After giving Ben's car away, she had spent a fair amount on cabs, but this should not be an expense in Florida (−$1,000). The CCRC director had told her the apartment she liked would cost $1,200 a month. This fee would include one meal a day, housekeeping and utilities (−$2,400). When she added these projected expenses, she came up with $32,200, which seemed like a lot of money.

Elizabeth decided to show these projected expenses and current income figures to Mrs. Greenfield, her accountant. She wanted her to help estimate her taxes if she moved and to review her proposed budget. She also showed her the latest audited financial statement from the CCRC. Mr. Grossfeldt had said that this statement was important because she needed to be sure that the community didn't go bankrupt if she was intending to live there the rest of her life, which might be 15 or 20 years. The director of the CCRC had also provided Elizabeth with a history of past fee increases at the community.

Mrs. Greenfield reviewed the financial statements as well as the history of past annual increases in fee. She explained that you would expect these fees to go up annually since costs increase, but she wanted to make sure the increases were reasonable and were not too high in any one year. She was pleased to see that this community was accredited by the American Association of Homes for the Aging (AAHA).

She also liked the fact that it had a nonrefundable entrance fee. Typically, the nonrefundable entrance fee is about half the amount it would be if it were refundable. Some retirement communities will refund your fee if you leave or if you want your family to inherit a larger estate. Since Elizabeth was already familiar with the retirement community and had no heirs except Abigail, a nonrefundable fee made more sense for her. This meant she did not have to put down as much money. The CCRC director had told her the entrance fee for the apartment she liked was $75,000.

Mrs. Greenfield told Elizabeth there were tax advantages to her if she moved to Florida because Florida had no state income tax. That was a nice contrast to the high taxes in Massachusetts. Although Florida did tax assets such as the value of her portfolio, the taxes would be much lower than they would be if she were a Massachusetts resident. Also, part of her monthly fee would be considered a medical expense and would be deductible on her federal income tax return.

From an estate planning point of view, Florida did not tax estates, but any assets she owned in excess of $600,000 when she died would be federally taxed. Mrs. Greenfield suggested Elizabeth consult with Mr. Grossfeldt for more details about the legal issues of estate planning if she became a Florida resident.

Elizabeth called Mr. Grossfeldt and told him about her meeting with Mrs. Greenfield. He said if she became a Florida resident he would make sure that her existing living will and powers of attorney conformed with Florida state law. Since she had put most of her assets in a living trust at the bank, most of her estate would avoid probate fees. He advised her that eventually she should put all her assets in the living trust.

Mr. Grossfeldt asked Elizabeth if she had thought about to whom she wanted her assets to go when she died if her only heir, Abigail, predeceased her. This was a difficult question. She would like to give some money to her friend Mabel, but she really didn't have any other living relatives or close friends. Mr. Grossfeldt suggested she might consider dividing her assets between Pastor Appletorn's church and Ben's college. He pointed out this might be a good idea since anything she left to a charity approved by the IRS would not be part of her taxable estate. Although her current estate would not incur much in the way of federal tax, giving it all to charity after Abigail died appealed to Elizabeth.

Mr. Grossfeldt said she could arrange to have Abigail be the beneficiary of her trust when she died. When Abigail died, the assets in the trust would go to the named charities. If Abigail died first, the assets would go directly to the charities. Mr. Grossfeldt also told Elizabeth that, although she named these two charities now, she could add or subtract charities later or change the beneficiaries totally if she wished.

Elizabeth really liked these ideas and said she would consider them seriously. In the meantime, her conversations with Mr. Grossfeldt and Mrs. Greenfield were very reassuring. It appeared that the information she had gathered so far seemed to support the move to Florida. She could hardly believe she was considering such a monumental change.

CHAPTER 12

Protecting Your Assets

Woman must not accept; she must challenge. She must not be awed by that which has been built up around her; she must revere that woman in her which struggles for expression.

MARGARET SANGER

Introduction

As a widow, having sufficient income and investing wisely are of paramount importance to you. Of equal importance is insurance which protects the assets you have already acquired. Most people think of life insurance when they hear the word "insurance," but also to be considered are: health, long-term care, disability, auto, household and liability insurance.

Life Insurance

Traditionally, life insurance is something men know a lot more about than women. This is because until recently it was sold primarily to men, particularly husbands, as a way to protect their families should something happen to them. Non-working wives were overlooked as insurance candidates because the rationale was that widowers could afford to hire a housekeeper (or remarry). Today, with only approximately 20 percent of families having the traditional structure of the non-working wife, the value of insuring the lives of women is now appreciated, particularly for those women earning as much or more than their spouses. Thus, if the subject of life insurance confuses you, it is with good cause. It was probably never explained to you except as to its benefits.

Psychologically, many people resist the idea of buying life insurance because it is connected to the concept of death, and most people do not want to think about that inevitable event. They prefer instead to invest money in assets that provide current income or growth of principal, which they can see. The problem is that they may not have enough time to accumulate sufficient money to provide for their dependents or to provide estate liquidation should they die before they have amassed sufficient capital.

HOW MUCH LIFE INSURANCE DO YOU NEED?

The question most often asked is: How much insurance should I carry? You recently went through the exercise of determining if you have sufficient income on which to live. If you are over 65 and your children are relatively self-sufficient, you may feel you don't need any insurance. On the other hand, although you may not need insurance to support your children, your estate may be large enough so there will be substantial estate taxes due when you die. Under current law, estates worth over $600,000 have a federal estate tax liability. You have to decide whether you want to have enough insurance to pay these potential taxes or if you want your heirs to liquidate estate assets to pay them. Unless your estate is very liquid, this may be easier said than done.

If you are a younger widow with dependent children and limited assets, you will need to buy life insurance on your life so there will be enough money to take care of your children should anything happen to you. Ghoulish though it may sound, children may be reassured if you have life insurance.

There are other dependents to consider besides your children. You may also have siblings who are less fortunate than you are—or parents who are living in reduced circumstances and need your financial help. To determine how much you need, review your situation with your financial advisor so that you can determine the amount of life insurance coverage to carry.

WHAT KIND OF LIFE INSURANCE SHOULD YOU BUY?

Also entering into the decision of how much is enough is the cost factor. When you are younger, insurance is less expensive—logically so because the chances of your dying at this time in your life are less than when you are older. The cheapest form of insurance one can buy is *term* insurance. This will cover you for a certain time period—usually a year—and the cost will go up each year. For those of you who will have a cash need for a limited period of time—such as until your children are through college—term insurance might make the most sense.

There is a method of payment for term insurance called *level term*, where the insurance company calculates what the premiums would be for a longer period, for instance, ten years. They total these premiums and divide the total by ten to determine your annual payment. This means that you will pay the same amount each year for ten years. Many people prefer level term for budgeting purposes because they like to know what they will pay every year. Be aware that term insurance offers only a death benefit and has no cash value.

For those who want more than a death benefit policy, there is *whole life* insurance, *universal life* insurance and *variable life* insurance. With whole life insurance, you pay a predetermined premium presumably for the rest of your life. Part of the premium pays for the death benefit, and part is invested within the insurance policy. Whole life policies can be structured so that you make payments for a certain period of time (typically seven years) and then you borrow against the accumulated cash value of the insurance policy to cover future payments. If you build up sufficient cash value, you will be able to borrow against the policy at very competitive interest rates should you need some money at a later date.

Universal life is similar to whole life, but instead of the cash in the policy earning a fixed rate of interest, the rate varies according to what interest rates are available in the marketplace. Universal life is less expensive than whole life, but it is also riskier because the rate the cash value in the policy earns is not as predictable and the expenses are not guaranteed.

In a variable life insurance policy, the cash portion is invested in mutual funds, which in turn are invested in stocks and bonds. We don't think universal and variable insurance are best suited to widows because they involve more risk than we think is appropriate for your life insurance coverage.

WHICH INSURANCE COMPANY SHOULD YOU USE?

If you and your advisor determine you do need life insurance, then you should select what kind and which insurance company is best for you. Prior to the 1980s, few people were concerned about the economic viability of insurance companies. However, in the 1980s, in an effort to earn a higher return on their investments, some insurance companies invested in "junk" bonds (bonds of questionable quality) and risky real estate. This came back to haunt them in the early 1990s, when many of the tenants of the real estate properties stopped paying rent and the junk bonds defaulted.

Two primary indicators of a good mutual insurance company are its long-term dividend performance and the strength of its financial ratings. Probably one of the best indicators of a good mutual insurance company is comparing the dividends they actually have paid to that which they forecast. The reason this is important is that an insurance agent may give you sheets of paper showing you projections of how fast your cash value is going to increase in your policy. These estimates are based on higher rates of interest earned in the past by the company which may be difficult to achieve in the future. Always ask to see projections based on an interest rate comparable to what is paid by an A or better-rated corporate bond. For example, if these bonds are currently paying an average 8 percent, you should not expect more from your insurance company.

Insurance companies are rated by A.M. Best, Standard & Poor's, Moody's and Duff & Phelps. A.M. Best's annual rating guide is available at many libraries. Standard & Poor's will give you ratings for five insurers on the phone free of charge (212-208-1527).

Also be aware that rates may vary from company to company, even for term insurance. For instance, a company that wants to build its term insurance business might offer very low rates for these policies but may not be competitive in other kinds of insurance.

Another question to consider is whether or not you should buy a *waiver of premium*. This term means that if you become disabled and are unable to pay the premium, the insurance company will continue to pay the premium in order to keep the insurance policy in effect. This adds to the cost of your premium.

These are all issues your advisor should check before recommending the best company for your particular situation. As with other investments, a track record and a strong balance sheet are very important.

Health Insurance

This is the area of insurance about which widows are most concerned, particularly if they have witnessed the major expenses incurred by their husbands' illness. If your husband had health insurance through his employer, regulations issued by the Department of Labor (COBRA) require his firm to offer insurance coverage to you and your family for 18 months. You will pay a different amount for this coverage than your husband did. You will pay the group rate for you and your dependent children. However, after 18 months, you must find your own insurance, and this can be very expensive.

If your husband was retired, health insurance may have been one of his retirement benefits. If he was over 65, Medicare may have been covering him. He also may have had some kind of supplemental (Medigap) coverage.

What is necessary is to determine how much coverage you have, what it covers and what it costs.

WHAT COVERAGE SHOULD YOU HAVE?

As a general rule, if you are able to participate as part of a group, the rates are cheaper, the service is better and you have fewer problems with claims. As far as guidelines go, a comprehensive major medical plan should pay at least 80 percent of all medical bills after deductibles. As in other kinds of insurance, the higher the deductible (the amount you will pay out of your pocket), the lower the premiums you will pay. You can save quite a bit if you have a $1,000 deductible versus $200.

The lifetime maximum under the policy should be at least $1,000,000. The policy should be guaranteed renewable and noncancelable. All insurance is less expensive if premiums are paid annually. Be aware that having dental and psychiatric coverage raises your premiums.

In an effort to pay lower premiums, some people consider HMO (*health maintenance organization*) or PPO (*preferred provider organization*) coverage. The HMOs require you to use their doctors and their facilities. PPOs combine their doctors and facilities with your doctors and facilities (you pay more for the latter). There are advantages and disadvantages to each kind of plan. Above all, you want to make sure that, if you become ill, at least your major costs are covered.

MEDICARE/MEDIGAP INSURANCE

Understanding Medicare is not easy. The subject is covered thoroughly in a Medicare brochure available at your local Social Security office.

Medigap insurance is provided by insurance companies to cover what Medicare doesn't cover. When you turn 65, you have a six-month open enrollment to buy a Medigap policy. Under current law, Medicare pays all but $657 of hospital costs during the first 60 days. If you need to stay longer than 60 days, you run into trouble. With doctor's bills, you have an annual deductible of $100 and then pay 20 percent of the remaining fees (higher, if your doctor does not participate in Medicare).

Medigap policies must conform to ten standardized model coverages labeled A through J. Every insurer must sell the basic A coverage, which picks up most out-of-pocket copayments for hospital charges and doctor's bills. Policies B through J provide increasingly comprehensive coverages, such as for prescription drugs under plans H, I and J. As you might guess, the price increases as the benefits increase, and the rates differ between insurance companies, so comparison shopping is necessary.

We recommend comparing the coverage offered by three companies. Once you and your advisor have selected a company and you have paid the initial premium, you have 30 days to receive a full refund. There is a six-month "window" at age 65 when insurers must accept applicants regardless of existing health problems, so timely application is important.

Disability Insurance

Most people don't realize the frequency or impact of disability. It is the greatest cause of mortgage foreclosures in the United States. Each year, according to the Department of Labor, one out of eight Americans will be disabled for 90 days or longer. If you are working, we think disability insurance is as important as health or life insurance. It provides needed income during periods when you are incapacitated from sickness or injury. This coverage is particularly important if you are a younger working widow with limited resources.

Most employers provide disability benefits, but they are not generally sufficient to cover all your expenses. What is particularly important is the definition of disability. Would the insurance company refuse to pay if you could do any kind of work (such as sweeping floors)? The desired coverage, which is called *own occupation* coverage, would pay if you could not perform the duties of the profession for which you are trained.

Through your place of employment, you are usually provided with group disability insurance. Initially, this is inexpensive; however, the premium generally increases as you get older. Group coverage has very strict definitions of disability and can be canceled at any time. If you leave your job, it is no longer available to you.

You can buy your own disability coverage that is renewable each year at a cost fixed at the time of purchase and cannot be canceled by anyone other than yourself. It has a more liberal definition of disability and in most cases will pay benefits even if you are only partially disabled and working on a limited basis. This type of insurance is more expensive than group insurance, but the longer you wait before you receive the benefits (90 days vs. 30 days), the lower the premium will be. Coverage, whether group or individual, is usually limited to 60 percent of your current income. The amount of coverage depends on your occupation and income level.

When you are reviewing your other insurance needs, make sure disability is not neglected. It is more difficult to obtain if you are self-employed, but here again, if you are unable to find individual coverage, there is usually some association coverage available.

There are insurance companies that specialize in providing disability insurance. Your financial advisor will help you select the right one for your situation.

Long-Term Care Insurance

One of the major concerns among retirees is the possibility that failing health and dependency as they grow older will require long-term care either at home or in a nursing home. This is also an area of concern for adult children with elderly parents.

Statistics indicate that 90 percent of those now age 65 will require home care services during their lifetime. Of this same age group, 40 percent will need nursing home care. Despite popular misconception, Medicare pays only about 2 percent of costs, while out-of-pocket payments account for 43 percent. The balance of payments is paid mainly by Medicaid. Of course, to qualify for Medicaid, one must first have exhausted his or her personal resources.

One solution to this problem is to purchase *long-term health care insurance* before a crisis develops. You select the daily dollar benefit you want, the length of time it will be paid and how long you wait until payments start. You can also choose inflation protection that provides an annual increase in daily benefits.

This type of insurance is relatively new and thus is still in an evolutionary stage. Industry standards are changing, and policies are becoming quickly outdated because of competition among insurers. For this reason, it is particularly important to select an economically strong company that is committed to providing this kind of insurance over the long term. Here again, your advisor will help you select the right one for your circumstances.

Homeowner's Insurance

We recommend that you review your homeowner's insurance annually. It is important that you have your home (the physical structure) insured for 100 percent of the replacement value. If you have lived in your home for many years, your policy limits might no longer cover the actual replacement value. Your insurance agent can help you determine what your coverage should be. It is important to keep this replacement cost evaluation up to date. One way to do this is to add an inflation rider that will increase your coverage annually to keep up with increases in values.

We also recommend personal property replacement cost coverage. This means, if you have a fire and your sofa is destroyed, you will get enough money to buy a new sofa that is comparable to your original sofa.

Any truly helpful replacement cost rider requires a household inventory of each item you own, a description of it and its condition as well as snapshots of each room taken from different angles. If you do not own a video camera, you may wish to rent one to make an audiovisual record of your home. Keep the inventory in your safety-deposit box and hope you never need it.

To cover your valuables, you need an additional policy attachment called a *valuables floater*, which requires an appraisal of your collectible items (art, silver, antiques, stamps, jewelry or furs). If you do not have this rider, you will receive only partial reimbursement of the item's value. Many policies have a maximum reimbursement of $500 or $1,000.

To add insult to injury, if you do not have this coverage and lose a valuable piece of jewelry, not only would you not receive adequate compensation, but also it is unlikely that you would be able to deduct the loss on your tax return. Unreimbursed casualty losses must exceed 10 percent of your adjusted gross income to be deductible.

Automobile Insurance

There are five major areas included in your automobile coverage:

LIABILITY

Liability insurance covers injuries you cause to pedestrians and occupants of other cars as well as damages to someone else's property. We recommend you have $300,000 for bodily injury suffered by one person in each accident, $500,000 for injuries suffered by all persons in the same accident and $100,000 for damage to property. This will appear on your policy as 300/500/100. Some companies offer a more flexible single-limit policy covering total payments for both property damage and bodily injury that will show one number instead of three.

MEDICAL PAYMENTS

This insurance covers medical bills resulting from accidental injury to you or passengers in your car without regard to who caused the accident. It also covers you when riding in someone else's car or when you are out walking. If you have other medical insurance, you usually do not need this insurance.

Many states require *no-fault insurance*, which provides personal injury protection to you, your family and others riding with you no matter who causes the accident.

UNINSURED MOTORISTS

Accidents involving uninsured motorists are always a potential threat. Uninsured motorist coverage covers losses you incur when involved in an accident with a motorist who is uninsured. We recommend coverage of at least $100,000 per person, $300,000 per accident and $50,000 property damage (100/300/50). This coverage is inexpensive, worthwhile and mandatory in many states.

A variation on the same theme, underinsured motorist coverage protects you when you are involved in an accident with a motorist whose limits are too low to compensate you adequately for your damages.

COLLISION INSURANCE

This covers damage to your car as a result of an accident. You can collect no matter who caused the accident. This coverage usually does not pay more than the current value of the car. A higher deductible will reduce your premium, but it should be set at an amount that you are willing to pay in the event your car is damaged.

COMPREHENSIVE

This section of the policy insures you against theft as well as damage to your car from falling objects, vandalism, etc. Again, to keep premiums low, set the deductible at the highest level that you would be willing to pay.

Also keep in mind that a rental car collision damage waiver (CDW) is not necessary if your own auto policy covers you. Dull reading as it is, read your policy carefully or call your agent before you find yourself standing at the rental car counter faced with the expensive CDW option. Many credit card companies also offer collision damage protection with their gold cards.

Umbrella or Excess Personal Liability Policies

These policies protect you in the event of a claim against you by someone who holds you responsible for an injury. For example, a friend slips on a stair in your home, falls down the full flight of stairs and breaks both arms and legs. Even a good friend might sue you. These policies usually apply to family members and include residence and personal injury liability.

You may have limited personal liability coverage through your existing home or auto insurance. However, this coverage is usually insufficient. You should have a separate liability policy that provides supplemental coverage. We recommend you have total liability coverage equal to your net worth to reduce your risk against catastrophic contingencies. As your net worth increases, you should increase the amount of your liability coverage. This coverage is inexpensive and very cost-effective for reducing risk exposure. It is normally obtained from the carrier of your automobile or homeowner's insurance.

Increasingly, insurance companies are insisting on covering both your auto and home. Using the same company is often more convenient and less expensive. It also prevents duplications in your insurance.

Conclusion

As tedious as it is, making sure that you have enough insurance, the right kind, with the right kind of insurance company, is essential to your future financial welfare. We cannot emphasize enough how important it is to make sure your insurance coverage—all of it—is adequate in case you suffer any kind of loss—life, disability, health, home or auto. This is an area where many procrastinate. You may question whether you will really need this coverage, and the policies are too complex to read, but when disaster strikes, it is too late.

Diane: Reactions to Protecting Herself with Insurance

When Diane met with Dorothy about the implications of her new job, Dorothy suggested that they review her insurance in greater detail. Earlier, Diane had followed Dorothy's recommendation to buy a $1,000,000 policy on her life. The policy was owned by and payable to an insurance trust set up for the benefit of the children. At the time, Diane had agreed but really did not understand the implications of the trust, so she asked Dorothy to explain it to her again.

Dorothy told Diane that, when she died, any assets she owned that exceeded $600,000 would be taxed. Her assets were currently $1,261,845, and the federal estate taxes would be $260,593, leaving her children with about $1,000,000. If the $1,000,000 insurance policy were added to her estate assets, the taxes on her estate would jump to $716,304, leaving them with $1,545,541. In other words, despite the fact the policy was worth $1,000,000, the additional taxes would be $450,000. By having the trust buy the insurance policy and pay the premiums, this would remove the $1,000,000 insurance proceeds from her taxable estate. This way, they would inherit $2,000,000. Quite a difference!

The firm for which Diane was going to work had said they would pay half her medical insurance premiums. This was particularly helpful because Mark's firm's coverage would no longer be available to them. With Dorothy's help, she had looked into the costs of individual health insurance coverage and found that the premiums would double from the present levels of $500 to about $1,000 per month. When Diane started working, her premiums would be reduced to $3,000 annually. This meant, in addition to having additional income from her salary, Diane would lower her future expenses by $9,000 a year due to the firm providing her with group health insurance coverage.

Diane also asked Dorothy about her disability insurance. Dorothy told her this, too, would be available to her when she started working. She would be glad to review the coverage to make sure it was adequate for her circumstances.

Dorothy reviewed Diane's household, liability and auto coverage and recommended that she consider using the same company for all three. In this way, she might be able to lower the premiums. Diane reminded Dorothy that Erin was about to turn 16 and would need to be covered by Diane's auto policy. Dorothy told her that the increase in premiums would probably not be that great since Erin was a good student and would not have a car of her own. Her problem would be when Jeremy required car insurance. Based on accident statistics, the insurance companies considered young male drivers more of a risk than young females.

Diane was really pleased with her meeting with Dorothy. She felt that she understood her current insurance situation better. What a good feeling that was!

Susan: Reactions to Protecting Herself with Insurance

The benefits at Susan's new job were not as good as they were at her old job. Her former employer paid for all of her benefits. The new one paid only a part of her benefits. However, she still was earning $15,000 more, and if she had to spend part of it for benefits, so be it.

Both associations offered a 401(k) pension plan. She could contribute some of her own salary to this retirement plan, receive a tax deduction for the amount she contributed and this money would accumulate for her tax deferred. At her previous association, they matched her contributions. For every dollar she invested, they added 25 cents. Her new association did not match her retirement contributions, but still, she thought she should take advantage of contributing to the retirement plan on a tax-deductible basis. At this new job, she had to pay one-half of the medical premiums.

Susan saw little reason to buy additional life insurance besides the $50,000 coverage provided by the association since the only person she really had to worry about was her mother. If Susan died, it looked as if her other assets would be sufficient to take care of her.

When she called the household insurance agent to remove the coverage on the cottage, she remembered to ask if her current policy included replacement coverage on the contents of her apartment. After checking, it turned out it didn't. She asked him to take care of that, and he said he would. The agent asked her if she needed a valuable items rider on her policy. He explained if she owned any expensive jewelry, rugs or paintings, they should be separately insured. Susan and Lance had bought some paintings and an oriental rug when they were married. Lance had also given her a few pieces of jewelry, which she cherished. The agent told her to have these items appraised so he could provide her with coverage. He also told her she had no liability insurance. He said he could add this coverage to her existing coverage for $75 per year. In view of her financial responsibilities, Susan thought this was a good idea.

This was the sort of thing Susan had not been able to cope with in the early stages of her widowhood. It felt good once again to focus on these details.

Audrey: Reactions to Protecting Herself with Insurance

Audrey had been approached by an insurance agent to buy life insurance. The same agent had talked to her about purchasing long-term health care insurance. Since she really didn't know this agent, she decided to call Mr. Silver and ask him what he thought about these ideas. He suggested that she come in with the information the agent had provided to her and they could discuss the ideas further.

When they met, Mr. Silver said that for her the primary reason to purchase life insurance would be to provide a larger inheritance for the grandchildren. However, at her age—and he struggled to be diplomatic as he discussed this with her—it was expensive to buy life insurance. He thought it would be better to focus on building her current investments. He suggested insuring Joanne's life instead. If something happened to her, he wondered if Keith could financially take care of the children. Mr. Silver also suggested in view of Audrey's concern about Keith it might be a good idea to set up an insurance trust. If Joanne died, then the proceeds of the policy would go into a trust to be managed for the children, as Audrey had provided in her will. Audrey thought this was a good suggestion and decided to discuss it with Joanne. Knowing how tight their budget was, she would offer to pay the premiums, which wouldn't be too expensive for someone Joanne's age.

Next they discussed the long-term health care insurance. Audrey had excellent medical coverage through John's company. After hearing some of the horror stories of her other widowed friends, she was exceedingly grateful for this coverage. However, the idea of buying long-term health care insurance appealed to her because it would keep her from becoming a burden to her children if she needed nursing home care. Mr. Silver recommended she select a company that had been offering long-term care insurance policies for a while. He explained that several companies had stopped providing this kind of coverage. She needed to make sure the company she selected was committed to providing this insurance in the future.

He said he thought it was important for this insurance to cover her either in a long-term health care facility or for nursing care provided for her in her home. Some long-term health care facilities in her area cost $40,000 a year. He warned her that with inflation that cost would easily double by the time she might be in need of one. For this reason, he recommended she buy a policy that had an inflation clause. This would automatically raise the amount of income she would receive each year should she need those services.

He had obtained quotes from two different insurance companies. He requested $100 per day coverage that became effective 30 days after she entered a long-term health care facility or needed at-home care. The policy had an inflation clause and was noncancelable. Mr. Silver explained that one of the companies was very particular about whom it insured but had a good record of paying claims. If she had any concerns about her health, he would use the other company.

Audrey said that Dr. PaPadisio had told her she was in excellent health for her age. Her regimen of daily walks and weekly golf games had paid off, and she really felt quite good. Mr. Silver helped her fill out the application for this coverage. He wanted to alert her to the fact her premiums might increase in the future. He explained her premium would not go up unless they raised the premiums for everyone in her age group.

Audrey said a friend had told her she could qualify for Medicaid coverage if she needed to go to a long-term health care facility. Mr. Silver told her that she would have to give away most of her assets to qualify, and he wasn't really sure that she wanted to do that. He was also concerned that Medicaid might not offer the same coverage if and when she had to go to a long-term health care facility some 20 years hence.

Audrey decided to apply for the long-term health care insurance he had suggested, although she felt somewhat badly she had not bought it through the agent who had initially approached her with the idea. On the other hand, Mr. Silver had looked at several companies before selecting the right one for her situation. The other agent had showed her only one—the one provided by the company for which he worked.

When Audrey had moved into her new townhouse, she had obtained replacement value insurance on the house and its contents. At the same time, she combined this insurance with her car insurance and bought an umbrella liability policy for $500,000. It looked as if she had protected herself as well as she could with insurance. She was particularly pleased with the decision she had made about the long-term health care insurance. She was adamant about being able to take care of herself now and in her old age!

She had discussed this latter point with Joanne just this past week when they were at the spa—Joanne had actually jumped at the chance to go with her mother for the long weekend. She was exhausted from caring for her family and knew she was overweight. They hadn't had sufficient funds to take any family vacations in years. Her father's death had also taken its toll on her, and she missed him sorely. Earlier in her marriage, before he had become ill, he often gave her a little money to purchase something for herself because, as he used to say, she would always be "his little girl." Thinking of these days always brought tears to her eyes.

While they were away, Audrey made sure Joanne understood her feelings about being able to provide for herself. Even though it was a painful subject, she also shared with Joanne her feelings about her own life and why she had requested Joanne be given the health power of attorney. She told her daughter she trusted her to make the right decision regarding medical treatment should she be unable to do so. Joanne got all choked up at this thought but understood what her mother was telling her. Mother and daughter hugged each other and wordlessly acknowledged the significance of the moment.

Elizabeth: Reactions to Protecting Herself with Insurance

After reflecting on her conversation with Mr. Grossfeldt, Elizabeth had restructured the terms of her living trust at the bank so that Abigail would receive the income from the trust until she died. Elizabeth was told there was no good reason for her to have life insurance. If she predeceased Abigail, her sister would receive $30,000 annual income from the trust. The charities would receive the trust assets when Abigail died.

Elizabeth was covered by Medicare. She had read an article about Medigap insurance, which succeeded in thoroughly confusing her. She asked Sam Weatherly about it, and once again, he helped her. He patiently reviewed the article and recommended the comprehensive Medigap insurance coverage he thought appropriate for her needs. He had already reviewed the different levels of coverage for himself and his wife, so it was easy for him to explain the options to her.

Elizabeth also asked Sam about long-term health care insurance. He pointed out to her that it would be pretty expensive for her to buy it at her age. Further, if she went ahead with the move to the Continuing Care Retirement Community, this coverage would not be necessary because they would provide her with nursing home care if she needed it. Elizabeth realized the fact that CCRC would provide her with a home for the rest of her life was another reason to move to Florida.

CHAPTER 13

Maximizing Your Investment Options

You may be disappointed if you fail, but you are doomed if you don't try.

BEVERLY SILLS

Introduction

In chapter 8, you made a list of your assets and liabilities. Your financial advisor will take your asset list and divide it into retirement and nonretirement assets. Next he or she will group them under separate asset categories. The basic asset classes would be: cash, fixed-income, stocks, real estate and other. Then your advisor would total these assets to give you a picture of your overall investment situation. This list helps you identify the different types of investment assets you own. With this information, your advisor can recommend any changes which should be made to provide you with sufficient income now and in the future.

Although your primary residence, your cars and your furnishings are assets, we would not include these under the list of your investments because they do not provide current income and are not easily changed. For instance, even if you sold your house, you usually buy another one of comparable value.

The composite picture would look like this:

Assets	Nonretirement $	Retirement $	Total $
Cash	_____	_____	_____
Fixed-Income	_____	_____	_____
Stocks	_____	_____	_____
Real Estate	_____	_____	_____
Other	_____	_____	_____

The above summary can be prepared from the asset list you put together in Chapter 8. Here we will discuss each asset class in more detail.

Cash

Under this category, list your checking accounts, savings accounts and money market funds. Any short-term assets that will come due within a year, such as certificates of deposit, Treasury bills, short-term loans owed to you or the estate and life insurance proceeds due you, should also be included in this list.

When listing your assets, you may have found that you had accounts in several banks. It is a lot easier to consolidate them into one account as long as the amount in one bank does not exceed $100,000. If nothing else, it cuts down on the bookkeeping. The fewer accounts you have to keep track of, the simpler life will be.

Another choice would be investing your cash in a money market fund with check-writing privileges. These accounts usually offer a higher rate of interest than you can obtain from a bank. However, the principal is not insured by FDIC as it is in the bank. These money market funds pay taxable or nontaxable income. If you are in a higher tax bracket (28 percent or higher), investing your money in the nontaxable account would provide you with a higher after-tax income. If you establish a money market fund, you would still maintain a checking account to handle your smaller expenses.

In summary, consolidate your cash accounts, and consider using a money market fund for the bulk of your cash.

Fixed-Income

Any investment that pays a fixed rate of income for a year or longer is included in this asset category—bonds, preferred stocks, notes receivable, certificates of deposit, mortgages, insurance policies, guaranteed investment contracts (GICs) and deferred annuities.

The most common form of fixed-income investment besides certificates of deposit are bonds. There are three basic categories of bonds: government, municipal and corporate.

U.S. GOVERNMENT BONDS

Government bonds are considered the safest investment you can make because it is generally believed that the U.S. government will continue to pay interest and principal on its obligations. You can buy government bonds through your bank, your broker or direct from the Federal Reserve. This type of investment is usually well suited to a widow's portfolio because it provides a reliable stream of income. The interest from Treasury bonds is not taxed by your state, which gives them an advantage over bonds, where the interest is taxable.

U.S. government obligations come in various denominations called bills, notes and bonds. The difference among the three types is in the holding period. Bills come due in three years or less, notes mature in one to ten years, and bonds mature in ten to thirty years.

SERIES EE BONDS

Two popular government bonds are *EE and HH bonds*. Series EE bonds are bought in small denominations ($25 or more) and currently pay a 4 percent minimum rate if you hold them for at least five years. Interest isn't paid until the bond is redeemed and compounds in the bond. You can choose to pay federal tax (they are free of state and local tax) each year on the interest or wait until you redeem the bond. You must redeem these bonds after 30 or 40 years, when they stop earning interest. You can avoid paying tax on the accumulated interest if you choose to exchange them for Series HH bonds, which pay taxable income for ten years.

GINNIE MAES

There are also securities that look like bonds that invest in federally insured mortgages, where the interest and the principal are backed by the "full faith and credit" of the U.S. government. The most popular of these are issued by the Government National Mortgage Association (GNMA) and popularly called *Ginnie Maes*. The yield is usually higher than that paid by U.S. Treasury bonds. However, this investment has some disadvantages, so consult your financial advisor before purchasing them.

MUNICIPAL BONDS

Municipal bonds are IOUs from a state, a city or other local government agencies. Income from municipal bonds is exempt from federal income taxes and, if issued by the state in which you pay taxes, is also free from local taxes.

There are *general obligation* and *general revenue* municipal bonds. The difference between the two types depends on whether the income is backed by the credit of the state or city issuing the bond (general obligation) or is backed by the revenue of a particular project, like a toll bridge (general revenue).

Sometimes the bond is *insured*. This means that an outside group called the Municipal Bond Insurance Corporation (MBIC) guarantees that both the income and the principal will be paid to you. While the fact that the bond is insured is reassuring, insured bonds usually pay a slightly lower interest rate than noninsured bonds because the insurance feature costs money.

We recommend buying municipal bonds that are rated A or better by both rating agencies (Standard & Poor's and Moody's). If you are in a higher tax bracket (28 percent or above), municipals may be a better choice for you than Treasury or corporate bonds because the after-tax return will be higher.

For example, if your $10,000 IBM bond pays 8 percent ($800 per year) and you are in the 31 percent tax bracket, you would have to pay $248 in federal taxes. This would leave you with an after-tax return of $552, or 5.52 percent ($552 divided by $10,000). If instead you invested in a $10,000 municipal bond paying 6 percent, you would receive $600 income and would have to pay no federal taxes on this income, giving you a higher after-tax return of 6 percent. If the municipal bond was also tax free in the state in which you live, you would pay no state income tax as well, which would increase the advantage of investing in the municipal bond.

CORPORATE BONDS

Corporate bonds are issued by corporations. The interest they earn is 100 percent taxable. Again, the better the rating (highest is AAA), the less risk you are taking with your principal. However, the higher the rating, the lower the interest rate the bond will pay.

JUNK BONDS

In the 1980s, a new type of bond gained popularity in some circles which was called a *high-yield bond* or, more realistically, a "junk" bond. These bonds had lower ratings (below BBB) or no rating at all. They paid a higher rate of interest to the bondholder than better rated bonds because the investors were taking greater risks. The companies that issued these bonds were not as financially sound as higher rated companies; therefore, the investor accepted the risk that they might not be able to pay the income they had promised to pay. Or even worse, the company might go bankrupt, and the whole investment would be lost. Promising to pay a higher rate of interest was the only way they could get people to invest in these bonds.

As with any other kind of investment, there are gradations within the category. The lower the rating, the higher the interest rate and the higher the risk the investor takes, and vice versa. Some junk bonds are less risky than others. For instance, there are some junk bonds where the issuing companies are improving their earnings.

Generally speaking, this type of bond would not fit in a widow's portfolio. For the younger widow who is able to take some risk with a small percentage of her investments or for any widow who has ample resources, it might fit—but only in small quantities.

CONVERTIBLE BONDS

There is another kind of corporate bond that is a hybrid—a convertible bond. This bond pays a stated rate of interest (just like any other bond), but if you wish, you can convert it into shares of stock. A convertible bond pays a lower rate of interest than a nonconvertible bond because if the stock price of the issuing company goes up, the price of the bond will go up as well. Thus, a convertible bond gives you more potential for growth of principal than a nonconvertible. Investing in these bonds can work out very well but involves more risk. Thus, they are not best suited to the novice investor or new widow.

ZERO-COUPON BONDS

These bonds are issued by the U.S. government, corporations and municipalities to which there are no coupons attached, so they are called "zero-coupon" bonds. The term "coupon" derives from the small, detachable segment of a bond certificate, which entitles the holder to the interest due on that date. Although the bond earns a stated interest rate, the interest accumulates in the bond instead of being paid to you.

The drawback to government or corporate zeros is that you are taxed on the income even though you don't receive it. With municipal zeros, you don't receive the income, but you don't have to pay taxes on the income since they pay tax-free income. When the zero bonds come due, you receive the principal amount of the bond, which represents your original investment plus the accrued income. Because they don't pay current income, zero-coupon bonds usually are not the best choice for a widow.

INTERNATIONAL BONDS

You can also invest in international government or corporate bonds. These involve more risk because not only are you investing in foreign countries, but you have the currency risk as well. This means your bond might go up in value, but because of the relationship of the dollar to that country's currency at that time, you might lose money. Again, this is best suited to the person who can take a higher degree of risk.

HOW DO YOU BUY BONDS?

There are three basic ways to buy bonds: individually, in unit trusts or in mutual funds.

Individual Bonds

If you buy an individual bond, you usually invest a minimum of $5,000, and you know exactly which bond you are buying. It may be purchased from a stockbroker, banker or financial planner, and you will pay a commission. You may also purchase U.S. Treasury bonds directly from the Treasury Department. If you do so, you will avoid paying fees.

Unit Trusts

Unit trusts invest in a group of municipal bonds (20 or 30 different issues) at a particular time and then hold them until they come due. There is no management involved because the portfolio does not change over the holding period. Unit trusts appeal to smaller investors because they can achieve greater diversification than if they bought a single issue.

Mutual Funds

Mutual funds buy a group of different bonds that meet specific criteria. As contrasted with buying individual bonds or unit trusts, the mutual fund has a manager who monitors these investments after the initial investments are made. He or she buys and sells bonds in the portfolio as he or she thinks advisable.

Many different kinds of mutual funds invest in bonds. You can buy a fund that invests in government bonds, good-quality corporate bonds, municipal bonds, junk bonds or convertible bonds. You can also buy a fund that invests in bonds with similar maturities. A long-term bond fund would invest in longer term maturities (20 or 30 years) in order to get the highest yield available. An intermediate-term fund would buy bonds with three- to nine-year maturities in an effort to protect your principal against rising interest rates. A limited maturity fund invests in bonds with one- to three-year maturities.

Investing in bonds through mutual funds offers maximum flexibility for investors. They are particularly suited to widows because of the diversification you can achieve.

DEFERRED ANNUITIES

Deferred annuities are contracts issued by insurance companies that pay you income. If you don't currently need the income, then it will accumulate in the annuity, and this income will not be currently taxed. As soon as you start to receive the income from an annuity, then part of the income will be taxed.

There are two types of annuities: *fixed* and *variable*. Fixed annuities pay a set rate of return very similar to certificates of deposit. Variable annuities invest in mutual funds, and the return on your investment varies according to how well the funds perform.

You may be the beneficiary of a deferred annuity that your husband had bought. If so, you will be asked if you want to receive monthly income from this annuity or if you want to cash it in and make another investment. You may also be the beneficiary of a life insurance policy, and your agent might suggest that you invest the proceeds in an annuity.

An annuity can pay you a fixed monthly payment for the rest of your life. This payment is based on a number of factors, including the interest rate the insurance company thinks it is going to earn and how long the insurance company thinks you are going to live (based on actuarial tables). Be aware that the amount an annuity pays differs from company to company.

We are not enthusiastic about agreeing to receive lifetime income from a deferred annuity. Although it may be reassuring to know exactly what you will receive in monthly income, what seems to be a large amount now may prove not so attractive ten years hence due to rising costs of living. In order to receive the highest rate of monthly income, you have to agree that the payments stop when you die. This option is called *lifetime only*. If you select this option, your heirs are not entitled to receive anything should you die.

To avoid this, you can choose to receive income for your lifetime, but stipulate that your heirs will receive payments for a certain period of time after you buy the annuity—such as ten years—if you die. If you select this option, your monthly payments will be slightly reduced. We don't like the idea of a fixed income for a widow in view of the rising cost of living.

MORTGAGES AND SECOND DEEDS OF TRUST

If you buy a mortgage or second deed of trust, you are assuming the role of the bank and lending the money to the home purchaser. These investments will provide you with a competitive rate of return for a stated period of time. The risk in this investment is dependent on the creditworthiness of the borrower. Unless you are very confident of the good credit of the borrower, we do not recommend this type of investment.

In the early 1990s, a new type of investment became available called CMOs (*collateralized mortgage obligations*). These are complex investments that we don't consider suitable for widows.

Stocks

Common stocks represent ownership in corporations. In general, stock prices go up and down according to how well the company does. Outside factors such as investor perception of the general economy, political variables, technological advances or industry reversals may cause an individual stock to go up or down.

BLUE-CHIP STOCKS

Many think that investing in stocks is risky and it is, but as we have pointed out previously, every investment involves some degree of risk. This risk can be reduced by buying good-quality stocks, often called blue-chip stocks. A stock qualifies as good-quality if the company doesn't have too much debt in relation to its total net worth (just like individuals). A good-quality company has a history of steadily increasing its earnings over a period of years and shares its earnings with the stockholders. A good-quality growth company reinvests 60 to 70 percent of its profits back into the company and pays the shareholders the remainder in the form of dividends. In such a company, the profits should grow each year, and so should annual dividends.

INCOME STOCKS

For the widow who requires higher current income, income stocks may be a better choice. This kind of stock pays a higher percentage of its profits to the stockholders in the form of dividends. A good example of an income stock is a public utility company. If you select a stock primarily for income, there will be less growth of principal; however, there will be less price fluctuation.

PREFERRED STOCKS

Preferred stocks are like bonds in that they are issued by a corporation and pay a fixed rate of interest. They are unlike bonds in that they don't have a maturity date—that is, a predetermined time when the face value is paid to you. We are not particularly enthusiastic about investing in preferred stocks because they don't seem to be "fish or fowl." They aren't as safe as corporate bonds, nor do they offer the advantages of common stock. If you want a fixed rate of return, you should buy bonds; if you want potential growth of principal and income, you should buy common stocks.

INTERNATIONAL STOCKS

You can also buy common stocks of companies based outside the United States—these are called international stocks. Investing in international stocks is riskier than investing in United States stocks because investment information is harder to obtain and is less reliable than in the United States. Also, currency fluctuations affect the performance of these stocks, just as they do for international bonds. If investing internationally appeals to you, we think it is best to invest through mutual funds rather than individual stocks. This should protect you against some of the potential risks.

HOW DO YOU BUY STOCKS?

You can buy individual shares of stock through your stockbroker, financial planner or banker. Shares of well-established companies normally trade on the New York and American stock exchanges, and you can follow the price of your stock every day in the newspaper. You can also buy mutual funds which invest in stocks.

Mutual Funds

Mutual funds invest in diversified portfolios of stocks and/or bonds. There are several advantages to investing in mutual funds: diversification, professional management and ease of recordkeeping.

Most mutual funds confine themselves to companies based in the United States. There are also *international mutual* funds, which invest in stocks outside the United States, *global* funds, which invest in stocks and bonds anywhere in the world (including the United States), and *single country* funds, which invest in one country's stocks or bonds. Although we think it is important to own international and global investments, we don't recommend single country funds because they are too limiting.

Mutual funds are classified by their investment objectives. The basic groups are:

- income funds (invested primarily in bonds)
- balanced funds (invested in stocks and bonds)
- growth and income funds (invested in stocks that pay dividends)
- growth funds (invested in stocks with emphasis on growth of principal)
- aggressive growth funds (invested in stocks of younger, riskier companies)

Most widows would invest in the first three types of funds.

To add to the confusion, you will also hear the terms "large cap" and "small cap" used to distinguish kinds of funds. *Large cap funds* invest in larger, well-known companies (less risk), and *small cap funds* invest in smaller, lesser known companies (more risk).

There are *sector* funds, which invest in a particular industry, such as health care or energy. We would not recommend these funds since we think it is safer to invest in a diversified fund that selects those industries the manager thinks are going to do well and can change among industries when the economic picture shifts.

There are *index* funds, which hold all the stocks included in a given stock market index, like the S&P 500. The reason you buy a managed mutual fund is so that it will do better than the stock market averages. For this reason, we would not recommend buying an index fund.

There are *open-end* and *closed-end* funds. Most funds are open-end, and their price is based on the total market value of all the assets they hold. Shares of closed-end funds are priced based on the market's perception of their worth. This valuation is usually lower than the actual value of the portfolio. These shares are traded on a stock exchange. We prefer open-end funds, as they reflect what the portfolio is really worth.

HOW DO YOU SELECT THE RIGHT FUND FOR YOU?

Currently, there are over 3,600 mutual funds available, so selecting the right one is difficult. Financial advisors start by looking at the long-term performance record of the fund (ten years or more). Although a long-term record of good results is reassuring, it is important for the advisor to ascertain if the management team that built the record is still in place.

Select funds that have performed as well or better than other funds with a similar investment objective. Although there are many different funds available, there are fewer fund management groups. To simplify the selection process, many advisors recommend funds managed by a particular investment group with demonstrated superior performance records. From this group (sometimes called a "family" of funds), they choose funds that match the investor's risk tolerance and investment objectives.

WHAT DOES IT COST TO BUY A FUND?

There are two basic kinds of fees involved when you buy a mutual fund: the *purchase fee* and the *management fee*.

Purchase Fees

Front-end load funds charge an initial fee to buy their shares, which might be as high as 8½ percent of the amount you invest. These fees—or commissions, as they are called—decrease if you buy more of a particular fund or more within a family of funds.

Exit-load funds charge no initial sales fee, but if you sell the shares before a stated time period, such as five years, you will pay a fee when you sell. These are sometimes called *deferred sales charge funds.*

No-load funds charge no initial or exit fees. These shares are bought directly from the fund company or through some discount brokers.

Management Fees

In addition to the fees for purchasing or selling mutual fund shares, fund companies also charge for their management and marketing expenses. The marketing fees (called 12b-1 fees) can be as high as 1.25 percent of the assets managed. It is legitimate for a fund to have marketing expenses, but we think the fee should not exceed .25 percent. No-load funds often charge high 12b-1 fees. What you may have saved in initial charges, you may pay later in marketing fees.

Management fees are charged to operate the fund. We think that these fees should not exceed .50 percent. The exception is international funds, which involve higher costs. For these funds, we would prefer to pay no more than 1 percent.

All these fees are fully disclosed in the prospectus of the mutual fund. Ask your advisor to review the costs with you. We advise you not to be overly concerned with the fee structure. It is more important that your advisor select the right funds for you and monitor them after you make the investment.

Real Estate

DIRECT OWNERSHIP

You can own real estate directly or indirectly. Direct ownership would mean that you own an individual piece of property and either manage the property yourself or pay someone else to do so. This would include a second home or rental property. You may have been involved in managing such assets when your husband was alive, and it might be a good idea to keep them. However, you may discover that upon objective analysis the money tied up in these properties might grow for you more productively elsewhere.

INDIRECT OWNERSHIP

Many real estate investments are held indirectly. Two common forms of indirect ownership are real estate investment trusts (REITs) and limited partnerships.

Real Estate Investment Trusts

Real estate investment trusts are common stocks that invest in real estate properties. In order to retain their status as real estate investment trusts, these companies are required to pay you at least 95 percent of the net income they receive from properties they own. This method of investing in real estate is very appealing because you receive a higher return than you do from most other common stocks. Unlike other kinds of real estate investments, which usually take a while to sell, you can sell these shares at any time.

Limited Partnerships

In a *limited partnership*, you invest with others in a particular property or group of properties. A general partner selects and manages the property. You as a limited partner put up most of the money to buy the property and leave the selection and management of the properties to the general partners.

Limited partnership interests fell out of favor in the late 1980s because many were structured to give tax benefits and had little or no economic merit. Since 1987, most partnerships provide current income to investors. Often this income is partially or totally tax sheltered because of depreciation deductions. Although the general partners charge the limited partners for selecting and managing the properties, investing as a limited partner enables the smaller investor to own part of a larger property.

Many people do not like investing in limited partnerships because you cannot liquidate your interest quickly. The typical holding period for limited partnerships is ten years. On the other hand, this investment pays a higher rate of interest than you would receive from a more liquid investment. The income should increase annually with rent increases. This potential for an increasing stream of income that is partially tax sheltered can be very appealing to an income-oriented investor. In addition, when the property is sold, there may be a gain on the sale.

We would not recommend investing all your money in a limited partnership. However, investing a small percentage (5 to 10 percent) of your total money in an income-producing partnership might be appropriate for you. As with your mutual fund selection, your financial advisor will be invaluable in helping you select a financially strong general partner with a demonstrated successful long-term record investing in and managing this type of real estate.

Other

This catchall category includes investments such as collectibles, precious metals, commodities and ownership in privately held businesses. It also includes limited partnerships that invest in oil and gas production, leasing equipment, etc.

Collectibles include art, oriental rugs, antiques, stamp collections and coins. These items are not easily sold, so if you are trying to build a secure financial future, you should avoid this kind of investment.

In the past, investing in gold, silver and other precious metals as a hedge against inflation was popular, particularly outside the United States. If you want to invest in metals, you can do so either directly, by buying coins or bars, or indirectly, by buying mutual funds that invest in gold or silver mining shares. However, this type of investment is speculative, so we would not recommend it for widows.

Riskier investments include commodities, put and call options and penny stocks. Therefore, we would recommend avoiding these high-risk investments under any circumstances.

As a widow, you may have inherited shares in your husband's privately held business. If so, he probably established a method whereby your shares will be purchased.

We believe partnerships that invest in oil and gas production are too risky for most if not all widows. However, with prices at historically low levels, one could argue that this might be a good choice for those able to take such a risk.

Leasing partnerships buy and lease equipment to businesses. These partnerships invest in high-tech equipment such as computers or low-tech equipment such as office furniture or cargo containers. The low-tech equipment has a longer life, so it does not involve the same degree of risk as the high-tech equipment. Some low-tech partnerships provide an above-average tax-sheltered yield that could fit your circumstances. We would recommend this type of investment to the widow who has ample resources, is willing to take some risk with a small percentage of her money and has a good financial advisor to help her select one.

Widows are prime targets for those seeking loans. If family or friends believe you have inherited a considerable amount of money, they may ask you to lend them money for various purposes. For example, they may want you to help them finance a business venture, educate a child or help them purchase a new house. Although it may seem harsh advice, we believe you should lend only money you never expect to see again. Always make a loan with a written agreement as to interest rates and repayment terms. That way, if it is a business loan and you are not repaid, you can deduct it as a loss on your income tax return.

Conclusion

Now that we have described the various types of investments, in the next chapter, we will review the basics of investment management—that is, how to put together a portfolio that meets your investment objectives.

Diane: Reactions to Maximizing Her Investments

Diane had implemented Dorothy's earlier investment recommendations, but she had never really understood exactly what she did. At the time, Dorothy had explained her investment proposals, and her father had reviewed and approved them. However, Diane now wanted to have a better understanding of what she had done.

Dorothy had told her that she could obtain an 8.5 percent return if she invested all her money in bonds. The problem was if she did this, her principal probably would not increase in value. Initially, Diane did not understand why it was important for her principal to grow. Dorothy explained that although her mortgage payments would remain constant, her other living costs would increase each year due to inflation. Based on the past ten years, she should count on them increasing at least 4 percent a year. At this rate, her current expenses of about $59,000 (excluding the mortgage) would increase to $72,000 in only five years. The level of her income needed to increase to cover these higher costs.

To protect herself against these rising costs, she should make investments that offered some chance of appreciation. Diane had told Dorothy she didn't want to take any risk, but Dorothy explained that she was really taking more risk by not investing in some stocks. If she invested only in bonds, the chances her money would not increase in value were high. If she invested in stocks, she had a better chance of increasing her principal. She could reduce her risk of investing in stocks by selecting mutual funds that invest in good-quality stocks with long-term records of consistently competitive performance.

To demonstrate her point, Dorothy showed her some examples. These illustrations showed what would have happened if Diane had invested $100,000 in each of three funds 15 years ago and withdrawn $8,500 a year ($708.33 per month) from each one.

The first fund Dorothy selected was an income fund that invested primarily in A—or better—rated bonds. The second was a balanced fund invested in good-quality bonds and stocks. The third growth and income fund had been in existence over 50 years and was invested in blue-chip stocks. Knowing Diane's low risk tolerance, Dorothy had carefully picked a well-known group of mutual funds that had been in business a long time. The examples showed that after, distributing $8,500 of annual income for 15 years, the $100,000 investment in each fund was worth:

- income fund $117,410
- balanced fund $217,087
- growth and income fund $373,426

After seeing these numbers, Diane wanted to know why Dorothy didn't put all her money in the growth and income fund instead of dividing it equally among the three funds.

Dorothy laughed and told Diane that if you knew for certain that the stock market was going to do as well in the future as it had in the past, you would invest it all in the stock fund. However, you never know for sure what the stock market is going to do, so investing in a balanced group of funds like this reduced her risk.

Dorothy pointed out that another good feature of mutual funds was that you could adjust the amount of income you withdrew from the funds at any time. For instance, when the children finally completed college, Diane could reduce the amount of income she received from the funds. If she did that, her investments had the potential to grow more because she would be reinvesting the income rather than spending it. However, for the time being, it was obvious Diane needed as much income as she could get. Dorothy felt the 8.5 percent level of income was a reasonable amount of income to withdraw from her investments without taking undue risk to her principal.

DIANE'S ASSET ALLOCATION

	Personal	Retirement	Total	%
Cash	$ 40,000*		$ 40,000	4
Fixed-Income	367,500		367,500	36
Stocks	367,500	$250,000	617,500	60
Total	$775,000	$250,000	$1,025,000	100

* Diane spent $10,000 of her cash reserve the first year to cover her negative cash flow.

Susan: Reactions to Maximizing Her Investments

When Susan reviewed her personal assets, she realized she seemed to have more stocks than any other kind of asset. She did not include the trust assets because she did not control them.

Her 401(k) pension assets at her former association were invested in a fixed-income fund ($25,000). Lance's pension fund was invested $75,000 in fixed-income and $225,000 in stocks, reflecting his more aggressive investment objectives. After paying off her stepchildren, she still had $60,000 in Lance's stocks.

SUSAN'S CURRENT ASSET ALLOCATION

	Personal	Pension	Total	%
Cash	$ 30,000*		$ 30,000	7
Fixed-Income		$100,000	100,000	24
Stocks	60,000	225,000	285,000	69
Total	$ 90,000	325,000	$415,000	100

* Includes net cottage sale proceeds of $28,000.

Susan reviewed her situation with Bob O'Brien. He suggested she keep the current portfolio he managed in stocks. He told her she was now in a higher tax bracket due to her salary increase and the taxable trust income she was receiving, so he recommended putting her cash reserve ($5,000) in a money market fund that paid tax-free income.

With the remaining $25,000 cash, Bob suggested that she invest $10,000 in an intermediate-term tax-free bond fund and reinvest the dividends in additional shares. This fund could also be considered a backup cash reserve should she need extra cash for any reason. He recommended she buy a fund instead of individual bonds because this way she would own several different bonds as well as obtain professional management. In addition, he pointed out that since funds buy bonds in such large quantities, they are able to buy them cheaper than an individual could. He recommended an intermediate-term bond fund because he was worried about rising interest rates. If interest rates increased, her principal could decline, particularly if it was invested in long-term bonds. By investing in shorter term bonds, her principal was less vulnerable to price declines.

Bob recommended that she invest the remaining $15,000 in an income-producing real estate limited partnership. Susan was surprised at this suggestion, as she had heard that limited partnerships were risky. Bob explained that the one he had in mind was much more conservative. It paid cash for all its properties (thus avoiding the risk of a mortgage) and produced tax-sheltered income of about 8 percent.

He had reviewed the remaining stocks she had inherited ($60,000) and recommended selling about half the portfolio. These were the stocks Lance had selected because he had a "hunch" about them. Bob said he wanted her to own stocks he followed more closely so that if anything went wrong (or right), he would know why! He recommended that she invest the $30,000 proceeds in situations which he thought held excellent growth potential. Specifically, he suggested she invest $10,000 in an international stock mutual fund and $5,000 each in four different stocks.

He explained to Susan that in 1967 approximately 70 percent of the common stocks available for purchase worldwide were on United States stock exchanges, with the remaining 30 percent in Europe, the Far East and Latin America. Today the U.S. represents only 40 percent of the world's capital equities. The major international stock markets have outperformed the U.S. markets in 16 of the last 25 years.

As for Lance's pension plan, Bob suggested that she consider dividing the assets more evenly between bonds and stocks. Currently, they were invested 25 percent in bonds and 75 percent in stocks. He reminded her that income from bonds in a pension plan would not be currently taxed. He would be glad to discuss this recommendation with her in greater detail but thought she should focus on her personal investments first.

Susan thanked Bob for his advice and went home to review the material he gave her. There was a lot to read, and she wanted to make sure she understood what he was suggesting. In addition to all the information he had given her on the specific investments, he had provided her with his version of the investment pyramid and showed her where he was recommending she invest. She realized that he was suggesting a well-diversified, but still conservative, portfolio.

SUSAN'S REVISED ASSET ALLOCATION

	Personal	*Pension*	*Total*	*%*
Cash	$ 5,000		$ 5,000	1
Fixed-Income	10,000	$162,500	172,500	42
Stocks	60,000	162,500	222,500	54
Real Estate	15,000		15,000	3
Total	$90,000	$325,000	$415,000	100

Susan's Investment Pyramid

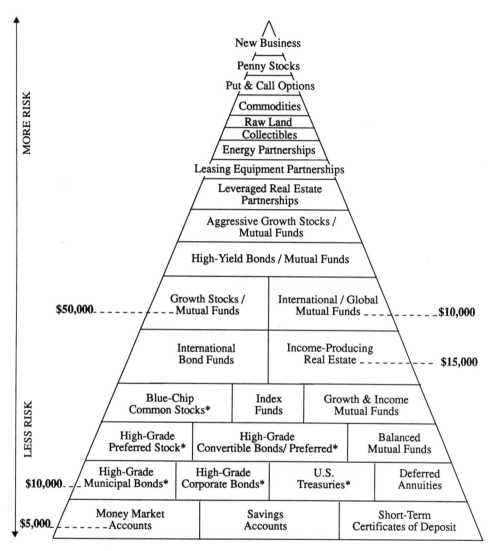

* or mutual funds that invest in this kind of investment

Audrey: Reactions to Maximizing Her Investments

Audrey realized that her current financial situation was not complex. She had sold her home for $225,000, netting $211,500 after Georgia earned her commission. Since her cost basis was $125,000 and she had used her one-time profit on her home sale exclusion of $125,000, she did not have to pay any tax on the gain she took. Her new townhouse cost $175,000, and she had paid cash for it. This left her with $36,500 net proceeds from the sale of her former home. She spent about $16,000 on curtains, rugs and new furniture, leaving her with $20,000 to invest.

She still had about $40,000 in her savings account. Adding the $20,000 from her house sale, she now had $60,000 in savings. Mr. Silver wanted her to keep a cash reserve of $10,000 in her savings account "just in case." This left $50,000 she could invest.

John's company stock was worth $200,000. Mr. Silver reiterated his recommendation that she sell at least some of it in an effort to diversify her holdings. She had been so busy with her family, her volunteer work and her golf that she hadn't done anything yet. He pointed out that the stock had not increased in value since she inherited it a year and a half ago, and if she was going to successfully combat inflation, she needed to have this money increase in value. This was cause for concern, particularly since the Standard & Poor's 500 Stock Index had risen 12 percent during this same period of time. Further, the company had not raised its dividend over the last three years.

AUDREY'S ASSET ALLOCATION

	Personal	%
Cash	$ 60,000	25
Stocks	$200,000	75
Total	$260,000	100

Because the stock had not gone up since it was valued in John's estate, Audrey would not have to pay any capital gains tax if she sold the shares.

Mr. Silver originally recommended that she sell about one-fourth of her stock, but in view of the fact it hadn't done anything in a good stock market environment, nor had it increased its dividend, he advised Audrey to sell at least half of her stock at this time. This was a big step for Audrey to take, but she thought that since Mr. Silver had consistently given her good advice in the past, it would be wise to listen to him this time.

He suggested she take the $100,000 proceeds from the sale of the stock and invest in a tax-free bond fund. Audrey thought that sounded contrary to Mr. Silver's previous advice. If he was seeking diversification, why wasn't he investing in a lot of different bonds? He explained that this fund invested in 20 or 30 different tax-free bonds throughout the country. Further, the fund invested in general obligation, revenue and insured bonds. All the bonds were rated A or better, and their average maturity was eight years. The fund paid 6 percent, which in her tax bracket (28 percent) was equivalent to 8.33 percent taxable income. Since Audrey currently was getting a 4 percent taxable return from her investments (which was 2.88 percent after tax), a 6 percent tax-free return sounded pretty attractive to her.

As for the $50,000 she had available in her savings account, he suggested Audrey buy shares of a balanced mutual fund. The particular fund he recommended was usually invested about 60 percent in stocks and 40 percent in bonds. The goal of this fund was to increase its dividend annually, and it had achieved that goal. Although it invested primarily in the United States, it could invest up to 40 percent of the portfolio internationally. The fund paid 5 percent in dividends and had increased in value, on average, 8 percent a year over the past five years.

Mr. Silver gave Audrey the material on both funds. This included the prospectus, as well as the most recent quarterly and annual reports. He recommended she read this information and then call him with any ques-

AUDREY'S RECOMMENDED ASSET ALLOCATION

	Personal	%
Cash	$ 10,000	4
Fixed-Income	120,000	46
Stocks	130,000	50
Total	$260,000	100

tions she had. He explained to her it was his intention to ultimately decrease her stock ownership in John's company to about 10 percent of her total portfolio. Making these investments would be the first step in that direction.

Elizabeth: Reactions to Maximizing Her Investments

Elizabeth continued to consider her potential move to the retirement community in Florida. She was concerned about how to obtain the $75,000 nonrefundable entrance fee.

The idea of a nonrefundable fee was somewhat scary to Elizabeth. However, when she considered the amount of time she had already spent visiting the CCRC, she couldn't imagine why she wouldn't like living there. After all, Abigail had lived there for several years and was very pleased with it.

Elizabeth had only $5,000 in her savings account and really didn't want to disturb her trust assets, so it appeared she would need to sell her house in order to raise the $75,000 entrance fee. According to the newspaper accounts she had been reading, houses in the Boston area were not selling easily due to the recession, but the REALTOR® she called, Mr. Winthrop, said there was a demand for houses in her price range in her quiet neighborhood. He came over to see the house and after inspecting it suggested she ask for $175,000, but be willing to settle for around $150,000. In fact, he knew of a young couple who would be perfect for this house.

Although Elizabeth thought she really wanted to move to Florida, when she was faced with a contract to sign by the REALTOR®, she got cold feet. It was a long form full of small print, and she thought she should have her lawyer read it before she signed it. She told Mr. Winthrop she needed some time to think over this idea. After all, this had been her home for most of her adult life! Mr. Winthrop said he understood perfectly, but he also knew of a couple anxious to buy a house before winter came and the snows started. He gave her his card and told her to call as soon as possible with her decision.

Thinking about selling the house reminded her of the land in Vermont, which she had ignored up until now. If this were sold, she would have those proceeds as well for the entrance fee or to invest. Besides, selling it would simplify her life, and she was interested in doing everything she could to make her life easier. She called the real estate firm in Vermont through whom they had bought the land and asked them to send her the appropriate papers to put this land up for sale. This was an easy decision for her to make because, even if she didn't move, she had no use for this land. The Vermont REALTOR® she spoke to said she thought she could sell it for $25,000, but not to expect a quick sale, as currently there seemed to be a lot of land on the market.

As she looked at her assets, she seemed to be in pretty good shape. She had $5,000 in her savings account. If she sold the house for $150,000, she would pay the CCRC entrance fee of $75,000 from the proceeds. Although she would have a profit when she sold her house, she had the $125,000 tax exclusion, which meant that she would owe no taxes on the sale. This would leave $75,000 to invest. When she sold the land, she would have $25,000 more, which would give her a total of $100,000 to invest.

ELIZABETH'S CURRENT ASSET ALLOCATION

	Personal	%
Cash*	$ 80,000	13
Trust Fixed-Income	250,000	41
Trust Stocks	250,000	41
Real Estate (lot)	25,000	5
Total	$605,000	100

* Savings plus house proceeds not needed for the CCRC entrance fee.

CHAPTER 14

Basic Rules of Investing

If I am not for myself, who is?

RABBI HILLEL

Introduction

There are many good books about investing, some of which we have listed in the bibliography. In this chapter, we will not try to cover everything you need to know about investment management, but rather will try to highlight what we consider to be the basic rules of successful investing.

Many of you have never been interested in investments, but now circumstances have forced you to manage your assets. We have seen widows express a high degree of frustration and anger because of their lack of financial knowledge. Acquiring knowledge about investments is just like learning in any field. At first, you start with a little information. After a while, you learn more, and as time passes, your overall knowledge increases. Unfortunately, this is a field that changes constantly. Just as you think you have grasped all you need to know, the tax laws change, a new kind of investment is introduced or your personal situation changes.

That's why it is important to be a knowledgeable investor and equally important to find a knowledgeable financial advisor who will keep you informed about any changes you should make. However, having said this, we do not recommend abdicating all responsibility to an advisor. We do encourage you to follow his or her advice. After all, it is his or her profession, not yours.

After your husband's death, you may have been overwhelmed by all you needed to know. Initially, you dealt with the basics—making sure you had enough income to cover your expenses and determining your assets and liabilities. Then you identified your financial objectives and selected investments to meet these objectives. In the process, some of you may have discovered you enjoyed managing your investments and actively pursued this new interest. Others of you tolerated it because you knew you needed to know enough to survive. Whichever group you fall into, let us share with you what we think are the 15 basic rules of successful investing.

Rule One: Have Sufficient Cash (Emergency) Reserve

The rule of thumb for the amount you should keep in a cash reserve is three to six months' expenses. This should be deposited in a savings account or invested in a money market account, where it is readily accessible and earning interest. This cash reserve would be available to cover any expected or unexpected large expenses, such as replacing your furnace or painting your house. Having this cash reserve prevents your having to liquidate an investment at an undesirable time. Besides, having a cash cushion should give you peace of mind.

Rule Two: Be Patient; Take the Long-Term View

The money you invest will probably be invested for the rest of your life. Unfortunately, whether or not your investments initially do well is really a matter of luck. Neither you nor your advisor can select the perfect time for you to invest so that you can make the maximum amount of money.

For example, on October 19, 1987, there was a stock market "crash," and the market averages plunged 508 points in one day, a drop of 22.6 percent. If you had made an initial investment the month before this crash, you might have justifiably panicked and called your financial advisor, asking him or her to sell your stocks. However, if your advisor had selected good-quality investments and had adequately diversified your portfolio, you had no cause to worry. In fact, a year later, the stock market averages were back to their pre-crash levels.

Keep in mind that you are investing for the long term, and don't worry about short-term volatility. (Sometimes easier said than done!)

Rule Three: Diversify To Reduce Risk

Most widows' first priority is to reduce risk. One way to accomplish this is to diversify among different kinds of assets. Many widows want only investments that provide current income. They confuse certainty with safety. The fact that a Treasury bond, a certificate of deposit or an annuity will pay a fixed rate of income for a certain period of time is very reassuring. However, it is important for your principal to continue to grow as your expenses increase over the years.

Ibbotson Associates compared an investment in long-term government bonds with an investment in stocks from 1926 to present times (a period that included the stock market crash in 1929, the Great Depression and World War II). If you had invested one dollar in long-term government bonds and reinvested all interest and repayment of principal into new long-term Treasury bonds, by 1992 your money would have grown to $21.94. If you had put the same dollar into a selection of well-known stocks in 1926 and reinvested all dividends in those same stocks, by 1992, your dollar would have grown to $675.59. This illustrates how important it is to have some stocks in every portfolio. The percentage of your assets invested in stocks and the individual stocks selected will vary according to your particular circumstances. Remember, there should be some growth potential in every investment plan.

Let us give you another example of how diversifying your investments reduces your risk. Compare two individuals who invest $100,000. The first person selects an investment that earns 8 percent annually. At the end of 20 years, his investment is worth $466,096. Not a bad record!

The second person divides her $100,000 among five different investments—$20,000 each. After 20 years, the first investment is a total failure, and she loses all her money. The second investment breaks even, and she gets her $20,000 back. The third investment earns 5 percent, the fourth

10 percent and the fifth 15 percent. Despite what it looks like, this person would have $534,947 at the end of 20 years—almost $100,000 more than the first investor. Diversification lowered the second person's overall risk while allowing her to realize an even higher total return than she would have otherwise.

	Initial Investment	*Average Annual Return %*	*Value after 20 Years*
Investor A	$100,000	8	$466,000
Investor B	$ 20,000	(total loss)	$ 0
	20,000	0	20,000
	20,000	5	53,066
	20,000	10	134,550
	20,000	15	327,331
Total			$534,947

You should diversify not only among *different kinds of assets* but also *within asset classes.* For instance, in the fixed-income asset category, you might own both government and corporate bonds. In terms of equities, you would select different kinds of stocks and/or different stock mutual funds.

Rule Four: Balance Your Investments

Although you don't want "all your eggs in one basket" (asset class), you should not over diversify. If half of a $100,000 portfolio is in two stocks and the other half is invested in 23 stocks, it lacks balance. If one of the smaller positions triples in value, it won't significantly impact the total portfolio value; but if one of the larger positions declines in value, it will have a disproportionate effect on the portfolio. Thus, you want to have balance between different kinds of assets and within asset classes.

Rule Five: Don't Chase Performance—Buy Good Quality

Some years the stock market does very well, and other years it doesn't. The same is true of every asset category. It is difficult to predict exactly when a particular asset class is going to do better than another. Therefore, to reduce risk, we recommend you diversify your investments, balance your assets and buy good quality. In the investment field, *good quality* refers to investments that have a demonstrable record of success.

If you are selecting a stock, you want to buy a company that has a history of increasing earnings and dividends. You also want a stock with a reasonable price-earnings ratio. (The P/E ratio is the current market price divided by the last 12 months' earnings per share.) As a general rule, the lower this number is, the less risk you are taking. The higher this number is, the more risk you are taking.

When you are buying bonds (either municipal or corporate), you are safest buying ones with a credit rating of A or better. If you buy less financially sound bonds, you will receive more income than you will receive from a better rated company, but you are also taking more risk.

Any time you receive a higher return from an investment than is available from another good-quality investment, you are taking a risk of losing all or part of your money.

If you are buying a mutual fund, then you want to look at its long-term record. Has it performed well in both good and (more importantly) bad markets? Looking at last year's record alone is not a reliable indicator.

Rule Six: Avoid Risky Investments

It is probably self-evident that you should avoid obviously risky investments, such as commodities futures, put and call options and penny stocks. What may not be as obvious is investing in collectibles such as coins, paintings, jewelry or oriental rugs. Collectibles do not pay you current income. They may or may not grow in value, but if you need money, you might have to sell them. There may or may not be someone who is willing to pay you what you think they are worth when you need the money.

Do not rationalize buying collectibles that give you pleasure as solid financial investments. It may not be much fun to look at stock or bond certificates, but properly selected, they will provide you with a comfortable life-style!

Rule Seven: Don't Get Emotionally Involved

There is a tendency for some investors to become attached to a stock. It might be the company your father worked for, a stock your mother gave you or one that did well for you in the past. The best test of whether or not you should continue to hold an asset is to ask yourself if you would buy it today if you had cash. If the honest answer is no, then you should sell it. A company that was wonderful in the past may not have kept up with the competition. It is important to recognize this, and if your advisor thinks it should be sold, sell it.

Rule Eight: Understand the Difference Between Total Return and Yield

The terms *total return* and *yield* are often used interchangeably, but this is incorrect. Yield is the annual income you receive from an investment each year divided by the current market price. For instance, a stock that pays an annual dividend of $1 and sells for $10 per share yields 10 percent. This concept is fairly straightforward. Let us take it a step further.

What if the same stock goes up from $10 per share to $12 per share during the first year you own it? If you sold the stock, you would have a $2 gain. For the purposes of this example, forget about taxes. If you divide this gain ($2) by the cost of the stock ($10), you would say you made 20 percent on your investment. In addition, you received the $1 dividend, or a 10 percent yield. The two added together (20 percent plus 10 percent) equal 30 percent. This number is your *total return*. Although you want total return from your investment, current yield is of primary importance to most widows.

Rule Nine: Spend Income (or Profits), Not Principal

When you first are widowed, you may inherit more money than you have ever had. You may be tempted to spend the money extravagantly. Don't yield to this temptation until you are absolutely sure you have enough income to cover your expenses for the rest of your life. If inflation continues to average 4 percent a year, as it has over the past ten years, your expenses will double every 18 years. Thus, if it costs you $50,000 after tax to live now, in 18 years, it will cost $100,000, and your income has to grow accordingly.

Thus, what seems to be a lot of money now may seem much less ten years from now. It is important to conserve and build your assets for the future. We have seen widows go through substantial sums of money in five or ten years by withdrawing $5,000 or $10,000 periodically. Your principal cannot grow, nor can your income increase, if you are spending it all.

Rule Ten: Don't Let Saving Taxes Dictate All Investment Decisions

There is a natural inclination for widows anxious to receive as much income as they possibly can to seek investments that provide tax-free income. This inclination is understandable but not advisable. Investing part of your money in tax-free bonds might be a very good idea, but investing everything in tax-free bonds—or in any asset category—is not a good idea from the standpoint of diversification, balance and growth of principal. After your advisor determines your tax bracket, he or she will tell you whether investing part of your money in tax-free bonds is advisable in your particular situation.

Taxes may also influence your judgment when your advisor says you should sell a position in which you have a gain. If you sell this asset, then taxes are due on this profit. Most people don't like to pay taxes. However, it gets back to sound investment advice: If this asset no longer looks as attractive as it was when you bought it and another asset appears as if it may do better for you in the future, then don't let paying taxes deter you. If you don't follow your advisor's recommendations to sell, you may find that a year from now you might not have the gain or any taxes to pay!

One strategy we recommend is, if you make a profit when you sell an asset, put aside enough money to pay capital gains taxes and reinvest the difference.

Rule Eleven: Invest in Mutual Funds

Just as your financial advisor might select individual stocks and bonds for you, he or she might choose instead to build a portfolio of different kinds of mutual funds. In this way, you are able to achieve maximum diversification and balance of investments.

For instance, you and your advisor may decide you need 10 percent of your assets in cash, 30 percent in income funds, 30 percent in balanced funds and 30 percent in growth and equity funds. Within the income fund category, you might invest in U.S. government, municipal and international bond funds. Within the balanced fund category, you might invest in three different funds, and the same for the equity income funds. This is just one example, but it conveys the idea.

Why would you choose mutual funds versus individual stocks? By investing in mutual funds, you are able to obtain diversification and the benefit of the thinking of different money managers. Further, most mutual fund management groups spend a lot of money on original research—that is, they visit the companies in which they invest and attend industry meetings. This amount of in-depth research may not be available from independent money managers.

Rule Twelve: Invest for the Long Term

Many investors worry about the market being "too high" when they invest. They are concerned that once they invest, the market might go down and they will lose money. This could happen.

There have been many studies of the timing of investments. One group took a 20-year period (1972–1991) and assumed that an individual invested $5,000 a year in the stocks in the S&P 500 Stock Index. Each year, she invested her money on the day the market was selling at its highest level. During the period studied, she invested $100,000. At the end of 1991, her investment was worth $464,243, which was an average compound rate of 13.67 percent.

This study also looked at what would have happened if the investor had made her investment each year on the day the market hit its low point for the year. In this case, her account would have been worth $593,127 after 20 years. She would have been happier with the second result but certainly should be pleased with the first result.

In summary, there are good times and bad times in the stock market, but over the long haul, any day is a good day to invest!

Rule Thirteen: Review Your Investments Regularly

You may have little interest in your investments other than in relation to the income they generate. You might be lulled into complacency if you are able to maintain a comfortable life-style. However, you must take the time to sit down with your advisor at least once a year to review your investments.

Economic conditions change, investment options change and your personal investment objectives may change during the year. It is important that your portfolio be adjusted accordingly. However, an advisor won't know your situation is different unless you tell him or her. If investments are not your strong suit, bring a more knowledgeable family member or friend with you to help you. Preservation and growth of your assets are the key to your comfort in the future, and you can't afford to ignore them.

Rule Fourteen: Educate Yourself

Regardless of your interest in investments, try to become more informed. There are various ways to become more knowledgeable.

If you go to your public library, you can find personal finance books. However, be sure they are fairly current. You might want to consider taking adult education courses on financial planning and investments offered by your local community college or university. You might also find it helpful to subscribe to a personal finance magazine such as *Money* or *Kiplinger's Personal Finance Magazine.* Read the business section of your newspaper on a regular basis, particularly the Sunday edition. Watching financially oriented television shows such as PBS's "Wall Street Week" is educational as well as entertaining.

If you want to learn more about stocks, if only to better understand what your advisors are telling you, consider joining an investment club. Here, in a social setting, you can learn more about the fundamentals of investing. It is a good way to meet other people who are interested in educating themselves, and the monthly expenditure is small. There is an organization called the National Association of Investment Clubs (NAIC) located at 1515 E. 11 Mile Road, Royal Oak, Michigan 48067. We recommend you contact them for additional information, (313) 543-0612. Their approach to investing is a very disciplined one. If you are not ready for a club, you can join the NAIC as an individual member and receive its monthly magazine, which focuses on stock investing. An informed investor is a better investor.

Rule Fifteen: Get Professional Advice

The field of finance is a complex one which is continually changing. It is not an area for amateurs, particularly when your future livelihood is dependent on your investment results. It is important to select an advisor who has experience, expertise, integrity and empathy. You need to have an expert to guide you, but it is important for you to take some responsibility for your decisions. Ask your advisor to put all recommendations in writing with supporting documentation. For instance, if the advisor recommends the portfolio of funds approach, the letter should tell you which funds are recommended, why these particular funds were selected and what income you can expect to receive from them (as well as when and how). The advisor should also tell you how often you will receive a written review of your investments (should be quarterly or semiannually) and what he or she will charge to monitor your investments.

If you find the recommendations confusing, sit down and have him or her explain them to you. If you are still confused, don't be intimidated; have them explained again. It is important to understand exactly what you are doing before you do it. After all, it is your money.

Conclusion

After a while, you may find you derive great personal satisfaction from participating in managing your assets. It is a great feeling to be in control of your finances, both present and future.

Diane: Reactions to the Basics of Investing

Diane spent a lot of time putting together a workable budget, deciding what to do about the children's schools and whether or not she needed to go back to work. These were all issues that required immediate action.

She had not yet addressed what to do with Mark's pension plan, handled by Scott Truitt, and it was time to do that. She had not liked Scott when she met him and had been intimidated by his glib manner. This led her to postpone dealing with the pension money.

Diane had been receiving monthly statements of the pension fund from Scott. When she last met with Dorothy, she had given her a copy of the most recent report. Dorothy asked to see all past copies of these statements so she could determine what progress, if any, had been made over the past year.

When Dorothy looked at the monthly reports, she was concerned about the amount of activity in the account. There had been five or six transactions per month, yet the account today was worth about the same as it was a year ago. This was during a period when stock market averages had risen 12 percent.

Dorothy showed this to Diane and suggested that Diane consider transferring the pension plan to an IRA account that Dorothy would manage. Since Diane would not retire until she was at least 62, Dorothy suggested Diane could invest more of this portfolio for growth than she had with her other money. She would recommend they invest this money in another well-established group of mutual funds. This way, they could reduce the risk by having a different group of fund managers managing her retirement money. She pointed out to Diane that although the stock market over the short term is very unpredictable, over longer periods of time, it is less so. She showed her a chart that demonstrated that the longer you left your stock investments intact, the better they performed. This chart, prepared by a group called Ibbotson Associates, covered a 65-year period.

Dorothy suggested they invest the $250,000 in a portfolio of funds—40 percent in bonds and 60 percent in stock funds. For the bond portion, she would invest $50,000 in a corporate bond fund and $50,000 in a U.S. government bond fund. For the stock portion, she would recommend

Diane's Pension Plan

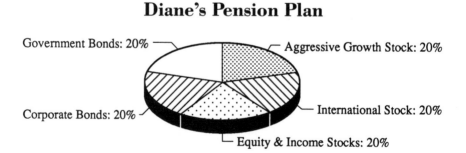

Government Bonds: 20% — Aggressive Growth Stock: 20%

Corporate Bonds: 20% — International Stock: 20%

Equity & Income Stocks: 20%

$50,000 in a good-quality growth fund that invests in stocks that pay dividends but where the emphasis is on growth of capital. She would balance that with $50,000 in an international stock fund that invests in established companies outside the United States and $50,000 in an aggressive growth stock fund. The latter would pay little in the way of dividends but would emphasize growth of principal.

Although Diane's risk tolerance initially had been very low (a "1"), now that she had a better understanding of her financial situation, she thought she was ready to take some risk with this retirement money—especially since she did not expect to use it for at least 19 years. Dorothy pointed out to her that since they were investing with a family of funds, they could move to a more conservative fund in the group at any time if she became concerned about the stock market.

Diane was pleased with this approach and decided to move the pension plan assets to Dorothy. She realized that only a year ago not only would she not have understood what Dorothy was talking about, but as her personality profile indicated, she would have lacked the courage to make this decision on her own. What a long way she had come!

DIANE'S RESULTANT PORTFOLIO

	Personal	*Retirement*	*Total*	*%*
Cash	$ 40,000		$ 40,000	4
Fixed-Income	367,500	$100,000	467,500	45
Stocks	367,500	150,000	517,500	51
Total	$775,000	$250,000	$1,025,000	100

Susan: Reactions to the Basics of Investing

In an effort to become more knowledgeable about investing, Susan had taken the adult education course on investing Bob O'Brien taught at the local community college. She had read some of the investment books from his recommended reading list and had subscribed to a monthly personal finance magazine. As a result, when Susan read the material Bob had given to her, she understood it and decided to follow his recommendations.

Now that her mother was settled in the retirement community, the cottage was sold and she had taken care of her own investments, she thought it was time to focus on Lance's pension account. She had left this pension fund at Lance's firm to be managed because she was overwhelmed by the amount of money involved. It was one thing to work with a $60,000 portfolio and quite another to manage a $300,000 pension fund.

Susan decided to take the big step and discuss this account with Bob O'Brien in greater detail. She liked the fact that he had been working as a broker with the same firm for ten years—it gave her a feeling of confidence in his abilities—and she had learned a lot from his investment class. What he said made sense to her.

He suggested that she take one of two approaches with this money. Since it was a larger amount of money, he would be glad to help her select a money manager who met a certain number of criteria, which they could put together. To have this manager handle this fund would cost her 2 percent of the assets a year. Bob was quite open with Susan, telling her that he would receive part of this fee; however, he would assume responsibility for monitoring the money manager's performance. If for any reason he thought she should change managers, he would tell her.

Alternatively, they could invest in a family of mutual funds, which he would select. The initial purchase fee would be 3 percent of the amount invested. After that, the mutual fund group would collect an annual management fee of about 3/4 percent of the assets managed. If she selected this second approach, Bob indicated he would provide her with semiannual written reports of how the funds were doing and would recommend any changes among the funds. If she decided to invest in these mutual funds, he would suggest she invest $100,000 in income funds, $100,000 in balanced funds, $50,000 in growth and income funds and $50,000 in aggressive growth funds.

Paying fees didn't particularly bother Susan. When she compared the cost of either of these approaches with the fees that the trust department charged her, they did not seem excessive. Susan remembered what she had learned in Bob's class and decided to compare the fees she would pay in each case.

Using her calculator, assuming each portfolio achieved a total return of 10 percent a year over a ten-year period, she worked out what the fees of each approach would be.

Year	Value	Money Manager	Mutual Fund
One	$300,000	$ 6,000	$ 9,000
Two	330,000	6,600	2,475
Three	363,000	7,260	2,723
Four	399,300	7,986	2,995
Five	439,230	8,785	3,294
Six	483,153	9,663	3,624
Seven	531,468	10,629	3,986
Eight	584,615	11,692	4,385
Nine	643,076	12,862	4,823
Ten	707,384	14,148	5,305
		$95,625	$42,610

By the end of the second year, Susan calculated that she would have paid more to the money manager than to the mutual fund group. By the end of the ten years, she would have paid $95,625 in fees to the money manager versus $42,610 for the mutual fund group—more than twice as much. She reasoned that if the money manager did much better than the mutual fund manager, then it would be worth the higher fee. However, she wondered how much better he or she would do given the past good performance record of the mutual fund group. Perhaps if she didn't have confidence in Bob O'Brien, she might select the money manager. Susan decided she would take the mutual fund approach. She realized that she could avoid the initial fees by buying no-load funds, but she did not feel sufficiently knowledgeable to take this approach. She preferred to have a financial expert such as Bob select and monitor her funds, and she was willing to pay him to do so.

She would reevaluate her decision periodically, but she liked the fact that she would be investing with a fund group that had been in business a long time and had a reputation for outperforming the market—particularly when the stock market went down. She didn't have a problem with taking some chances in her own account, but her retirement plan was a different matter.

Audrey: Reactions to the Basics of Investing

Audrey read the material Mr. Silver gave her. She liked the recommendation of diversifying her investments, and she certainly liked the idea that she would get higher income from the municipal bonds.

The idea of the balanced fund that could invest internationally as well as domestically also appealed to her. John's company stock hadn't done anything in the past year and a half. She had been pleased that she hadn't lost any money, but Mr. Silver had put that into perspective when he pointed out what the stock market had done in the same period. Since the market had gone up and John's company stock had not, she was not satisfied. To add insult to injury, the company hadn't even increased its dividend.

Audrey appreciated Mr. Silver's sensitivity to the fact she might be sentimentally attached to the stock because it was John's company. Actually, she was never that happy with the company when John worked there, and if they weren't doing well, then she thought she should sell most of the stock. She would keep $10,000's worth for old time's sake and sell the rest.

When she called Mr. Silver with her decision, he was surprised but pleased. Indeed, he was trying to move her in this direction but was prepared to do it gradually. He said that his test for whether or not he would hold a stock was: would he want to buy it if he had cash? This stock was not one he would recommend for purchase to anyone.

The next question was what to do with the proceeds ($190,000) as well as the $50,000 cash available to invest. Mr. Silver said he would revise his original recommendations and reduce the amount in the municipal bonds to $80,000, raise the amount invested in the balanced fund to $80,000 yielding 5 percent and put $80,000 in a growth and income fund that invested in blue-chip stocks yielding 3 percent. This left her with $10,000 in John's company stock. She would then be invested about equally in stocks and bonds.

Mr. Silver advised Audrey to take the income from her municipal bond fund in cash. However, since it appeared that she would not need the income from the other two funds, he suggested she reinvest this income back into additional shares of the funds. In this way, she could build these assets. If she needed this income in the future, she could stop reinvesting and start receiving it.

Audrey was much happier with this recommended plan. It seemed to offer diversification as well as balance. The funds she was buying were good quality, and it appeared they should grow in value over time. This was important because she wanted to use this money primarily to educate her grandchildren now and in the future. The way college costs were increasing 10 percent each year, this might be difficult to do.

AUDREY'S RESULTANT PORTFOLIO

	Personal	%
Cash	$ 10,000	4
Fixed-Income	120,000	46
Stocks	130,000	50
Total	$260,000	100

Although Audrey was very happy with the investment program Mr. Silver had put together for her, she decided she really would like to learn more about investing. One of her friends from the golf club, Janet Pine, told her about an investment club she belonged to and how much she enjoyed participating in the monthly meetings.

Apparently, members of this club did not have to invest that much money—$50 per month—and this group of 15 women met regularly for lunch and to discuss their portfolio. The club had been in existence for five years and had purposely stayed small, but one of their members was moving to Florida.

Audrey thought she would like to participate in such a group but wondered how they would feel about having such a novice join them. She decided to ask Janet if they would consider letting her replace the person who was leaving. Janet suggested she attend the next meeting as her guest. This would give her an idea of whether she would like to join.

Audrey attended the next investment club meeting and found she was fascinated. You could not be a passive bystander at this meeting. The money you invested was the smallest part of the commitment. The group started by reviewing the ten stocks they had in their portfolio and looked at whether they should make any changes. Next they reviewed the amount of cash they had and discussed what they should buy. They had selected an industry they thought held potential for growth, and then five of the members had prepared reports on the primary companies in the industry. After a long debate, they finally picked a stock they liked and decided to buy 100 shares.

Audrey knew she was overcommitted with her other activities—the symphony, Reading Is Fundamental and golf—but she knew it was hard to find one of these clubs to join, and she really wanted to learn more about investing. It looked like a fun way to increase her investment knowledge in a nonthreatening environment. Besides that, it seemed like an interesting group of women. She thought about her strong interest in the investment club and contrasted it to her feelings about the weekend she had just had with Lionel. She realized it wasn't Lionel, but rather she was not enthusiastic about that type of involvement.

He had done everything he could to please her. He had brought her a beautiful plant and had complimented her on the way she had decorated the house. They had gone out to dinner alone on Friday evening. On Saturday, they had joined the Lyons, her oldest and closest coupled friends, for dinner. She could tell that they liked him a lot. The evening went very smoothly, with no awkward moments. The men split the bill when it came, and it was like old times.

When they got home, Lionel took her in his arms and told her how much he liked her and her friends. She understood by his body language that he wanted to sleep with her. Her instinct was to say no, but another side of her thought she really ought to see how she felt about having sex with a man other than John, and she was attracted to Lionel. She allowed herself to walk upstairs to her bedroom with him, still feeling indecisive, but lulled by the wine, the dinner and the comfort level of the evening. It had been so long since she had been held and kissed by a man. She did miss that type of physical closeness.

Lionel was very considerate of her sexually, and she appreciated it. It was easier than she had imagined. However, she slept fitfully and spent a good bit of the night thinking. If she were going to attach to someone, it would be Lionel. By morning, she had reached a conclusion. She knew she had to talk to Lionel and share with him her feelings. She told him he was the first man she had slept with since John's death. Certainly, it wasn't anything Lionel had done, but she didn't feel right about what had transpired the night before and wasn't sure she would feel right about it with anyone. She acknowledged to him her recognition of his need to have a permanent relationship with someone and her respect for this need. It was just that she didn't feel she was seeking the same thing.

Lionel, the charming southern gentleman that he was, verbalized his disappointment but assured Audrey that he appreciated her being honest with him.

The remainder of the weekend was very pleasant and smooth except that Lionel slept in the guest bedroom and gave her a warm, friendly kiss on the cheek prior to retiring for the evening, in contrast to the long, passionate kiss of Saturday night.

By the end of the weekend, she was convinced that she valued her current life-style and wanted to maintain it rather than become involved with a man, even one as nice as Lionel. She realized that aspect of her life was over, at least for the present. Right now, she wanted to concentrate on her volunteer work, her female friends, her golf and, above all, her children and grandchildren. She thought that most women would jump at the opportunity for a relationship with someone as considerate and warm as Lionel, but for her it was not right. She had bittersweet feelings, but in her heart of hearts, she knew she had made the right decision.

Elizabeth: Reactions to the Basics of Investing

With each person she spoke to, Elizabeth grew closer to making a decision about moving to Florida. Mrs. Greenfield had told her that the retirement community was financially sound and she had adequate income to cover her expenses. Mr. Grossfeldt had reviewed the legal aspects of the move, and there seemed to be no obstacles there. Sam Weatherly had told her she didn't need to buy long-term care insurance because this facility provided nursing home care if needed. Mr. Winthrop had told her she should be able to sell her house for about $150,000, and, despite the difficult real estate market out there, he had a potential buyer. Although it might take some time to sell the Vermont land, she did not need that money right away.

Elizabeth was still reluctant to sever her ties with the church. She thought she should talk this over with Pastor Appletorn. He was as sensitive as ever to her concerns. He assured her that they would miss her at the church but that it seemed that a move to Florida would be good for her. After all, Florida was not that far away, so she could come back and visit.

While she was meeting with Pastor Appletorn, she asked him about a brochure she received from the church a couple of months ago. It described something called a "pooled income fund." As she understood it, she could transfer some money to this fund and it would give her income for the rest of her life. When she died, her designated beneficiary (she had in mind Abigail) would receive income from this fund for the rest of her life. After she and Abigail died, the church would receive the amount left in her account in the pooled income fund. The brochure she was looking at said the current income from the fund was 8 percent. That sounded attractive to her, particularly when compared to the income she received from other investments.

Pastor Appletorn told Elizabeth that this pooled income fund was quite popular with retirees. They liked it because they could have their cake and eat it, too—that is, they could receive a competitive level of income for their lifetime and that of a designated beneficiary, and ultimately, the church would benefit. He emphasized that this was an "irrevocable" gift. In other words, once Elizabeth invested in the pooled income fund, she couldn't change her mind. He explained the level of income she would receive would change periodically based on the income that the assets in the pooled income fund were earning. In addition to regular monthly income, she would also get an initial charitable deduction on her tax return. This deduction would not be as high as it would be if she donated the money outright, but it was based on her age and the age of her designated beneficiary.

Pastor Appletorn said he would be glad to give her an estimate of how much the deduction would be if Elizabeth wouldn't mind giving him her age and that of Abigail. Elizabeth had no trouble doing so. She was 77, and Abigail was 79. Pastor Appletorn checked the chart he had and told her if she gave $25,000 to the pooled income fund she would receive a current deduction of $8,853. He explained that this deduction changed monthly based on IRS rates. He suggested she review the idea with her accountant. He would be glad to answer any questions Mrs. Greenfield might have.

Although Pastor Appletorn used an example of a $25,000 contribution, he told Elizabeth that the contribution could be as little as $5,000. Elizabeth thought this information was very helpful. She did not want to tell Pastor Appletorn without first discussing it with Mrs. Greenfield and Mr. Grossfeldt, but she was thinking of investing the rest of the proceeds of the house ($75,000) plus the land ($25,000) in this pooled income fund. If she planned for the church to ultimately inherit part of her estate, why not give it now so she would derive a greater current benefit from it?

Mrs. Greenfield ran a taxable income estimate for Elizabeth that incorporated all the information Elizabeth had given her, including the sale of the house and the land and the contribution of these proceeds to the pooled income fund. She told Elizabeth that although she would be entitled to a total deduction of $35,412 for contributing $100,000 to the pooled income fund the IRS limited the maximum deduction she could take each year. However, whatever she couldn't deduct in the first year she could carry over to the next five years.

Elizabeth took these statements to Mr. Grossfeldt and asked him for his opinion about the idea of contributing to the pooled income fund. He agreed that since she expected to give the church at least that much ultimately, this contribution would fit into her overall estate planning.

Mr. Grossfeldt reminded Elizabeth that if she predeceased Abigail, Abigail would receive income from the trust as well as from the pooled income fund. When Abigail died, the trust assets would be split equally between the church and Ben's college. All in all, he thought it was a good idea and recommended she do it.

CHAPTER 15

Establishing Your New Identity

Life can only be understood backwards; but it must be lived forwards.

SOREN KIERKEGAARD

Introduction

The need to cope with the immediate demands of widowhood does not allow time for reflection on where you are on a personal level following this traumatic event in your life until several years later. Our conversations with widows indicate somewhere between two and five years after the death of their husbands they are ready to undertake this process. At this point, time has softened the acuteness of the pain experienced, and you have made a number of important decisions. This has allowed you to feel you are beyond simply responding to one demand or another. You have caught your breath and are now able to begin planning for the future.

For some of you, major changes will have taken place, and you will feel you are living a life quite disparate from the one you shared with your husband, while for others of you, the changes will be much less dramatic and more subtle. It is time to give some thought to where you are on a personal level today and where you would like to be in the future. What steps need to be taken to enable you to achieve that which you desire to achieve? What, if anything, do you want to change? Are you content with

312

your present life-style, or do you feel you have resigned yourself to just existing?

At this point, regardless of your previous patterns, it is likely you have become more self-reliant. You are undoubtedly familiar with check-writing, tax forms, estate matters and other aspects of life in our times. If you had feared making a mistake of some sort in the past, you should now be well beyond that stage of your widowhood. As you have mastered these areas and become more secure handling various unfamiliar matters, you should have developed greater self-reliance. With self-reliance comes improved self-confidence and a better self-image.

Establishing Personal Goals

You are now ready to give some thought to what you might like for yourself in the future. Are there areas of your life you would like to explore that you have never dared to consider? This might sound trite, but it's often never too late to try to realize a dream. Obviously, your future plans will be impacted by your health, age, financial status and family situations. However, the time has come to think about you and your personal goals.

If you had always thought it would be fascinating to explore a certain subject, take a chance and enroll in a class in the subject area you always felt was outside your realm. Investigate a sport you've always wanted to try. Consider a hobby. Take a trip. Perhaps you'd like to get involved in some volunteer work you had always been reluctant to express an interest in because you anticipated a negative response from your husband. Now is the hour for you! At this moment in your life, primary consideration for the welfare of others, parents, mate and children should be placed aside in favor of you and your needs. For some, this may be a foreign and uncomfortable role because you have grown up believing it was your responsibility to put the needs of others before your own. This may have worked for you in your married life, but it is not constructive in your present state, which requires you to make and implement decisions for yourself.

All too often, at this point in your life, you will have time to think about the choices you made and possibly the choices you didn't make. Were you an active decision maker, or were the decisions you made in response to what you thought was expected of you or accepted by others as the appropriate path for you?

Remarriage: Issues to Consider

For some of you, a new path will bring a new relationship. If so, give some thought to the way in which you would like to see this relationship evolve. Would your first choice be marriage? If so, what do you need to consider? It is likely that the man with whom you become involved now has previously been married. His marriage ended either as the result of divorce or with the death of his former wife. What are his family obligations? Does he have children for whom he is financially responsible? Is he the personal representative of his wife's estate? Does he have debts, and if so, to what extent? There are innumerable questions to be asked and answered in order for you to make the best determination for you.

If you are an individual who feels it is necessary to be married if you are going to be involved with a man, you need to seek advice from your lawyer and accountant as to the implications of such a move for you and what issues need to be resolved before taking that step. Do not feel that there is something wrong with the relationship if you are concerned about financial matters. Most likely, you are not at the place in life where you were when you married your husband. If the person with whom you are involved is a substantive individual, he will welcome your questions and appreciate your need to deal with these issues in a responsible manner. Addressing necessary financial issues should not detract from your emotional or physical relationship; it should increase this individual's respect for you. Clearing the air about these matters often allows for a deepening of a relationship. If the man in question is put off by your inquiries, you need to give some serious thought as to the desirability of marrying this man. He, too, should have a need to have the area of finance clarified.

If you decide to marry, you might want to sign a prenuptial agreement. Such a document outlines how your existing assets are to be handled after you are married. In it, there should be provisions as to how future income and assets are to be treated and what your financial rights will be once you are married.

If you have established a committed relationship with someone new, you will want to evaluate the pros and cons of either maintaining your present single state or remarriage. A number of factors need to be weighed prior to making this decision. Whether or not you ultimately choose to live together, one or both of you may feel it is preferable to maintain your single status for legal or tax reasons. Other considerations include your emotional state, your view of the role of a wife, your religious or spiritual values, your age, your finances, your health, your responsibilities, if any, for a child, children, parents or another relative.

In today's world, an individual has several choices as to how to establish and maintain a relationship with a new significant other. There are few givens. What is important here is for you to make a decision about what feels right for you at your present juncture. Do not allow yourself to be persuaded that there is only one course of action.

Whatever your decision, examine your motivations. Although there are many factors to consider, we would like to draw specific attention to your motivation to reattach. Your need might be healthy and appropriate, but some women choose this route out of habit and fear of being alone. If so, reattaching to replace your loss may only lead to new problems. You may anticipate replacing your husband and returning to the familiarity and safety of your previous life-style. This is not possible. The new potential mate is undoubtedly an individual in his own right, with his own set of habit patterns, needs and expectations. You cannot replace your husband, but you can establish a new, rewarding relationship.

If you are uncertain as to your reasons for reattaching, feel uncomfortable, or in any way insecure about your motivations to reattach, seek help from a mental health professional. If you saw someone at the time of your loss, consider some additional sessions with this person to help you clarify and understand what you are now feeling and experiencing. If you did not see anyone, consider doing so now. Ask a friend or your physician for an appropriate referral.

If you developed new, solid friendships in your widow support group, discuss with these friends your feelings in relation to your new relationship. Sometimes these friends have impressions of you that are very helpful, given their knowledge of you.

Do not hesitate to discuss the decision to marry or live with someone with an appropriate relative, sibling, child or children or even a parent. Also, consider such discussions with long-standing close friends. Hopefully, these people will be honest with you and respond with consideration and compassion to your questions and concerns. They will not be able to make any decisions for you, but hopefully, they might provide you with some insight and make observations which will be helpful to you in making your own decision.

Whatever you decide, your choices run the gamut, from a valued, platonic friendship with a man, to a physical and emotional relationship in which you each maintain separate households, to the full commitment of marriage. The key again is to select the best path for you.

Work: Volunteer or Salaried

For those widows whose situation and age preclude the need to find salaried employment, there are a host of worthwhile activities available to you to which you might like to devote some time. These range from volunteer work at a hospital or another medically related facility, to organizations such as the Red Cross, and civic and cultural groups. Some communities have foster grandparent programs that many individuals find to be a most gratifying experience.

Some areas have Volunteer Service Bureaus that are usually listed in the phone book under Social Services in the County Services listing. They can tell you which groups are seeking volunteer assistance and something about each organization. Make an appointment to meet with someone at the Volunteer Bureau to discuss your interests, availability and to learn more about specific organizations seeking such help. The extensiveness of the list will surprise you.

On the other hand, if you need or want to have a salaried position and have never worked or not worked in a long time, consider beginning this activity gradually. For some of you, now is the hour to become recertified in a field in which you have already been employed. If you are able to locate a part-time position in this field, take it and see if it works for you at your present stage of life. The job exposure may allow you to better identify what you might like to do. While working, you may be able to obtain some training that will enable you to get a better job in the same field or in another field.

Retail sales and reception work often offer entry-level employment for various ages. Entry level means no previous experience is required. Training is usually provided on the job. These areas appeal to many widows as a means of reentering the job market.

For others, it might be a time to obtain some training in a field in which you are interested and where there is the likelihood for employment at your age. For example, if you had done secretarial work prior to or earlier in your marriage but have not worked in ten or more years, you would need to brush up on your existing skills and acquire new computer skills in order to be employable. You can obtain information about training programs in your area from a community college, university or perhaps in the Yellow Pages of your phone book.

In many metropolitan areas, a given university will offer assessment programs for women desirous of returning to the job market who are uncertain as to where to turn. These programs provide a counselor who will meet with you to obtain both a job and experiential history. This latter refers to activities performed while you were married, such as organizational work related to the P.T.A. at your children's school, Girl Scout leader or other volunteer work. They will also have you take a number of aptitude and interests tests. At the conclusion of this process, they will help you to identify ways in which you can couple your interests with those activities you successfully accomplished during your marriage in a manner that has application to the current job market. The key is to determine what might be right for you. In some fields, weekend internships and/or part-time work is available on an initial basis. It is not unusual for this type of work to lead to more full-time employment should you so desire.

If you are not anxious to return to the world of work but need some additional income, there are other routes to consider. It might be possible for you to perform a service from your home, such as typing, general clerical, child care, pet walking or house sitting. You might decide to rent out a room in your home or garage space if it is available. These are some suggestions, but we'll leave to you the task of identifying what might work for you. If you have an idea, ask questions, make calls, follow leads and see what comes of it! Many have found the book *What Color Is Your*

Parachute? to be helpful in identifying heretofore unrecognized talents and interests.

To identify employment areas that are expected to grow in the future, consult the U.S. Department of Labor's *Occupational Outlook Handbook* and other resources in your local library. Also read books and recent magazine articles on this topic. For instance, one area expected to expand is home repairs. Another obvious growth field is the area of computers. With the aging of America, there increasingly is a need for individuals willing to work in these fields. Here, too, individuals possessing a range of skills are needed.

Location or Relocation

For whatever reason, at this point, too, you reconsider your living space. Some of you have already moved, but for others, this is the time you should review your long-term living situation. Should you move to a smaller place? Is your home too large? Do you eventually want to make a move to one of a growing number of facilities for the older population? Should you consider returning to the place where your primary family is or was located? Should you move closer to a child or children? Should you move to a warmer or drier climate? What are the advantages and disadvantages of such a move?

Based on where you are and what your long-term goals and needs might be in relation to your life-style, now might be a good time to investigate alternate housing as well as location. For example, if you have friends in Florida and children in St. Louis, you will probably want to visit both places to see what is available for you and which location appears to offer the most support.

If you have reattached, you and your new mate may want to establish a home in a new location after disposing of your individual homes, condos or apartments. In this manner, you will be creating a new beginning with its own identity. For others, the preferable decision may be to combine resources and maintain one of the existing households.

Conclusion

Again, depending on time of life and individual circumstances, allow yourself to identify where you hope to be in the future and how to get there. Whatever you decide, be clear on the degree to which the decision is your own and one that is right for you.

Diane: Reactions to Establishing a New Identity

As Diane cleared the dishes this Wednesday evening, she realized that in a few days it would be three years since Mark had suddenly died. She couldn't believe how much her life had changed since that fateful day.

She was working nine to five most days, again as a paralegal for a law firm. She now viewed her job very differently, in contrast to when she had been previously employed. Nowadays, it was important to her, while earlier, it was something to occupy her time prior to having children and staying at home. She took pride in her skill level with regard to estate planning. This type of work had personal meaning for her. She knew she made a contribution to the clients with whom she met because of her own life experience.

She was also able to acknowledge to herself the assistance she provided to the estate lawyer with whom she worked. He counted on her and often asked for suggestions on ways to approach a particular client based on her knowledge and experience. Sometimes he asked her to share with a client the danger of ignoring a given issue.

She recalled how difficult it was for her to think about working when Dorothy had finally gotten across to her it was essential for her to be employed. She had reluctantly agreed to take the refresher course she had located at the University of Maryland. The director of the paralegal program had really been very helpful. When the topic of specializing in some aspect of that work was introduced, she encouraged Diane to consider taking an elective in estate planning. At first, Diane was hesitant. She thought it would be boring and scary because she didn't like working with numbers. However, the more thought she gave to it, the more she realized it would be right for her.

She had dreaded the thought of having to let go of the life-style she had enjoyed so much as Mark's wife. Yet here she was three years later somewhat resentful of the various demands made on her time because of the need to work, but feeling good about being productive and appreciated by her employers. She took pride in the way she handled her work and knew she had a reputation as one of the firm's best paralegals. It was not uncommon for her to overhear one of the other lawyers commenting to her lawyer on how lucky he was to have Diane working for him. The various raises and performance evaluations she had received reflected the firm's recognition of the contribution she made to the firm.

Diane told Alice she would finish the dishes by herself tonight. Alice was delighted. Diane was not being solely considerate of Alice. She really wanted a few minutes to reflect upon her life without interruption. The end of the year seemed to lend itself to this process. Erin had begun her first year of college this past year. She had not been able to go away to any college she chose without regard for cost, but she had been able to attend a state school and live on campus. She was enjoying college, had made many new friends with a broad range of economic backgrounds and was doing well academically. The strong private school background she had received in the academic area had definitely helped her get off to a good start at college.

Jeremy was now in eighth grade in junior high and Alice in fifth grade in elementary school. Both of them attended the neighborhood public schools. They, too, seemed to be making satisfactory progress in the academic area.

Of the children, Jeremy seemed to have had the most difficulty dealing with the loss of his dad. She felt he increasingly missed the one-on-one male activities that some of his friends had with their dads. She guessed it was what was referred to as male bonding. Everybody was good to him. His grandfather and uncles spent time with him and included him when possible in all of the sports activities they attended. His friends' fathers were also sensitive to his situation. She was watching Jeremy closely and discussed him regularly with Robyn.

Alice seemed to love being in public school. She could walk to school with her friends. She was in the school band and Girl Scouts, both of which took place at school. She was also a crossing guard, which is a rather prestigious assignment for someone in fifth grade.

All in all, Diane was comfortable with the way the children were developing. The most striking difference from the days before Mark died, which was how Diane viewed life, was the way they functioned as a family. They were now a unit. Any important decision was discussed. Diane weighed carefully the children's situations prior to arriving at a family decision. She knew with certainty that this aspect of their lives was healthier and the bonds among them were stronger than at any time when Mark was alive. Diane hoped they would carry the present mode of problem solving into their personal relationships in the future.

After finishing the dishes, Diane moved to organizing the kids' lunches for the next day. She missed Erin's help in so many ways, yet the family seemed to function more smoothly when she was at school.

Tomorrow evening, Robyn was coming over to dinner so they could discuss the three-day weekend they were planning together. She made a list of things she needed to purchase on her way home from work tomorrow for dinner. As Diane completed her jobs in the kitchen, she realized that the weekend she was about to spend with Robyn would be the first weekend she had spent in her adult life going someplace without her parents, her spouse or another family. She guessed she was finally growing up at the age of 45.

She glanced at herself in the hall mirror as she was about to go upstairs and see how Jeremy and Alice were making out with their homework. She felt pleased with herself for managing to keep the house. She loved it, and its decoration represented her major accomplishment in life prior to Mark's death. She had agonized over every piece of furniture she'd purchased and spent hours debating between this wallpaper pattern or that and whether or not she had selected the perfect fabric. She could hardly relate to the former Diane. She couldn't imagine having the time to spend in this manner. What a luxury!

She also thought she was in better physical shape now than she had been in those days, thanks to Robyn's insistence on her joining a health club. She practically dragged her there in the beginning, but now it had become a valued part of her week's routine. She made a point of going there at least two times a week and often was able to get there three times a week.

She smiled to herself as she walked upstairs, for it was at the health club, about three months ago, that she met Tom. They had gone out several times now, mostly informally, and really gotten along well. She thought about a coworker telling her, when she had said she worked out at the health club, that health clubs were the singles bars of the nineties. She had laughed at the time and said, "Not if you saw what I look like when I'm working out." Yet here she was dating someone she'd met at the club. She hoped things would continue to go well between them. She and Tom talked so easily. She also found herself very attracted to his quiet strength. She thought in a kind of disbelief that she'd had more significant conversations with Tom in three months than she'd ever had with Mark. She was now a different person. She would always wish the tragedy of suddenly losing her husband and children's father had not occurred, but she was able to readily acknowledge she liked the Diane of the present better than Mark's wife Diane.

There was no way to compare her present and past levels of understanding regarding financial matters. Prior to Mark's death, she had comprehended nothing and, in addition, chose to have it that way. This was one area for which she held her parents or her father responsible. Her parents had indirectly encouraged her to believe such matters were truly best left to men to handle. She now viewed herself as childlike in the way she had asked Mark if she could spend money on this or that and didn't like that image at all.

As she had gained financial knowledge, she had been very clear with her dad about his role. She usually had him review Dorothy's recommendations. This was an adjustment for him because, like Mark, he was accustomed to making all family financial decisions. But Diane knew her dad had greater respect for her now than he had in the past, and their relationship was consequently stronger. There was no question she liked herself better for taking charge of her financial life. Taking charge was probably not quite accurate. She still relied heavily on Dorothy for guidance, and finances were clearly not her favorite subject, but she no longer abdicated responsibility when it came to decision making.

Susan: Reactions to Establishing a New Identity

Susan reflected on how much her life had changed since she last found herself on a flight winging her way to Minneapolis for an ASAE convention. The previous ASAE convention in Minneapolis was the first one she attended following Lance's death. At that time, she never could have imagined how much her life would change. The self-assured executive of today had not even been glimpsed in the frightened, uncertain, menopausal widow of five years ago.

Now, as the plane carried her toward Minneapolis, she was the director of a relatively small association that had done well under her leadership. The therapy she had undertaken with Dr. Coleman to help her deal with Lance's sudden and untimely death had resulted in her exploring many aspects of her own psyche. She would never have sought therapy for herself since she had no conscious awareness of needing to do so. However, looking at those aspects of her personality had provided her with a much greater understanding of those factors that had impacted the way she viewed life, made decisions and interacted with others.

When Lance died, she suffered a major loss. There would always be an empty place in her heart for him because he was no longer in her life; however, she rarely dwelt on her loss anymore. She was alive and leading an active, productive life. She understood her financial position and was satisfied and comfortable with the accountant, attorney and investment advisors she had selected. She had renewed her social contacts with some of the friends she had lost touch with when she had been married to Lance. She had formed new friendships which were important to her. Perhaps most significant and gratifying was her relationship with Sean.

About a year ago, she had met Sean at a local ASAE meeting in Seattle. He was an attorney who had made a presentation to the group. During the social hour which followed the meeting, Susan found herself talking at length with him about a particular concern of hers within her association and the potential legal ramifications. She asked if he would be willing to consult with her further on a professional basis about the matter. He had indicated his willingness to do so, and they had exchanged business cards.

Susan's secretary had contacted his office and scheduled a meeting with him for the following week. At the conclusion of their business meeting, Sean had surprised her by asking if she would have time to join him for lunch. She did and proceeded to take the longest lunch hour she had ever taken—three hours.

Sean was an interesting man. Rather dissimilar to Lance in appearance, he had been a widower for the past three years, attempting to raise his daughter, Melissa, a freshman in college. Although she didn't like to admit it, she saw him as more open and somewhat warmer than Lance, particularly when he described his relationship with his daughter. By the time they had finished lunch, it was clear to both of them that there was a degree of attraction between them, and they arranged to go out to dinner the following Saturday. In the course of the evening, he was very up front about his worries about getting into a relationship with a woman because of a bad experience he had following his wife's death from cancer. Susan was equally honest with him about her doubts as to whether or not she could ever allow herself to have a relationship with a man who had an adult child. She described the personal pain she had experienced as an outgrowth of the rejection she felt from Lance's children both while he was alive and after his death. Just remembering the way Adam and Leslie had treated her made her shudder. Sean was quick to pick up on it and suggested they allow themselves to continue to date and see what materialized.

In the course of the next month, she saw Sean about twice a week. She was pleased to learn that he, too, was a committed bicyclist. He had not taken any long bicycle trips as she and Lance had done, but he was equally enthusiastic. He owned a small motor boat, which he used on a lake not far from where she and Lance had had their lake house.

After seeing each other regularly for about six weeks, Sean asked her to have lunch with him and Melissa the following Saturday. Melissa was very interested in contemporary art and had prevailed upon him to accompany her to the current exhibit in a particular downtown gallery. He thought it was important for Susan and Melissa to get acquainted. With considerable reluctance and trepidation, Susan agreed. Their relationship was progressing; they were increasingly enjoying the time they spent together; and both knew this was a critical factor in whether or not they should allow themselves to maintain and pursue their present path.

Susan was amazed at the openness with which she and Sean communicated in view of the limited time they had known each other. When she was being totally honest with herself, she realized she and Sean were better able to share ideas, feelings and thoughts with each other than she had ever been able to do with Lance. In part, she recognized it was an outgrowth of her work with Dr. Coleman. Sean, too, had had some therapy and was good at identifying his feelings and expressing them. They had explored so many ideas and feelings in such a short time.

She remembered how she had agonized over her first meeting with Melissa. She couldn't even decide what to wear and must have put on and discarded five different outfits before she settled on a silk blouse, slacks and a scarf. She expected the worst but hoped they would respond well to each other. Melissa was medium height with relatively long blonde hair and large deep brown eyes. She had a warm smile and an openness that Susan found very appealing. She could see how fond father and daughter were of each other and how comfortable they were with one another. Susan didn't ever remember the same comfort level evident between Lance and Leslie, although perhaps at that point in her life, she was less aware of interpersonal relationships.

Lunch was pleasant, and conversation didn't lag. Both women were relieved that they didn't instantly dislike each other. Both were aware of the importance to Sean of their responding positively to one another. Susan was surprised at Melissa's ability to mention her mother in a way that introduced no discomfort to any of them. Melissa asked Susan many questions about her work and her background. At this juncture in her life, Melissa was unsure of her own professional goals and had not even selected her undergraduate major. Susan had astonished herself when she suggested to Melissa that perhaps she'd like to spend a day with her at the association getting a firsthand idea of what work of this nature was all about. Melissa was truly pleased by the invitation, and they arranged to do so within the next two weeks. At the conclusion of the lunch, all three of them were aware of just how pleasant everything had been.

Susan smiled to herself as she recalled it was on the occasion of her next date with Sean following this lunch that she allowed herself to sleep with him. She had been so fearful of this aspect of their relationship not working out and of failing to meet Sean's expectations. She thought she was more nervous about this than her first sexual experience. Perhaps it had something to do with her feeling less feminine because she viewed herself as being in the midst of menopause. She had heard horror stories about women having a variety of difficulties with sex, from a loss of a sense of sexuality to being nonorgasmic. She had been a wreck about introducing this dimension into her budding relationship with Sean and had delayed addressing it with him. She rationalized that she was worried about becoming attached to a man with a child. However, after that critical lunch, she knew she could no longer avoid her own anxieties and would have to address them. When it actually happened, it just felt natural and wonderful.

Sean had taken her to dinner and talked her ear off about how positive Melissa was about her. Susan was very pleased but also felt good about her own positive response to Melissa. All of this was so different from her experience with Lance and his children. Adam and Leslie never allowed themselves to get to know Susan as a person. They acknowledged her as their father's wife, but knew very little of what she did or how she felt about things or what she thought. Melissa probably knew more about her after one lunch than Leslie and Adam had known about her in the 12 years she was married to their father. Later that evening, when Sean took her back to her condo, he held her in his arms and kissed her gently as he had before. This time, Susan allowed herself to respond. She was unprepared for the strength of her body's response to Sean. She didn't know if it was what she had read about menopause, her fears about Sean's daughter or Lance's memory that had prevented her from allowing herself to respond physically to him before this night. Whatever it was, it melted away as she found herself responding to him. She no longer felt the need to work everything out in advance and was ready to explore this relationship on all levels.

Within the past year, their relationship had developed into a very solid one. They had a mutual respect and an acceptance of each other as equals. They shared some common interests and enjoyed participating in them with one another. Above all, they were able to talk to each other in an open and frank manner that was new to Susan. Just this past week, they had made the big decision to marry. Susan was so excited she could hardly believe it was real!

She realized the plane had begun its final descent and roused herself from her musings. She wondered if Andrew would be here. If he was, he'd be surprised to see how much she had changed and grown. She'd have a lot to tell him.

Audrey: Reactions to Establishing a New Identity

It was well past midnight when the chauffeur-driven car John Jr. had hired for the occasion pulled up to her front door following the 65th birthday dinner the children had arranged for her. It had been a wonderful evening. She always savored these moments as times to reflect upon where she was in life. She seemed to view the present in relation to the past and also the future. She was pleased with her decision not to pursue her relationship with Lionel. It would have been so very nice to have had him as an escort this evening.

She knew her decision not to move forward with Lionel was right for her, but she did question her motives. Part of it was the geographic distance between them, but it was more than that. Basically, Lionel met all of her requirements: He was charming, in good shape, physically attractive and financially secure. Yet she had been reluctant to move the relationship forward in the manner Lionel would have liked. Something was missing for her. She continued to feel it was connected somehow to the way she felt about her marriage to John. Was she simply afraid to try marriage again? In her present widowed state, she felt less encumbered than when she was married. It was a feeling she valued. Her experience with married life and that type of commitment felt like a trap to her. There were many excuses which came to mind, but Audrey was honest enough with herself to admit she enjoyed the companionship of men but did not want to remarry and risk falling into old patterns.

She enjoyed all of her present activities and couldn't imagine giving any of them up, although she knew she was losing weight again. She was certain Dr. PaPadisio would scold her about doing too much and not eating properly when she next saw him. She knew she had to pay more attention to her eating patterns. It was just that when she got caught up in an activity, it was not uncommon for her to forget about eating. She was clearly in danger of being overcommitted. Asking herself why she had allowed herself to take on so much was really unnecessary. She knew the answer. It was primarily a reaction to everything she had not been able to do when she was married to John. For the first time, she was doing what she wanted to do, not what a good wife was supposed to do to help her husband. There was so much out there to be done, and she enjoyed so many different things. It wasn't even that she hated all of the entertaining she did for John. It was just that her current endeavors represented her own choices, and that meant so much to her.

The Reading Is Fundamental work was particularly gratifying, and she found herself giving more and more time to this organization. As she watched her grandchildren develop and knew how much time Joanne spent reading to them and playing educational games with them to expand their verbal skills, she doubled the hours she gave to her work with this program. She felt so badly for those children less fortunate than her grandchildren.

Sometimes she wondered if she just kept herself so busy because she didn't want to think about anything or be alone. This thought didn't feel right to her. If anything, she spent too much time evaluating what she was doing and the reasons for it. She wouldn't change anything about her relationship with her children and grandchildren. She felt fortunate and thought that few women had the kind of substantive ties she did with her family. It was one of mutual respect. All of them felt comfortable living their individual lives, yet there was a richness to the quality of the times they had together. When possible, they rotated the celebration of major holidays among the three houses. Keith's parents usually joined with her in celebrating the holidays, but her daughter-in-law's family was large and they had long-standing holiday traditions of their own, so John Jr. usually alternated spending the holidays between the families, which was fine with all concerned.

Her financial situation was very stable, and Audrey was grateful for that. She met regularly with her advisors and was pleased with the way her money had been invested and managed. She had joined the investment club and remained active in it. In fact, she had been elected secretary this past year. She had learned so many things on a financial level and done so many different things on a volunteer basis she could hardly believe it.

She wondered how John would respond to the Audrey of today, yet if he were alive, she knew she wouldn't be this person. Perhaps these were strange thoughts, yet she wondered if he would like her in her present mode. She really believed he would prefer her as she had been and would have something negative to say about women who committed themselves to all these outside activities. All in all, at 65, she was very positive about the quality of her life.

Elizabeth: Reactions to Establishing a New Identity

Twenty months after Ben had died, Elizabeth found herself ready to make a decision on her living situation. Fall was always beautiful to Elizabeth in New England, and this morning, it seemed exceptionally so. However, with fall came the thought of winter, and Elizabeth didn't know if she was up to facing another winter in Boston on her own.

Last winter, there were times when she could not leave her house for days. The neighborhood was also changing, and the young boys she had counted on to mow the lawn and shovel snow were off at college or launching careers and living on their own. The few houses which had been sold had been sold to young couples with small children not yet ready to take on these jobs.

She had spoken at great length with Pastor Appletorn, the Weatherlys, Mabel and her other friends about relocating to Florida. Being in the same retirement community with Abigail was really appealing. She had visited Abigail in Florida three times, and each time, it seemed more desirable. She had met so many people with whom she enjoyed spending time. There were so many things to do she was rarely by herself.

She also questioned her purpose in life. The majority of her life was behind her. Was she being foolish to look forward to something—sort of a new beginning? Who needed her anyway? Did she have anything to give to anyone, and did it matter? These were grim thoughts that made her feel empty and hopeless. At the same time, she wasn't ready to sit around and wait to die. What would be gained by settling in a retirement community in Boston? The residents of Abigail's retirement community were productive and displayed that productiveness in a number of ways. Some of the residents made craft items, which were offered for sale on special occasions; others volunteered their time to the foster grandparent program at the local elementary school. Most important, she thought, was the enthusiasm for life she felt when she visited there. She had no dependents, so it didn't matter where she lived. There was nothing wrong with wanting more out of life at her age. Pastor Appletorn had stressed to her the appropriateness and positive aspects of wanting to lead a productive life. She no longer felt guilty about those feelings or disloyal to Ben for having them.

Elizabeth looked at the kitchen clock. It was already 10:30. Where had the morning gone? She was beginning to get somewhat concerned about her feelings of fatigue. She felt tired a great deal, was sleeping more and was having a harder time mobilizing. She didn't like feeling this way. If she stayed in Boston, she thought she might become more of a recluse. When she was in Florida, she felt more alive and more anxious to participate in the activities available to the residents of the community. From a health standpoint, the move might be a good idea.

Her only reluctance about moving to Florida was the finality it represented. It would be closing a door on her life with Ben. Yet Ben was dead now, and she was alive. What did it say about her marriage to be facing a Boston winter and feeling alone and afraid to leave her house? Did it make her less of a wife to Ben? She didn't think so. If she went into the Continuing Care Retirement Community at this point in her life, with her health stable according to her doctor, she would be eligible for the lifetime continuing care program, which would take a great burden off her shoulders. She had no one to care for her the way she had cared for Ben if she became incapacitated.

After her visits there, she had developed several new friendships and maintained these contacts through the mail and even on the phone when she was in Boston. Her new friends were trying to persuade her to relocate, citing their own experiences weighing the pros and cons of the move for them. None of them seemed to have any regrets, and all encouraged her to move to Florida.

As Elizabeth looked around the familiar kitchen with its somewhat faded wallpaper, she realized that there really was not enough available to her in Boston to warrant staying through the winter. She had basically had a good life with Ben in this house, but it was time to move. A tear slid down her cheek as she realized she had made the decision to close this chapter of her life.

She felt fortunate knowing she had no financial concerns. She had already spoken with Mr. Samuels, the trust officer at her bank, and learned she could maintain her present trust or transfer it, should she so desire, upon getting settled in Florida. For the present, she would leave it in the hands of Mr. Samuels at her present bank because she felt comfortable with him. Too much change at one time would be unsettling.

Elizabeth called Pastor Appletorn and told him of her decision to move to Florida. She also told him that she had finalized her estate planning with Mr. Grossfeldt. She had designated the church as the ultimate beneficiary of her trust after she and Abigail died. Meanwhile, she intended to put $100,000 in the pooled income fund offered by the church. This way, she could ultimately benefit the church but receive more income now. Pastor Appletorn was overwhelmed with her generosity and thanked her profusely.

After she hung up the phone from talking with Pastor Appletorn, she felt ready to make the move to Florida. Elizabeth knew exactly which apartment unit at the CCRC she preferred. She would contact Abigail to get the purchase process started. She thought she would like to be able to leave Boston by the first of December at the latest.

In a way, she felt fortunate that she was capable of living on her own. Many women her age were not in as good shape physically, financially or mentally. Although she was somewhat nervous about all of the change she was about to introduce into her life, she found herself looking forward to it.

When she allowed herself to think about it, she realized she acted differently in Florida than she did in Boston. She participated in many more activities there, and all of the trips available to the community seemed like so much fun. She knew she would join both the bridge club and the sewing club as soon as she had her furniture in place. She had attended a few of their meetings and enjoyed them immensely. The members had all been welcoming and fun.

Most surprising to her was her present correspondence with Abe, a member of the community she met through Abigail. He was nothing like Ben. He talked a great deal, played a lot of golf and seemed to love to take trips. Their mutual interest in travel led to their initial conversation. She couldn't believe he had taken the time to write to her, but he had, and he always included the latest community trip information. He told her he was sure these trips would help convince her to make the move.

She felt a little disloyal to Ben being attracted to this casual, relaxed lifestyle, but what harm was it for someone going on 77? In fact, if anyone had told her she would be excited about embarking on a new phase of life at 77, she would never have believed it. Abigail would be especially pleased to learn she had finally made her decision to move to Florida.

She would contact a real estate agent in the morning and discuss when to put the house up for sale and at what price. Her life as Ben's wife had just ended, and she was ready to be what she now was—a widow by the name of Elizabeth who was ready to start a new life.

Epilogue

There was that law of life, so cruel and so just, which de-
manded that one must grow or else pay more for remaining
the same.

NORMAN MAILER

Undoubtedly, you have had many experiences since the death of your
spouse that have contributed to the person you are today. However, the loss
of your spouse was probably the most painful experience of your life to that
point. There will be times when you reflect upon the range of emotions you
experienced during that traumatic time in your life as though it were
yesterday—the tangible pain, the agony, the fears about the present and the
future, the sense of being bereft of purpose, the vulnerability, the loneliness, the anger, to name some of the more common ones. But most
importantly, you should now have a sense of having experienced on a
personal level the rhythm of life: birth, childhood, adulthood and death—a
growth process in which all living things participate. As a widow, you have
firsthand knowledge of this life process—its forming, molding, reforming
and remolding.

Few of the widows with whom we have spoken did not feel they were a
different person ten years after the loss of their spouse. Many were more
pleased with the person they were today than they were with their former
selves. Others acknowledged that they had coped as best they could with
their loss but never felt quite the same or as though life held much pleasure
for them following this event. You had no choice in determining when your
spouse would die, thereby leaving you "On Your Own"; however, having

by this time coped with the emotional upheaval and the financial responsibilities that accompanied your loss, you have grown. One grows from all of life's experiences. We therefore encourage you to be all that you can be. Following an appropriate recovery period from your loss, move forward. Life progresses for all of us, including you, and you need to allow yourself to drink of its waters.

Diane: Ten Years Down the Road

Diane, now 52, found herself daydreaming while the family watched with intensity the latest efforts of the Redskins in their bid to play in the Super Bowl. She had been reminiscing about the time five years ago when, after considerable thought, she had decided to accept Tom's proposal of marriage. For several reasons, she had initially found herself ambivalent about his proposal. To her surprise, she had realized she enjoyed being independent and wasn't sure how she felt about giving up this independence. Also, although responsible when it came to most matters, Tom's attitude with regard to money management could best be described as casual. He didn't have anywhere near as much ambition as Mark had, but did well and was well thought of by his company. Additionally, she wasn't sure how his two grown children would blend with her three children in a combined family unit.

She remembered conspiring with Dorothy about various approaches to involve Tom in the financial planning process. She didn't want to alienate him, overwhelm him or suggest that she didn't love him, but she knew she would not marry without a premarital agreement. She and Dorothy had finally decided that a straightforward nonstrategical approach was best. After all, Tom was 55, and it was time for him to pay some attention to retirement planning. As Dorothy had said—they might be retired for 25 or 30 years, and Diane wanted to make sure they had enough money. Even now, five years later, Diane smiled to herself when she recalled that conversation. It certainly had been a reversal of roles. There she was, convincing her fiancé that financial planning was important, when five years before that, she didn't even know what financial planning was.

Tom had agreed to meet with Dorothy since what Diane had said about planning for retirement did make sense. When they met, he liked Dorothy but was a little taken aback by everything that was involved in a premarital agreement. However, he knew how important the children were to Diane and realized that both the shock of unexpectedly being widowed and the financial circumstances that accompanied this event had made her very aware of the need for financial planning. As for himself, a recent round of early retirements at his company had made him more aware of retirement issues. Although his job had not been affected, he had some apprehension about the future he had not had before—since he had worked for the same company for 30 years. He had come to truly appreciate Diane's concerns about their financial future.

She had been musing about the time, following their first meeting with Dorothy, when they had drafted a joint budget as well as an asset statement. There had been surprises for both of them. Diane discovered that Tom had accumulated little in the way of assets other than the equity in his home and his pension plan. On the other hand, Tom was unprepared for the amount of money Diane had invested and realized why the premarital agreement was important to her.

In putting together the budget, they were able to determine what made the most sense for them as a couple. They had decided it would be best for them to live in Diane's house at least for a while. In this way, Alice could complete high school with no disruption. Tom suggested that he sell his house. When he knew what he would realize from the sale of his house, then they could come up with a budget that would include his contribution to the household as well as to a retirement plan. Planning in this way had been the first step in a truly joint endeavor. It had represented growth to both of them. It felt symbolic of their future together.

She roused herself from her musings. It was almost halftime, and she was going to put more food out for Tom and the assorted guests—from Alice's friends to a few of Tom's coworkers in the football pool. She could hardly believe Tom was almost 60. She had a hard time accepting that Erin, now 25, had not only graduated from college but had earned a master's degree. Jeremy, now 21, was in his junior year of college majoring in economics, and Alice was a junior in high school. She didn't feel the way 52 sounded. She certainly felt younger than she had the first year following Mark's death.

She valued her marriage to Tom. He treated her as an equal, was loving and tried to be sensitive to her needs. Their ability to communicate with each other was excellent, and they shared mutual interests. He had no problem with her doing things with her women friends or coworkers. The female friends with whom she was close meant a great deal to her. Before Mark's death, she had not had these types of friendships, and after she remarried, she worked at maintaining them, as did her friends.

Diane thought she was as extroverted as she had previously been, although better organized. Juggling work, her marriage, the children, her parents and friends was not easy, but being able to handle it all gave her a great deal of satisfaction. She regularly used the stress reduction techniques she had learned in the special class offered by the health club. The deep breathing and visualization techniques she had learned had been particularly helpful. She tended to practice what she had been taught and found it helped her to solve problems better and in fact to function better in all areas. She thought they had also enabled her to gain better control of her emotions. She didn't think she'd ever cry at the drop of a hat the way she once had, nor did she think she "wore her heart on her sleeve." Sometimes she could hardly recognize the Diane of ten years ago. She was so much more self-sufficient now. She had been through the worst type of personal tragedy she could envision for a woman, and not only survived, but thrived.

Susan: Ten Years Down the Road

Susan and Sean were now enjoying their fifth year of married life. They both valued their relationship and felt lucky to have found each other. Neither had expected to find another who would provide the pleasure and closeness they clearly shared. For both of them, the relationship was different from the one they had with their former spouses. They worked at not making comparisons and were successful in doing so.

The aspect of her present life that surprised her the most was her relationship with Sean's daughter, Melissa. Their initial positive response to one another had been expanded. The two women genuinely liked each other and had grown to love each other. Susan had never dreamt of being so close to a stepchild and so was unprepared for the rewards of such a relationship. Melissa had graduated from college with a combined graphic arts/business major. While at school, she became involved with a wonderful young man to whom she was now married. She and Susan had planned the wedding, thoroughly enjoying the experience and their collaboration. They had married during Melissa's senior year, two years ago, and had just had their first child, a boy. Susan adored her grandson. She proudly showed her Grandma's brag book photo album to all her friends, coworkers and acquaintances. They all teased her about it and tolerated it fairly well. She enjoyed every minute of it.

Susan's mother was still living in the nursing home she had found for her around the time of Lance's death. Her brother, much to her surprise, had married a woman with three children and appeared to have quite a full life. He had maintained his involvement with their mother and had increasingly assumed responsibility for making small purchases for her and driving her to various doctors' appointments and the hairdresser when he was able to do so. Mom seemed to thrive on his attention, making an effort to look good when she knew he was coming for a visit. Susan thought this had been beneficial for both of them. She wondered what would have happened if she had not modified her behavior and encouraged Ron to become more active with their mother. Both of them would have lost out on something that had become meaningful and special to them.

Susan realized that the Susan of today was a much softer woman than the Susan of ten years ago. Although she continued to be organized, efficient and dependent on list making to prioritize what she needed to do, she felt she was less pragmatic and more in touch with her feelings than at any point in her life. She was also more tolerant and accepting of others, more secure and less intense. She didn't feel 60, but that was in fact her current age. On rare occasions, she would find herself musing about her life with Lance and the person she was at that point in her life. She wondered if the Susan of today would have been attracted to Lance, and yet she would have described herself as happy with him. It was just that now she realized both she and Lance were uncomfortable with feelings and thus had never adequately shared them with each other. So much had happened to her in the years since Lance had met his tragic death. If Lance had not died, the Susan of today would not exist. It was a sobering thought to Susan. Without any reservations, she liked herself better today.

On a recreational level, bicycling had been a favorite activity for Susan when she was married to Lance. She had many fond memories of these excursions with Lance and had been very uncertain about how she would feel sharing the same activity with Sean. As with everything else, they talked about it and, for starters, decided to try it out, not revisiting the places she had frequented with Lance. This worked well, and most recently, they had combined a camping and bicycling trip in Canada, which both of them had thoroughly enjoyed. Sean had had a great deal more experience with camping than Susan had, but she was a willing student and had come to truly enjoy it.

On a professional level, her association had grown under her direction. She had received appropriate recognition for her accomplishments and had even been approached by a larger association to assume the same role with them for more money. She had gone back to Dr. Coleman for a few sessions to discuss the advantages and disadvantages of the new job offer. She had turned them down because she felt comfortable managing the various aspects of her current life and at this time was not anxious to take on any more responsibility.

Over the years, Susan had increased her investment knowledge. She continued to work with Bob O'Brien, who gave her sound advice. They had built Lance's pension assets up to a nice amount. This account, together with her retirement plan from the association and Sean's assets, should provide them with a comfortable income when they retired.

Sean and Susan had been thinking more and more about their retirement. They had even considered moving to a warmer climate, but as they really liked the Seattle area, they had decided not to move. They felt the apartment they lived in was ideal for the present as well as the future. Susan and Sean had even attended a retirement lecture Bob O'Brien had given and had started to complete the worksheets he provided. They weren't ready to retire yet but wanted to be prepared when the time came.

It was hard to believe how content she was only ten short years after Lance's death. Then, she had trouble envisioning life without him. Now, here she was with a better job, physically active, financially secure and emotionally content. She was truly a fortunate person.

Audrey: Ten Years Down the Road

Audrey took a long, luxurious bath prior to dressing for the Reading Is Fundamental gala scheduled for this evening. She was one of the honorees in recognition of her contributions to the organization over the past nine years. She had done such an excellent job of chairing their fundraising luncheons in the past three years that her chapter had raised more money than at any time in its history. She didn't feel that she had done anything extraordinary, but the numbers spoke for themselves. Everybody with whom she worked was very impressed.

Naturally, her children and grandchildren would be present. J.T., now 24, was in graduate school working toward a master's degree in business administration, and Casey was in a combined master's and doctoral program in environmental sciences. Both had told her they would make every effort to attend this event in honor of their very special "Gran Gran." Of course, it was no problem for Joanne's children since they were all still living at home.

Audrey looked in the mirror and thought she looked pretty good for a 72-year-old woman. She was slim and paid meticulous attention to her appearance. It was now ten years since John had died, and she had a hard time remembering what it felt like when she was married to John. She had done so much in the past ten years. She also felt lucky to be alive.

Almost four years earlier, during her routine physical, Dr. PaPadisio had identified what he thought was a small lump in her left breast. The mammogram she had the next day confirmed his fears. She had a biopsy shortly thereafter, and Dr. PaPadisio had told her that it confirmed a malignancy. However, he was quick to assure her that the type of cell identified was a slow-growing type and not at all comparable to John's situation. She really didn't believe him about the prognosis but determined to go along with the recommendations of the surgeon to whom he referred her. This surgeon recommended Audrey undergo a mastectomy and breast reconstruction immediately thereafter. Audrey reviewed all of this with John Jr., who agreed with the treatment plan after looking at the X-rays, lab reports and talking to both of her doctors. Everyone had been very supportive. She had the surgery, and things went well. She was fortunate because her recuperation was smooth. She had heard nightmare stories from her friends about their experiences with breast reconstruction. In fact, for whatever reason, her weight stabilized following her surgery. Even Dr. PaPadisio had commented on it. She had not had any health problems since that time, and she had regular six-month checkups.

She was totally committed to her walking routine. Achilles had died of old age, and she had debated for some time about replacing him. She didn't know if she wanted the responsibility of a new dog but missed the companionship of Achilles. Finally, she broke down and bought an irresistible German shepherd puppy. She called him Zeus. She decided she was more likely to maintain her walking routine if she had a dog to walk. Zeus was a handful, but she really got a kick out of him. He was just adorable.

After her initial visit with Joanne to the spa so many years ago, she had purchased a Stairmaster for use at home. She used it regularly and thought the combination of the Stairmaster and her walking kept her in good physical shape. She had actually enjoyed the spa so much she made it a practice to go every year with her daughter. Both mother and daughter valued these trips. She sometimes wondered why she hadn't done anything like that prior to John's death. It was just one of many things she had never thought about doing when John was alive.

Going to the golf clinic with her married friends had also become an annual event. Only, now, there was another widow among them. Actually, she had met Lionel again at one of these clinics. He had remarried and told her that he was happy with his new wife. He went on to say she would always be very special to him and he held her in the highest regard. It was a good experience for both of them. Both knew what might have been, yet both were satisfied with their present life-styles. Audrey was so glad their paths had crossed again. It confirmed for her the correctness of her decision to remain unattached, yet it reaffirmed her fondness for him.

She had also taken trips with different groups. She was still active in the investment club and had attended a couple of their international meetings. She had also taken some trips with her friends sponsored by the symphony. Her horizons had widened considerably.

Audrey had her annual visit with Mr. Silver last week and was very pleased with the current status of her portfolio. Just as Mr. Silver had originally told her, the municipals had not grown much in value, but they had provided a steady stream of income. Her two mutual funds had more than doubled in value over the past ten years. She had finally sold the rest of John's company stock and invested in a couple of stocks she had researched in her investment club. They had done quite well.

Although she certainly maintained an active life-style, she had not had any difficulty keeping within her budget. She had been able to maintain her gifting program with John and Joanne and felt it had helped stabilize Joanne's marital situation. Keith had finally found a job he liked and had been working for the same company for five years. Now that the children were in school full-time, Joanne had gone back to college to get her degree and was teaching in a local elementary school.

As she put the final touches on her makeup this evening, Audrey thought she was fortunate to have had a husband who provided her with the financial resources to develop a life of her own after his death. He could not have related to the Audrey of today, yet he had contributed to her creation.

Elizabeth: Ten Years Down the Road

Elizabeth smiled as she opened her mail. There was the familiar anniversary card sent to all the members of the retirement community to recognize the number of years they had been in residence. My, my, eight years! It didn't seem that long, and yet it seemed even longer. This certainly was not a new feeling; so many things seemed both forever and yet fleeting. If she had been in the retirement community for eight years, that meant it had been ten years since Ben passed away. She didn't think about him that much these days, although she did have fond memories of her married life. It was a different time and place, and she was different.

She often thought about her present life in contrast to her life with Ben. She could accept it was a much fuller one. She continued to be an active participant in both the sewing and bridge clubs she joined upon moving to Florida. Fortunately for her, she had experienced very little memory loss and didn't have a hard time keeping track of the cards—except when her mind wandered and she allowed herself to daydream, usually about an upcoming trip. Elizabeth was continually surprised at how important travel had become to her. She never thought she would be so interested in going to different places. She always took at least one trip a year, and she especially enjoyed the cruises. She was hooked on "Loveboat." She guessed this wanderlust was an aspect of her personality that laid dormant throughout her marriage to Ben because he had no interest in travel.

She had better stop daydreaming and get moving. She had to attend a meeting of the welcome committee, of which she was the past president. Over the years, the committee had incorporated some of her suggestions into the standard welcoming package presented to all new residents. She was pleased with her contribution and derived considerable satisfaction from it.

She also wanted to stop and spend some time with Abigail before the meeting. Abigail had suffered a mild to moderate stroke several years ago and had limited mobility. She had residual partial paralysis of the right side, which particularly affected her right leg. She was therefore some-what invalided and could only really get about in a wheelchair. Elizabeth was pleased that she could be with her now. She knew it meant as much to Abigail as it did to herself.

While getting dressed to see Abigail, Elizabeth listened to the morning news. According to the weatherman, Boston had six inches of snow. She certainly didn't miss those winters. The warm Florida weather had really agreed with her. Initially, she had been concerned about the humidity, but it had not turned out to be a problem. Last summer, when she had visited Boston to attend Pastor Appletorn's retirement dinner, some of the parish-ioners told her she looked younger and was more animated than when she left Boston eight years earlier. She got tired of hearing, "My, that Florida life certainly agrees with you. I've never known you to be this talkative."

It had been good to see so many of the church members. Unfortunately, Mabel and some of her other acquaintances had died. She missed them, but she enjoyed reminiscing about them with mutual friends. The church even formally acknowledged her attendance, and Pastor Appletorn expressed their appreciation for her generosity to the church. She was able to stand and smile when she was asked to do so in recognition of her contribution. Ten years ago, she would have wanted to hide under a table if so recog-nized, but now, although she was somewhat embarrassed, it posed no problems.

She had affiliated with a church in her present location. She enjoyed it and the people, but this affiliation didn't feel quite as rewarding to her as her church in Boston. Perhaps this was the result of all the support she had always felt was available to her there and her long-standing ties with the church and the congregation. In fact, the only void in her life as a result of the move was the loss of Pastor Appletorn and other church members, such as the Weatherlys. In the overall scheme of things, she thought it was a relatively small price to pay for her otherwise presently happy life.

Thanks to Ben, she had no financial worries. Elizabeth was pleased with herself for having made the time to see Mr. Samuels at the bank in Boston and tell him how much she appreciated how well he had managed her account. About four years ago, after talking to several friends in her new location and listening to a lecture by a trust officer from a local bank in Florida, she had decided to transfer her trust account to Florida. It seemed to be the right thing to do based on her current residency. As always, Mr. Samuels had been very helpful and reassuring to her regarding the advisability of this decision. She was especially thankful to him for never making her feel stupid or unimportant. She wanted to express her gratitude in person.

In her new setting, she had developed many rewarding friendships. She thought it was the first time in her life people related to her for herself. She had a hard time expressing this feeling to anybody, including Abigail, but she thought it was true. Abe, the man with whom she had corresponded eight years ago, before deciding to relocate, had become a valued, special friend. They really enjoyed each other's company. They both loved to travel and always took the same trips offered by the retirement community. They had structured their lives so they could spend time together every day. Neither she nor Abe ever openly discussed it, but what they shared was comparable to married life. At the end of the community activities each evening, they would retire to her apartment, she would prepare something to drink, such as iced tea, and they would have a snack. They would watch TV and talk. She thought he seemed to have more respect for what she thought than Ben ever did, but she didn't allow herself to dwell on such thoughts. Abe was also very complimentary, always remarking on a new outfit or her hair or something. Sometimes in Boston with Ben, she had felt she was invisible or like a piece of furniture.

As she thought about her new life, now not so new, in Florida and the agony she went through in making the decision to relocate, she wondered what her problem had been. The move to Florida had been very positive. It had been a wonderful idea, and she was so pleased she had acted on it. She had no regrets. She was more self-confident and more outgoing than she had ever been in her life. She had discovered things about herself she had never imagined were there. She discovered that she truly enjoyed people and was more adventurous than she had realized. She had a hard time fathoming that in her eighties she was still discovering facets of her personality that had been dormant all of her adult life. But such was the case. There was no question in her mind but that her present life was fuller and more rewarding than most of her previous existence.

Bibliography

Bolles, Richard Nelson. *What Color Is Your Parachute?* Berkeley, Calif.: Ten Speed Press, 1970–1993.

Blau, Anne Kohn. *The Sex of the Dollar*. New York: Simon & Schuster, 1988.

Brothers, Dr. Joyce. *Widowed*. New York: Ballantine Books, 1992.

Brown, Judith N., LLB, and Christina Baldwin. *A Second Start*. New York: Simon & Schuster, 1986.

Caine, Lynn. *Widow*. New York: Bantam Books, 1974.

DAWN—Divorced and Widowed Women's News. Founder: Sharon Grinage, Suite G., 455 DeVargas Center, Santa Fe, NM 87501.

Foehner, Charlotte, and Carol Cozart. *The Widow's Handbook: A Guide for Living*. Golden, Colo.: Fulcrum, 1988.

Gates, Philomene. *Suddenly Alone*. New York: HarperCollins, 1990.

Ginsburg, Genevieve Davis. *To Live Again*. New York: Bantam Books, 1989.

Grollman, Earl A. *Living When a Loved One Has Died*. Boston: Beacon Press, 1987.

Jackson, Edgar N. *When Someone Dies*. Philadelphia: Fortress Press, 1971.

Jones-Lee, Anita. *Women and Money*. Haippauge, N.Y.: Barron's Educational Series, 1991.

Kleiman, Carol. *The 100 Best Jobs for the 1990s and Beyond*. Chicago: Dearborn Financial Publishing, 1992.

Koumanelis, Samantha. *More Power to You! The Personal Protection Handbook for Women*. Chicago: Round Lake Publishing, 1993.

Krause, Lawrence A. *Sleep Tight Money*. New York: Simon & Schuster, 1987.

Kubler-Ross, Elizabeth. *On Death and Dying*. New York: Macmillan, 1969.

Kushner, Harold S. *When Bad Things Happen To Good People*. New York: Avon, 1981.

Lawrence, Judy. *The Budget Kit: The Common Cent$ Money Management Workbook*. Chicago: Dearborn Financial Publishing, 1993.

Loeb, Marshall. *Marshall Loeb's Money Guide*. Boston: Little, Brown, 1993.

Loewinsohn, Ruth Jean. *Survival Book for Widows*. Washington, D.C.: AARP; Glenview, Ill.: Scott, Foresman, 1984.

Lynch, Peter. *One Up on Wall Street*. New York: Simon & Schuster, 1989.

Lynch, Peter. *Beating the Street*. New York: Simon & Schuster, 1993.

Magee, David S. *Everything Your Heirs Need To Know: Your Assets, Family History and Final Wishes*. Chicago: Dearborn Financial Publishing, 1991.

Martin, Mary E., and J. Michael. *Home Filing Made Easy!* Chicago: Dearborn Financial Publishing, 1993.

Miller, Theodore J. *Kiplinger's Invest Your Way to Wealth*. Washington, D.C.: Kiplinger Books, 1991.

Miller, William A. *When Going to Pieces Holds You Together*. Minneapolis: Augsburg, 1976.

Neeld, Elizabeth Harper, PhD. *Seven Choices*. New York: Clarkson N. Potter, Inc., 1990.

Nudel, Adele Rice. *Starting Over: Help for Young Widows and Widowers*. New York: Dodd, Mead, 1986.

Parkes, Colin Murray, and Robert S. Weiss. *Recovery from Bereavement*. New York: Basic Books, 1983.

Rando, Therese A. *Grieving: How to Go on Living When Someone You Love Dies*. Lexington, Mass.: D. C. Heath & Co., 1988.

Savage, Terry. *Terry Savage Talks Money*. Chicago: Dearborn Financial Publishing, 1990.

Schiff, Harriet Sarnoff. *Living Through Mourning: Finding Comfort and Hope When a Loved One Has Died*. New York: Viking, 1986.

Sheehy, Gail. *The Silent Passage*. New York: Random House, 1991, 1992.

Sinclair, Carol. *When Women Retire*. New York: Crown, 1992.

Temes, Roberta. *Living with an Empty Chair*. New York: Irvington, 1980.

Truman, Jill. *Letter to My Husband: Notes about Mourning and Recovery*. New York: Viking Penguin, 1987.

Viorst, Judith. *Necessary Losses*. New York: Fawcett Gold Medal, 1986.

Wall, Ginita. *Our Money, Our Selves*. Yonkers, N.Y.: Consumer Reports Books, 1992.

Weiss, Geraldine, and Janet Lowe. *Dividends Don't Lie*. Chicago: Dearborn Financial Publishing, 1988.

Westberg, Granger E. *Good Grief*. Philadelphia: Fortress, 1962.

Worden, J. William. *Grief Counseling and Grief Therapy*. New York: Springer, 1982.

Index